Organizational Lear
Competitive Adv...

Organizational Learning and Competitive Advantage

edited by

Bertrand Moingeon and Amy Edmondson

SAGE Publications
London • Thousand Oaks • New Delhi

First published 1996

Reprinted 1998

SAGE Publications Ltd
6 Bonhill Street
London EC2A 4PU

SAGE Publications Inc
2455 Teller Road
Thousand Oaks, California 91320

SAGE Publications India Pvt Ltd
32, M-Block Market
Greater Kailash – I
New Delhi 110 048

British Library Cataloguing in Publication Data

A catalogue record for this book is
available from the British Library

ISBN 0 7619 5166 0
ISBN 0 7619 5167 9 (pbk)

Library of Congress catalog card number 96–069126

Typeset by Photoprint, Torquay
Printed and bound in Great Britain by Biddles Ltd, Guildford and King's Lynn

Contents

Notes on the Contributors

Rafael Andreu is Professor of Information Systems at IESE, Barcelona. He holds a Doctor's degree from UPC and a PhD in management from the Massachusetts Institute of Technology. He has written articles in leading journals and is co-author of the book *Information Systems Strategic Planning: A Source of Competitive Advantage.*

Chris Argyris is James Bryant Conant Professor of Education and Organizational Behavior in the graduate schools of Business and Education at Harvard University. He has also served as a faculty member and chairperson of the Administrative Sciences Department at Yale University. With Donald Schön of MIT, he has developed a theory of individual and organizational learning that sets the standard for depth of insight and focus on action. He is author of thirty books and three hundred articles.

Philippe Baumard is Assistant Professor at the University of Paris-XII and Lecturer in Strategic Management at the École des Hautes Études Commerciales (HEC). He holds an MSc in economics (University of Aix-en-Provence) and a PhD in management (University of Paris-Dauphine), and has published three books about knowledge and competitiveness and is currently publishing a fourth. Philippe was a Visiting Scholar with New York University (1993–1994).

Michael Beer is Professor of Business Administration at the Harvard Business School, where his research and teaching have been in the areas of organization effectiveness, human resource management, and organization change. He received a PhD in organizational psychology and business from Ohio State University. Prior to joining the Harvard faculty, Mike was Director of Organization Research and Development at Corning Glass Works. Mike Beer has authored or co-authored several books and many articles.

E. Ralph Biggadike is Vice-President of Strategic Management at Becton Dickinson and Company. Formerly, he was Group President in charge of the company's drug delivery business. Prior to joining Becton Dickinson, he was Paul M. Hammaker Professor at the Darden Graduate School of Business Administration, University of Virginia, where he headed the Business Policy and Political Economy area.

Claudio Ciborra is Professor and Head of MIS and Organization Department at Theseus Institute and Associate Professor of Information Systems and Economics at the University of Bologna, School of Political Sciences.

He received his degree in engineering at the Politecnico of Milan. He has been Visiting Professor at the University of Aarhus and NYU Stern School of Business Administration.

David Collis is an Associate Professor in the Business, Government and Competition area at the Harvard Graduate School of Business Administration. He is an expert on global competition and corporate strategy. His work has recently been published in the *Harvard Business Review, Strategic Management Journal, European Management Journal*, and in several books. He graduated as a Baker Scholar from Harvard Business School, MBA, and received a PhD in business economics from Harvard University, where he was a Dean's Doctoral Fellow.

Anthony J. DiBella holds a PhD in management from the MIT Sloan School of Management where he is a Visiting Scholar in the Center for Organizational Learning. His applied research and consultation focus on the interplay of culture, change and learning in organizations. Dr DiBella has conducted fieldwork worldwide and consulted for many companies, including AT&T, EDF, Exxon Chemical, and Fiat.

Amy Edmondson is an Assistant Professor in the Technology and Operations Management group at the Harvard Business School. She received her PhD in Organizational Behavior from Harvard University. Her current research explores organizational learning and work team effectiveness, and she has published both empirical and theoretical articles in scholarly journals. Previously she was Chief Engineer to the late architect and inventor, Buckminster Fuller, and author of a book about Fuller's mathematical ideas, entitled *A Fuller Explanation: The Synergetic Geometry of Buckminster Fuller*.

Russell A. Eisenstat is an independent consultant specializing in the mnanagement of large scale organizational change and innovation, strategic human resource management and strategy implementation. His prior work experience includes six years on the faculty of the Harvard Graduate School of Business Administration. Dr Eisenstat received his PhD in organizational psychology from Yale University, and his BA from Harvard University.

Janet M. Gould is Director of the Organizations as Learning Systems Project at the MIT Center for Organizational Learning and co-founder of GKA Associates, an INC 500 consulting company. Her research focuses on managers' understanding of complex systems and the transfer of learning. Ms Gould is an Associate Editor of *Systems Dynamics Review* and a Vice-President for the Systems Dynamic Society.

Bertrand Moingeon is an Associate Professor in the Strategic Management Department at the HEC Graduate School of Management – Paris. He received a postgraduate diploma in strategy and management (HEC Doctoral Program), a PhD in sociology from Besançon University, and a postdoctoral diploma in management (Aix-Marseille University). He is the author of several publications in the area of socio-economics, strategic management and organizational learning. In 1994, he was a Visiting Research Scholar at the Harvard Business School.

Ashish Nanda is an Assistant Professor at the Harvard Business School. He teaches courses in general management, administrative theory and joint ventures. He received a BTech in electrical engineering from the Indian Institute of Technology and a postgraduate diploma in management from the Indian Institute of Management. He was awarded a PhD in business economics from Harvard University in 1993. He has written numerous monographs, articles, case studies and teaching notes at Harvard.

Edwin C. Nevis recently retired from the MIT Sloan School of Management, where he was a faculty member in the Organization Studies Group, Director of the Program for Senior Executives, and a member of the Center for Organizational Learning. He has also practiced organizational consulting for forty years. His newest book, published in April 1996, is entitled *Intentional Revolutions: A Seven-Point Strategy for Transforming Organizations*.

James A. Phills Jr is an Assistant Professor at Yale University's School of Management, and received the Yale Alumni Association Award for excellence in teaching in 1995. His research focuses on strategic change and organizational learning. Phills received his PhD in organizational behavior from Harvard University. He has consulted to a wide array of organizations for over ten years and has written extensively about the consulting process and the development of client–consultant relationships.

J. Douglas Orton is an Assistant Professor in the Strategic Management Department at the HEC Graduate School of Management – Paris. His 1994 dissertation at the University of Michigan was an analysis of reorganization decision processes in the 1976 reorganization of the US intelligence community. At HEC he teaches courses in strategy, strategic redesign and organization theory, and recently received a grant from the HEC Foundation to study the 1996 reorganization of US intelligence.

J.-C. Spender is Professor of Strategy, Chair of Enterprise and Small Business and the Director of the Rutgers Center for International Business Education and Research. He studied engineering at Oxford, worked in the nuclear engineering and computer fields before doing his PhD in strategy at Manchester (UK). He has taught on four continents and has published three books.

Prologue:
Toward a Comprehensive Theory of Management

Chris Argyris

There are two requirements that I believe are important to make further progress in managerial theory and practice. The first is a greater emphasis on integrating the managerial functional disciplines into a coherent, actionable whole of managerial governance. The second trend is incorporating into the more comprehensive theory knowledge about causes of barriers to the implementation of such a theory and how to overcome them. The chapters in this volume provide many important insights in how to make progress in both of these requirements.

The Features of a Comprehensive Theory of Management

In order to indicate how the integration of the various managerial functional disciplines can be achieved, we begin by stipulating the basic features of managerial theory.

First, all management theories are about taking action to achieve goals, objectives, or intended consequences. This volume focuses on such goals, especially producing competitive advantage. A major claim is that organizational learning is key to achieving these goals.

Organizational learning is important because no managerial theory, no matter how comprehensive, is likely to cover the complexity of the context in which the implementation is occurring. There will always be gaps and there will always be gap-filling. Organizational learning is critical to detecting and filling the gaps.

Second, all managerial theories are normative because the ultimate goals they are intended to satisfy and the values upon which action is based are choices made by human beings. At the core of all managerial theories is the concept of effectiveness. Effectiveness is accomplishing the goals or objectives in ways that they persist and do not destroy the present level of effectiveness.

Third, all managerial theories contain propositions describing causally what is required to produce the intended consequences. All theories that are based on causal explanations must also contain rules to test the validity of the causal claims.

Fourth, all managerial theories about action should be testable in the world of action which they claim to understand and explain. Moreover, the processes of testing should be so explicit and user-friendly that practitioners should be able to use them in everyday practice. Managerial theories that claim to understand causality and to generate predictions useful in the world of practice, must contain testing procedures that are producible under the conditions of everyday practice.

Fifth, managerial theories are designs about effective action. At the outset, the designs are espoused theories of action. That is, they contain propositions of the form, 'if you behave A then B is likely to follow, given certain defined conditions'.

The creators of these espoused theories strive to make the propositions so clear that anyone educated in the concepts will be able to produce them. For example, the theory of activity-based costing specifies the actions to be taken in order to identify cost drivers. This is an espoused theory because it is a design for action not yet implemented in an actual situation.

All creators of managerial functional disciplines strive to define their espoused theories so that they work as advertised. For example, if an individual follows the specification of how to identify cost drivers, the cost drivers will be identified. The specifications are so explicit that if two individuals use the same numbers, arrive at different conclusions about the cost drivers, an error has been created. It is possible to trace backwards the steps taken to identify where the error was made.

Sixth, the aspiration is to define the espoused theories rigorously enough so that individuals can produce the results with a low likelihood that the espoused theories (that is, their specifications) are wrong. This feature may be defined as internal validity. The validity is internal in the sense that it represents a test of the causal claims embedded in the theory of activity-based costing.

Seventh, theories of managerial functional disciplines also contain claims about the relevance of its idea to consequences that matter such as contribution to profit. In the case of activity-based costing, the external validity of the theory can be tested by observing if the reduction of costs does lead to predicted consequences such as contribution to profit.

Eighth, put simply, internal and external validity are about making sure that we are not blindly kidding ourselves or others. This concern is as salient for the creators as well as the users of the theories.

Producing internal and external validity requires a particular type of reasoning. I call it productive reasoning. Productive reasoning specifies the premises, the inferences that can be made from the premises, and the conclusion that can be derived. These specifications are necessary because they are the foundation for thought and action. Productive reasoning therefore requires that the users make their premises explicit. The inferences made from the premises should also be explicit. The conclusions arrived at should be crafted in ways that the claims made are testable preferably as rigorously as possible. For example, the tests should allow for falsification or disconfirmation, not simply confirmation (Popper, 1959).

Integrating Functional Theories of Action

In order to accomplish integration, we must first identify the concepts to be integrated. But, in order to identify them we must understand them. This is usually a simple task if one remains within one's own discipline. I, as an organizational theorist, find it very difficult to identify the correct concepts from fields such as accounting, finance, and so on. What makes the task even more difficult for individuals like myself is the fact that in most functional fields there may be several different concepts purporting to be relevant to the same empirical phenomena. In order to help me to choose I must understand the ways in which these concepts are used in their respective domains. I must also understand the history of the use of these concepts. Most of the chapters in this volume provide such information and indicate how the concepts may be organized into a more comprehensive theory of management.

The Implementation of Newly Integrated Theories of Action

Integration will take time. It will be incremental because it will be driven by lessons learned as we try to use the theories. One set of lessons has to do with what is required to fulfill the criteria of internal and external validity described above.

There is another set of lessons that is relevant to implementation. The world of practice, I believe, is full of examples where clients agree with the recommendation of studies that they have commissioned, yet they do not implement them effectively. The cause of the lack of effective implementation has less to do with the internal and external validity of the analysis. It has more to do with the fact that those who are to implement the findings, find doing so, for a whole set of reasons, embarrassing and threatening (Argyris and Kaplan, 1994).

The commonly accepted answer to this problem is to involve the client early in the design. One meaning of involvement is to generate, through joint participation, a sense of commitment for the implementation of the recommendations. Unfortunately, in too many cases this means genuine participation until one engages individual, group, or organizational defensive routines. Involvement now takes on an additional meaning, namely, that of bypassing the defensiveness and covering up the bypass. This not only inhibits effective implementation, it also reinforces the existing defenses.

In order for progress to be made in implementing the new, more comprehensive theory of management, we require that it contain a body of propositions about how to deal with defensiveness effectively at all levels of the organization.

Behavioral Theories of Action

It is time to introduce a distinction. The basis of the managerial functional disciplines is their objectives and their propositions about how to achieve them. For example, individuals trained in activity-based costing will know how to discover cost drivers. The ideas, rules and procedures that they use come from the technical theory of action called activity-based cost accounting.

I call such theories technical because their underlying intellectual architecture is in the service of objectives and values that are embedded in technical theories of management. Finance, marketing, operations and strategy are other examples of technical theories.

Another feature of such technical theories is that the major role they require of human beings is to act consistently with the technical imperatives embedded in them. Human beings can accomplish this requirement by knowing technical theories and procedures. Technical theories, in other words, do not require human involvement beyond that needed to make them 'implementation clones' of the theory.

There is very little attention paid by the creators of technical theories to the problem of barriers to implementation, especially when everyone involved accepts the recommendations developed from the technical analysis as valid. I am aware of two exceptions. One is the work of Professor Michael Jensen in his economic-financial theory of governance. He has introduced the concept of Pain Avoidance as part of the intellectual structure of his theory in order to explain such phenomena as defenses. Professor Robert Kaplan has taken on the task of dealing with defenses by making the concept of organizational defenses a part of implementing the technical theory of activity-based costing. Many of the chapters in this volume provide further illustration.

The moment that implementation of any technical theory requires actions that go beyond the required routines of that theory because of embarrassment or threat, the greater the likelihood that individuals will activate their personal theories of action about how to deal with embarrassment or threat. I call these behavioral theories of action because they are based upon theories of human intention, learning and action.

These theories of action differ from the technical theories of action described above in several ways. First, they require the use of defensive reasoning. Individuals are advised to keep their premises tacit and to make their inferences tacit. More importantly, they craft conclusions that are not easily testable by logic independent of that which they used to create the conclusions. The testing is often self-referential and self-sealing.

Second, it is not possible to correct error by tracing backwards to identify the point of deviancy. The reason is that each actor believes that his or her theory of action is correct. If there are differences, they are based on different views of reality and different values.

Third, there are discrepancies between the theories of action they espouse and the ones that they use. For example, many individuals espouse the value of productive reasoning and tough tests, yet they use defensive reasoning and soft tests. The defensive reasoning they use helps them to be unaware of the gap between their espoused theories and their theories-in-use. Indeed, it also helps them to be unaware of the defensive program in their heads that keeps them unaware.

The unawareness is caused by the fact that the behavior to deal with embarrassment or threat is learned in early life. Hence the behavior is highly skilled. All skillful activity is so automatic that it is taken for granted. It becomes tacit.

Organizational Defensive Routines

The use of defensive reasoning results not only in skilled unawareness of the gaps between espoused theories and theories-in-use; it also leads to skilled incompetence. Individuals skillfully follow the dictates of their defensive reasoning which leads them to become highly limited learners and to create organizational learning systems that are also highly limited in learning.

Organizational defensive routines are the most powerful learning systems that limit learning at all levels of the organization. Organizational defensive routines are any actions, policies, or practices that prevent the experience of embarrassment or threat, and at the same time prevent discovery and reduce the cause of embarrassment or threat. Organizational defensive routines limit learning; indeed they are often anti-learning.

Learning and its Relationship to Competitive Advantage

Learning occurs when errors are detected and corrected. An error is any mismatch between intention and what actually happens. Learning therefore does not occur when an error is discovered (or a new insight is obtained). Learning occurs when the discovery or insight is followed by action.

There are at least two kinds of learning. Single loop learning occurs when the mismatch is corrected by altering behavior or actions. Double loop learning occurs when the underlying values are changed and then new actions follow. The chapters by Andreu and Ciborra; Beer, Eisenstat and Biggadike; Edmondson and Moingeon; and Phills illustrate the differences between single loop and double loop learning. They also cite many examples of how single loop learning is likely to lead to information processing and dialogue (by individuals, within groups and between groups) that will make it difficult to implement an effective problem solving process as required to produce competitive advantage that persists. In every chapter, the reader will find contributions that indicate limits of single and double loop learning and contributions of new ways to conceptualize features of organizational learning.

The chapter by Collis re-examines some basic economic concepts and suggests ways that they may be redefined in order to be more clearly related to competitive advantage. Nanda's chapter helps to define the steps that would have to be taken for a resource-based view of organizations to become more implementable. Andreu and Ciborra describe how information technology can be used to formulate and implement features of a more comprehensive theory of management.

There are several chapters that make contributions to the behavioral theories of action, especially about organizational learning, and show how they are related to competitive advantage. They are the chapters by Beer, Eisenstat and Biggadike; Orton; Edmondson and Moingeon; DiBella, Nevis and Gould; Phills; and Spender.

In conclusion, I believe that two important requirements for producing effective theories of management are, first, to integrate the existing managerial functional disciplines into a more comprehensive theory that is actionable in everyday practice. This will require some alterations in the internal structure of the theories as well as explicit ways to connect them to each other.

The second requirement is a theory of effective implementation, where the effective use of the technical theories is adequate for effective implementation. This volume of readings is an important contribution to these two challenges.

References

Argyris, Chris and Kaplan, Robert S. (1994) 'Implementing new knowledge: The case of activity-based costing', *Accounting Horizons*, 8(3): 83–105.
Popper, K. (1959) *The Logic of Scientific Discovery*. New York: Basic Books.

Introduction:
Organizational Learning as a Source of Competitive Advantage

Amy Edmondson and Bertrand Moingeon

Organizations facing uncertain, changing, or ambiguous market conditions need to be able to learn. Few managers or organizational scholars would disagree with this statement; however, most are aware of the difficulty of taking action based on this as a prescription. For over a year, the editors of this book have been engaged in a spirited transatlantic dialogue focused on furthering linkages between strategic management and organizational behavior. Bertrand Moingeon is a scholar of sociology and strategic management at Groupe HEC in France and Amy Edmondson is a scholar of social psychology and organizational behavior at Harvard in the United States. Our collaboration began in early 1994 when Moingeon was a visiting professor at Harvard Business School, and since then we have spent many hours teaching each other the latest (and the earliest, or classic) findings in our own areas of interest. Our initial goal for collaborating was to demonstrate with empirical data from some of Edmondson's field research that organizational learning is a source of competitive advantage. However, we soon found that this initial goal pointed to an area of investigation that might occupy us for years, and we identified opportunities to conduct further empirical research on this subject together, as reported in our own chapter in this volume. Thus, despite the inconvenience of being separated by an ocean, our enthusiasm for this ongoing dialogue shows no signs of waning. We continue to seek examples and to develop arguments to understand and show how learning processes can provide competitive advantage for organizations.

The editors' collaboration is almost incidental in terms of the timing of this book. The two streams of research that we represent appear to be on a (mutually productive, in our view) collision course, hardly needing our facilitation. In this introduction, we provide some context to show how two streams of research are coming together – each encroaching upon territory previously claimed by the other field – in ways that we believe will be of interest to scholars and practitioners working in the areas of organization theory and management.

Developing a Comprehensive Theory of Management

In the prologue, Chris Argyris proposes that developing a *comprehensive theory of management* requires integration between technical theories in management and the behavioral theories that delineate barriers to their implementation. As he notes, the contributors to this volume – coming from both strategy and from organizational behavior – have begun to forge such an integration. In this introduction, we describe how the field of strategic management is shifting to embrace a dynamic view that calls attention to issues of learning. We also note that many organizational learning and organizational development (OD) theorists are increasingly paying attention to technical disciplines such as strategic management. As described in the next section, in the field of strategy, a new emphasis on organizational capabilities raises the question of how to develop them. Similarly, in OD, a new awareness of the limitations of ignoring substantive business issues has led to an interest in integration. However, in both fields, these shifts have led very few researchers to alter their approaches substantially enough to use many tools and definitions from other disciplines. The strategy literature stops short of examining actual learning processes, and the organization development literature contains few examples of collaboration or integration across research traditions (Edmondson, 1996).

This book represents a step toward such integration. Its aim is to bring together perspectives from two streams of management research – strategy and organizational learning and development. Ten original chapters, both theoretical and empirical, have been contributed by seventeen authors from the two fields. Each of the chapters lives at or near the boundary between these fields, and each thereby makes a contribution toward building what Argyris has called a comprehensive theory of management.

To develop management theory that is more comprehensive – or less fragmented by disciplinary boundaries – we first must engage in cross-disciplinary dialog to become familiar with other perspectives. This strategy is based on the premise that different theoretical approaches can each provide a valuable lens through which to view an organization, and that by using multiple lenses a more complete understanding of organizational phenomena will be achieved. In this view, describing the 'elephant' of an organization's behavior requires more than one lens (Adams, 1994; Waldo, 1961). Ultimately, out of such dialogue, a new or meta-theory may be constructed (such as a comprehensive theory of management, as Argyris suggests), that weaves other theories together to specify a set of propositions that are all integral components of producing organizational effectiveness. Thus, as an initial step toward strengthening relationships between strategy and OD, this book presents a multiple-lens view of organizational phenomena related to achieving competitive advantage through learning processes. To provide a context for these different lenses, the next section describes current changes in strategy, followed by a description of similar shifts in OD.

Strategic Management: An Emerging Dynamic View

The aim of strategy theorists is to explain sustained superior performance, or above average profitability, of companies (Bowman, 1974; McGrath et al., 1995). For years the dominant view – derived from the industrial organization (IO) theory framework – explained superior performance through structural features of industries such as barriers to competition (Porter, 1980). In this view, industry characteristics explain much of the variance in firm performance, and industry analysis is the means by which managers can attempt to improve their company's competitive advantage. Nanda, in Chapter 5, describes this emphasis on the external environment at the expense of a firm's internal activities as a persistent 'bias' in the strategy field.

An alternative view proposes that firm-specific resources and competencies are critical factors enabling firms to achieve superior performance in the market. This perspective can be traced back to Selznick (1957) who proposed that organizations each have 'distinctive competence' that allows them to earn superior profits, and to Penrose (1959) who described the firm as a 'collection of productive resources'. More recently, Wernerfelt (1984) and Barney (1991) have proposed that analysis of a firm's skills and capabilities is of greater strategic value than analysis of its competitive environment. Subsequently, an empirical study found that stable differences across business units accounted for more variance in returns than industry effects (Rumelt, 1991), and a 'resource based view of the firm' began to earn increased attention by strategists. The resource-based view does not represent a pendulum swing to an opposing view, but rather explicitly calls for a dual focus on industry analysis and firm capability (Collis and Montgomery, 1995). In his chapter in this volume, Nanda describes the history and implications of the resource-based view in some detail, and this introduction does not attempt to do the same, but instead focuses on drawing connections to organizational learning.

Two implications of the resource-based view of the firm make it relevant to organizational learning research. First is the recognition that resources encompass both tangible, material assets as well as intangible and tacit assets (Prahalad and Hamel, 1990). Idiosyncratic bundles of knowledge and skill – clearly within the domain of organizational learning (e.g. Huber, 1991) – can be legitimate firm-specific resources. In Chapter 7, Collis formalizes the argument that tacit collective knowledge can be a source of profit or economic rent. Second, as firm-specific resources receive more emphasis, questions of how they can be acquired and developed become increasingly relevant, which is the domain of learning. Thus, as Nanda (in this volume) points out, the resources perspective views firms as learning organizations that improve their capabilities through experience. This is a shift toward a dynamic rather than static view of strategy (McGrath et al., 1995).

How does possessing a capability become a source of competitive advantage? Organizational capabilities are bundles of resources – capital assets, human know-how, and routines – combined in path-dependent ways that make them difficult to unbundle or decipher (see chapters by Nanda and by Collis). Sociologist Pierre Bourdieu proposes that a given capability functions as *capital* in contexts in which it is valued; in other contexts the same capability may not be valued and is thus simply a *feature*, as discussed by Edmondson and Moingeon in Chapter 1. Similarly, Collis (1994) calls attention to the context-dependent nature of capabilities as sources of economic rent. Thus, in strategic terms, a capability may be a source of advantage or else simply be a feature of the organization that possesses it, depending upon whether that capability is valued in the market in which the organization competes. The dynamics of markets are therefore critical, as a given capability may initially be highly valuable in a market but later become commonplace and thus simply a feature. Henry Ford's introduction of mass production into the automotive industry provides a well-known historical example, which illustrates additionally that features fall into two categories; one is essential capabilities such as mass production in the automotive industry, which function as 'the price of entry' – and the other is an activity or resource not directly relevant to an organization's ability to compete in its market.

In the field of strategy, this increasing emphasis on capabilities and learning is not limited to academic journals. A highly successful strategic consulting firm, The Monitor Company – founded over ten years ago to implement Michael Porter's industry analysis framework – has undergone a profound shift in emphasis from a sole focus on technical excellence in strategic analysis to incorporating an organizational learning capability based on the work of Chris Argyris. Monitor consultant Roger Martin (1993) describes the behavioral and cognitive barriers to implementation of technically excellent strategies that led his company to begin to examine how people learn or become willing to embrace new perspectives. Ultimately, working closely with Argyris in an intensive multi-year developmental process, Monitor's senior consultants learned to address their own and their clients' *defensive routines* in a way that helps them and their clients avoid predictable implementation failures. From this investment, the company is developing an integrated consulting practice that combines technical excellence in strategic analysis with a rigorous behavioral practice called *productive reasoning* (Argyris, 1993). In this example, strategy and learning come together in two ways. First, a model of strategic consulting is being expanded to incorporate behavioral tools developed from the organizational learning perspective to provide added value for clients. Second, it illustrates Monitor investing in the development of an organizational capability that can provide competitive advantage for the firm (for additional discussion, see the chapter by Edmondson and

Moingeon). This dual focus runs through this book; several chapters illustrate the integration of behavioral and technical disciplines (such as those by Phills: Chapter 10; Beer, Eisenstat and Biggadike: Chapter 8; and Andreu and Ciborra: Chapter 6); others examine tacit knowledge or learning processes as sources of competitive advantage (such as those by Collis: Chapter 7; Spender: Chapter 3; and Baumard: Chapter 4).

As alluded to above, the line separating strategic approaches is blurred, and *static* versus *dynamic* is not a clear-cut distinction. For instance, the capability of analysing industry forces and generating new insights provides one of the ways a firm can achieve competitive advantage (Collis, 1994). Diagnosis can be an organizational capability, and thus *process* (learning to analyse) and *framework* (Porter's five forces) coexist in the resource-based view. In sum, questions of how to manage the development of new capabilities are becoming increasingly relevant to strategy research as knowledge and capabilities are recognized as potential sources of competitive advantage. However strategy researchers have stopped short of focusing directly on learning processes and how to encourage them. Thus, we turn to research in organizational learning and development to explore these issues.

Organizational Learning: Toward an Integrative Approach

Recently, both academic and popular management writings have emphasized people and knowledge as determinants of organizational competitiveness. Pfeffer (1994) argues that effective management of people – including developing and empowering people, sharing information, creating self-managed teams, training and cross-training people – is a more important determinant of competitive advantage than industry analysis and structure. CEO Ray Stata (1989) describes employee learning as critical to Analog Devices' success, and Senge (1990) drew widespread attention to the notion of *the learning organization* in his management bestseller *The Fifth Discipline*. As part of this trend, organizational development (OD) consultants are widespread in companies, as are discussions of such intangibles as excellence, vision and corporate culture (e.g. Deal and Kennedy, 1982; Peters and Waterman, 1982). Much of the focus of OD has been on inspiring commitment and participation by people throughout the organization.

Despite the increased awareness and legitimacy of behavioral issues, OD practices have been thwarted by organizational resistance to change, and by other sources of ineffectiveness. Beer, Eisenstat and Biggadike (in this volume) describe traditional OD as being plagued by a weakness of remaining too focused on behavior and thus disconnected from substantive issues of business strategy. They argue that OD methods fail in part due to management resistance to naive prescriptions for openness, participation and teamwork across all situations regardless of task or strategy, and in part due to a focus on interpersonal behavior without sufficient connection to strategy, customer and task as driving forces for change. Other scholars have criticized OD approaches as being too focused on motivation and self-actualization (for instance, Perrow, 1986) and as ignoring how organizations function as systems (Blake and Mouton, 1988).

In recent popular management literature, learning is presented as a source of competitive advantage (e.g. Redding and Catalenello, 1994; Senge, 1990; Stata, 1989), but definitions and mechanisms involved in achieving this advantage are not specified. Moreover, little empirical evidence has been presented to support this claim. Meanwhile, recent research in the strategy field has shown, for example, that tacit, behavioral features of total quality management (TQM) programs such as executive commitment and employee empowerment are associated with superior firm profitability, while the technical features of TQM such as quality training and benchmarking do not seem to produce competitive advantage (Powell, 1995). Other strategy research has shown that firm identity and culture can limit the effectiveness of new strategic initiatives such as firm mergers (Moingeon and Ramanantsoa, 1995). One of the aims of this volume is to promote active sharing of definitions and research questions across management disciplines, to support further integrative research; more will be said about this below.

There is preliminary evidence that integrating technical and behavioral theories is both possible and worthwhile. Argyris and Kaplan (1994) have collaborated across the disciplines of organizational behavior and accounting to explore the implementation of *activity-based cost accounting* in the face of organizational *defensive routines*. And, a recent study of organizational learning at Monitor illustrates how technical expertise alone is insufficient to produce desired organizational outcomes; new behaviors and skills must be learned to supplement the organization's competency in strategy consulting (Argyris, 1993). Similarly, Andreu and Ciborra (in this volume) explore organizational resources and competencies in information technology as outcomes of learning processes.

Overview of the Book

The first part – Learning Processes and Competitive Advantage – examines organizational learning processes and tacit knowledge as potential sources of competitive advantage. Edmondson and Moingeon (Chapter 1) propose that different kinds of learning processes are appropriate in different environments, and DiBella, Nevis and Gould (Chapter 2) show in a multi-company empirical study that organizations differ from one another based on the kinds of learning processes they employ. Spender (Chapter 3) explicates how tacit knowledge can function as a source of competitive advantage, and Baumard (Chapter 4) conducts case study research to elucidate some of the mechanisms by which this occurs.

The second part – Organizational Learning and Strategic Capability – examines the resource-based view of the firm in some detail. Nanda (Chapter 5) provides a thoughtful review of definitions and terms, and describes the importance of the resource-based view for current strategic thinking. Andreu and Ciborra (Chapter 6) show, through a study of information technologies, that capabilities and competencies are outcomes of learning processes, and are sustained by the organization's structure. Thirdly, Collis (Chapter 7) presents a formal economic argument that learning and tacit knowledge can provide economic rent or profit for firms. The shift toward a learning perspective is evident in each of these three chapters.

The final part – Strategic Change and Organizational Learning – focuses on implementing new strategies. The chapter by Beer, Eisenstat and Biggadike (Chapter 8) presents an innovative systems-based intervention methodology designed to enhance organizational learning and strategic change; it is a process designed to help executives align the corporate strategy with organizational structure. Orton (Chapter 9) operationalizes many of Weick's (1979) process categories, and explores the implications of a process view for managers and scholars interested in reorganizing and restructuring organizations. Finally, Phills (Chapter 10) explicates four cognitive processes in which strategy consultants engage as part of their efforts to help clients. Each of the three parts of the book includes a short introduction to provide further description of the papers and the relationships between them.

Conclusion

This book is a first step in promoting interdisciplinary thought and research aimed at understanding the role of organizational learning in achieving competitive advantage. The concept of organizational learning has received growing attention as a source of competitiveness in both academic and popular management literatures over the past few years. Meanwhile, assessment of competitive advantage traditionally has belonged to scholars and practitioners in the field of strategy. The purpose of this volume is to focus explicitly on the link between these constructs by presenting a variety of papers by scholars whose work bridges the two areas of research. Finally, given the preliminary nature of this endeavor, this book presents a variety of perspectives, often with very different views, research methods and styles. Some chapters are theoretical, some are empirical; some present formal academic arguments, others embrace a more informal accessible style. We hope that its diversity will allow *Organizational Learning and Competitive Advantage* to appeal to a range of readers, and that it will inspire further work in this promising new area of inquiry.

References

Adams, G.B. (1994) 'Blindsided by the elephant', *Public Administration Review*, 54(1): 77–83.

Argyris, C. (1993) *Knowledge for Action: A Guide to Overcoming Barriers to Organizational Change*. San Francisco, CA: Jossey-Bass.

Argyris, C. and Kaplan, R. (1994) 'Implementing new knowledge: The case of activity-based costing', *Accounting Horizons*, 8(3): 83–105.

Barney, J.B. (1991) 'Firm resources and sustained competitive advantage', *Journal of Management*, 17(1): 99–120.

Blake, R.R. and Mouton, J.S. (1988) 'Comparing strategies for incremental and transformational change', in R.H. Kilmann, T.J. Covin et al. (eds), *Corporate Transformation*. San Francisco, CA: Jossey-Bass.

Bowman, E.H. (1974) 'Epistemology, corporate strategy and academe', *Sloan Management Review*, 15: 35–50.

Collis, D. (1994) 'Research note: How valuable are organizational capabilities?', *Strategic Management Journal*, 15: 143–152.

Collis, D. and Montgomery, C. (1995) 'Competing on resources: Strategy in the 1990s', *Harvard Business Review*, July–August: 118–128.

Deal, T.E. and Kennedy, A.A. (1982) *Corporate Cultures: The Rites and Rituals of Corporate Life*. Reading, MA: Addison-Wesley.

Edmondson, A. (1996) 'Three faces of Eden: The persistence of competing theories and multiple diagnoses in organizational intervention research', *Human Relations*, 49(5): 571–595.

Huber, G. (1991) 'Organizational learning: The contributing processes and a review of the literature', *Organization Science*, 2(1): 88–115.

McGrath, R.G., MacMillan, I.C. and Venkataraman, S. (1995) 'Defining and developing competence: A strategic process paradigm', *Strategic Management Journal*, 16: 251–275.

Martin, R. (1993) 'Changing the mind of the corporation', *Harvard Business Review* Nov.–Dec.

Moingeon, B. and Ramanantsoa, B. (1995) 'An identity study of firm mergers: The case of a French savings bank', in H.E. Klein (eds), *Case Method Research and Application*. Needham, MA: WACRA. pp. 253–260.

Penrose, E.T. (1959) *The Theory of the Growth of the Firm*. White Plains, NY: M.E. Sharpe.

Perrow, C. (1986) *Complex Organizations: A Critical Essay*, 3rd edn. New York: Random House.

Peters, T.J. and Waterman, R.H. (1982) *In Search of Excellence: Lessons from America's Best Run Companies*. New York: Warner Brothers.

Pfeffer, J. (1994) *Competitive Advantage Through People*. Boston, MA: Harvard Business School Press.

Porter, M.E. (1980) *Competitive Strategy: Techniques for Analyzing Industries and Competitors*. New York: Free Press.

Powell, T.C. (1995) 'Total quality management as competitive advantage: A review and empirical study', *Strategic Management Journal*, 16(1): 15–37.

Prahalad, C.K. and Hamel, G. (1990) 'The core competence of the corporation', *Harvard Business Review*, May–June (68): 79–91.

Redding, J.C. and Catalenello, R.F. (1994) *Strategic Readiness: The Making of the Learning Organization*. San Francisco, CA: Jossey-Bass.

Rumelt, R.P. (1991) 'How much does industry matter?', *Strategic Management Journal*, 12(3): 167–185.

Selznick, P. (1957) *Leadership and Administration*. New York: Harper and Row.

Senge, P. (1990) *The Fifth Discipline: The Art and Practice of the Learning Organization*. New York: Doubleday.

Stata, R. (1989) 'Organizational learning: The key to management innovation', *Sloan Management Review*, 12(1): 63–74.

Waldo, D. (1961) 'Organization theory: An elephantine problem', *Public Administration Review*, 21 (Autumn): 210–225.

Weick, K. 1979 *The Social Psychology of Organizing*. New York: Random House.

Wernerfelt, B. (1984) 'A resource-based view of the firm', *Strategic Management Journal*, 5(2): 171–180.

Part 1

LEARNING PROCESSES AND COMPETITIVE ADVANTAGE

Scholars, consultants and managers who advocate organizational learning as a source of competitive advantage confront a notable lack of empirical data to support their case. The four chapters in this part are thus of particular interest, as each presents some empirical evidence to support the argument that learning processes can provide competitive advantage for a range of different kinds of organizations. Three of the chapters present new data from the authors' current field research efforts, and one (the chapter by Spender) reviews previously published research to shed new light on the way different types of knowledge are put to strategic use in organizations.

In the first chapter, Edmondson and Moingeon review the range of existing perspectives on organizational learning, and propose a clarification of terms to facilitate further discussion of learning and strategic advantage. They also distinguish between 'learning how' and 'learning why', and maintain that in some market environments, *learning how* is needed, while in others, *learning why* is more appropriate. Examples of both types of learning processes are used to illustrate ways in which learning how and learning why each can generate advantage in different corporate settings. Similarly, the chapter by DiBella, Gould and Nevis proposes that organizations have different learning styles, and that these can be modified to fit the demands of different market environments. These authors identify five distinct organizational learning styles based on extensive field research in four international corporations, as described in this chapter.

Learning can generate more than one kind of knowledge. The third chapter presents a careful analysis of the types of *tacit knowledge* in organizations. Spender reviews different ways of classifying knowledge and considers recent evidence of different ways of knowing. He maintains that there are three types of tacit knowledge, each with different strategic implications. The experience of an organization called EMI with CT scanning is re-examined to illustrate the interplay between these different types of knowledge. In the final chapter, Baumard builds on Spender's typology to understand how organizations use tacit knowledge to deal with ambiguity. Brief case studies illustrate how tacit knowledge provided a tangible source of advantage for two very different organizations.

1

When to Learn How and When to Learn Why:
Appropriate Organizational Learning Processes as a Source of Competitive Advantage

Amy Edmondson and Bertrand Moingeon

Scholars and practitioners have pursued the elusive phenomenon of organizational learning for a number of years (for instance, Argyris, 1982; Hayes et al., 1988; Huber, 1991; Jones and Hendry, 1992; Levitt and March, 1988; Schein, 1993b; Senge, 1990; Stata, 1989). In a world characterized by rapid change and ambiguous signals, the ability of organizations to decipher the environment and to respond accordingly is of considerable theoretical and practical interest. Many researchers, including those referenced above, have made significant contributions to understanding these processes. However, the term itself, which dates back at least as far as March and Simon's (1958) *Organizations*, is the only point of broad agreement. Organizational learning is presented in the literature as occurring at different levels of analysis – from individuals (Argyris, 1982) to organizations (Levitt and March, 1988) – and as applying to such disparate processes as diffusion of information within an organization (Huber, 1991), individual interpretive processes and interpersonal communication (Argyris and Schön, 1978; Daft and Weick, 1984; Weick, 1979), and the encoding of routines in an organization (Cyert and March, 1963; Levitt and March, 1988; Nelson and Winter, 1982). In some conceptions, organizational learning is prescriptive and thus viewed as manipulable (for example, Argyris, 1993; Hayes et al., 1988; Senge, 1990) and elsewhere is the basis of descriptive theory, documenting factors influencing or impeding organizational adaptation (see Huber, 1991; Levitt and March, 1988).

Given the variety of definitions of organizational learning and the different processes described in this literature, skepticism must accompany the simple proposition, 'organizational learning is a source of competitive advantage'. In this chapter, we review existing ideas about organizational learning, including contributions from both academic and business authors, and present a new framework with which to think about empirical research and managerial practice. We propose that different types of learning identified in the literature are appropriate in different situations, and therefore that timing and choice may be critical elements of gaining advantage from organizational learning processes.

The first part of the chapter organizes different approaches to organizational learning into four categories. Themes that run through these approaches are then highlighted, and a new framework, which attempts to sharpen an existing distinction between different levels of learning, is proposed. The focus of the last part of the chapter is on describing and operationalizing 'learning how' and 'learning why', toward developing the utility of these different processes for different organizational settings. Two brief case studies are used to illustrate the framework.

A Fragmented Construct

Defining Organizational Learning

Several theorists have noted that the organizational learning literature is fragmented, consisting of multiple constructs and little cross-fertilization among pockets of scholars (see Fiol and Lyles, 1985; Huber, 1991; Shrivastava, 1983). The following review will not avoid re-emphasizing this point; however, observations also will be made about common themes across the different treatments. Definitions of organizational learning found in the literature include: encoding and modifying routines, acquiring knowledge useful to the organization, increasing the organizational capacity to take productive action, interpretation and sense-making, developing knowledge about action–outcome relationships, and detection and correction of error. In this array of definitions, some primarily involve individual human actors, while others take place at the organizational level of analysis. Some are the basis of intervention models, while others are components of descriptive theory.

Thus, primary unit of analysis provides one critical distinction in the organizational learning literature; research objective provides another. Some researchers study how *organizations* learn – that is, how these social systems adapt, or change, or process incoming stimuli; these outcomes are typically functions of individual cognitive properties or of organization policies or structures. Other researchers primarily examine how *individuals* learn – that is, how individuals embedded in organizations develop, adapt, or update cognitive models. Although they study organizations, the starting point for their analysis of organizational phenomena is individuals. At the same time, some of each of the above groups primarily attempt to describe factors influencing these adaptive processes, or to document phenomena such as dilemmas or sources of gain. The desired research product, in this case, is a precise description and/or a robust model of causality. Others undertake research primarily aimed at improving organizations. Their research objective is to identify managerial actions to improve organizational effectiveness. A two-by-two matrix depicts the resulting categories of learning phenomena (see Figure 1.1). These are: (1) organizations as embodiments of past learning; (2) individual learning and development in organizations; (3) organizations increasing their capacity for change through active, intelligent participation, and (4) individuals gaining awareness of personal causal responsibility and developing inter-personal skill (see Figure 1.2). Theorists in the first two categories tend to describe how organizations or individuals learn whatever it is they learn, while those in the latter two view learning as something to be encouraged or initiated.

Organizations as Embodiments of Past Learning

Descriptive research at the organization level of analysis includes approaches stemming from behavioral theories of the firm and from theories of social construction. Thus a range of phenomena, from the role of routines to the role of interpretive processes in shaping organizations, are described as organizational learning.

Routines   Learning processes such as imitation and trial and error have been viewed as explaining existing behavior in organizations. In contrast to normative approaches, learning is viewed here as a faulty mechanism that leaves organizations dominated by routines – in which 'action stems from a logic of appropriateness or legitimacy, more than from a logic of con-sequentiality or intention' (Levitt and March, 1988: 320). Organizational actors are more habit driven and imitative than rational. Behavior in organizations is thus highly dependent upon and structured by routines (Cyert and March, 1963; Nelson and Winter, 1982). Learning, in this view, is the accumulated residue of past inferences, which are encoded into routines; the focus is on how these routines are formed and how they change. How routines are transmitted among actors is viewed as comparat-ively straightforward – occurring through such phenomena as socialization, education, imitation, and professionalization (Levitt and March, 1988), mechanisms similar to those described by institutional theories (Powell and DiMaggio, 1991). Finally, representing an inventory of past learning, routines in organizations can make new learning especially problematic.

This perspective is explicitly based at the organizational level of analysis, focusing on how routines are encoded and selected. A central message is that learning from experience leads to predictable traps; when organiza-tions build up experience in given routines, they become less likely to actively seek better alternatives. These dynamics create built-in barriers to learning at the organizational level, such as 'superstitious learning' and 'competency traps' (Levitt and March, 1988). In superstitious learning, organizational members erroneously believe desired outcomes to be results of well-honed organizational activities. Similarly, a competency trap occurs when accumulated past experience leads an organization to favor the continuity of inferior work processes. In both cases, current paradigms and

The two dimensions

1 Primary unit of analysis, or starting point for analysis: Some researchers study how *organizations* learn (behave, adapt, process stimuli) as a function of inputs such as structures, design, or cognitive properties. Others focus primarily on how *individuals* learn (develop, adapt, acquire knowledge and skills) in organizational settings.

2 Research objective: Some researchers are primarily analytic, attempting to model adaptive processes and/or document dilemmas, traps, or sources of gain. The desired research product is a robust model of causality or precise description. Others undertake research primarily aimed at improving organizations; they seek policies and processes that will enhance organizational effectiveness. The desired product from this kind of research is managerial actions to improve organizational effectiveness.

		PRIMARY UNIT OF ANALYSIS	
		Organization	*Individual*
	Descriptive research	Levitt and March: competency traps. Huber; Cyert and March; Nelson and Winter: routines. Shrivastava: individual learning as poor metaphor for organizational learning. BCG, Epple et al.: learning curves. Weick: organizations as interpretive systems. Daft and Weick; Duncan and Weiss: language and interpretation.	Brown and Duguid: becoming an insider is learning. Pedler et al.: flatter organizations create a tension that elicits new learning and personal development. Pettigrew and Whipp: widespread individual learning is a kind of organization capability. Stata: individual learning makes organization more flexible and responsive.
RESEARCH OBJECTIVE	*Intervention research*	Hayes et al.: institute 'people first' assumptions. Ciborra and Schneider: question formative context to enable organizations to adapt. Schein: culture as learning and as malleable.	Senge: individuals can learn to experience awareness of personal causal responsibility. Isaacs and Senge: simulations that help individuals diagnose causality. Argyris: understand and change individuals' theories in use to promote effectiveness.

Figure 1.1 *A typology of organizational learning literature*

	PRIMARY UNIT OF ANALYSIS	
	Organization	*Individual*
Descriptive research	(1) Organizations as embodiments of past learning	(2) Individual learning and development in organizations
Intervention research	(3) Organizations increasing the capacity for change through active, intelligent participation	(4) Individuals gaining awareness of personal causal responsibility and interpersonal skill

RESEARCH OBJECTIVE

Figure 1.2　*Categories of organizational learning research*

practices have staying power, and sensitivity to indications of the need for change is low. Only exceptionally inappropriate routines are likely to lead to a perceived need for change. This phenomenon is described as a product of organizational characteristics.

Acquiring and distributing knowledge　Several theorists have defined organizational learning as a process by which an organization expands its repertoire of actions. Citing behavioral learning theory, Huber (1991) defines *learning* as a process that enables an entity to increase its range of potential behavior through its processing of information. *Organizational learning* is then defined as occurring when any of an organization's units acquires knowledge that the unit recognizes as potentially useful to the organization – an explicit attempt to avoid 'narrow conceptions' that 'decrease the chances of encountering useful findings or ideas' (Huber, 1991: 89). Because the organization is the potential beneficiary of the knowledge, this learning is organizational. These concepts remain at a high level of abstraction, and lack attention to ways organizational actors can put the new potentially useful knowledge to use.

Learning curves have been studied extensively in manufacturing environments (see Epple et al., 1991). The conventional 'learning curve' indicates that the number of labor hours per unit produced can decrease rapidly with cumulative output. The resulting curve represents an exponential increase in productivity, some of which is attributed to the effects of learning. As discussed by Bruce Anderson of Boston Consulting Group, there is also an experience curve effect in these reductions; that is, other aspects of cumulative production experience such as economies of scale and improved technology also contribute to decreasing costs. However, increased knowledge and skill are important components of such improvements. This learning, which constitutes the refinement of routines (Cohen, 1991), is transferable within and across plants in the same company; it becomes a kind of stored knowledge that is useful to the organization. Recent researchers have proposed ways to enhance learning curves to increase competitive advantage (for example, Hayes et al., 1988, whose work will be revisited below).

Interpretative processes   Organizations are interpretive systems (Daft and Weick, 1984), in constant flux – artificially stabilized through interpretive processes, routines and standard operating procedures. Thus, referring back to psychologists' 'traditional definition of learning', Weick finds learning in organizations rarely able to satisfy its conditions of producing a 'different response' in the 'same situation' (1991: 116). Shrivastava (1983) also finds individual learning a poor metaphor for organizational adaptive processes. Defining organizational learning instead in a 'nontraditional way' favors an information-processing view of learning, in which stimuli are not actual physical events but are interpretations of events (Weick, 1991). Similarly, organizations have been viewed as shared agreements, with a primary organizational activity being sense-making (Duncan and Weiss, 1979).

Individual Learning and Development in Organizations

Some organizational learning theorists examine processes of individual adaptation or development in organizational settings. For example, Brown and Duguid (1991) describe learning as becoming 'an insider' by acquiring tacit or 'noncanonical' knowledge. Although these researchers studied how work groups became communities of learning, it is the individuals who learn, become insiders, and contribute to differences among groups. Ray Stata, CEO of Analog Devices, describes individual learning as a source of competitive advantage for his organization (Stata, 1989). Descriptive theory at the individual level of analysis includes models that specify conditions which elicit employee learning, as well as models that describe beneficial outcomes of an organizations' individuals engaging in learning activities.

Personal and interpersonal development   Flatter organizational structures create a tension that elicits learning and personal development by employees (Pedler et al., 1990). New interpersonal challenges encountered in less hierarchical, more team-based organizations encourage individuals to engage in developing their communication and other interpersonal skills. Organizations can implement activities that develop the knowledge and skills of the individual, creating a kind of institutionalized learning or 'organizational capability' (Pettigrew and Whipp, 1991). Here the learning of its individual actors constitutes an enhanced capability of the organiza-tion. These authors suggest that explicit plans and structured processes contribute to effectiveness, and that individual learning in organizations is relevant in the degree that it does so. However, these studies can be distinguished from intervention research in that, despite explicit concern about effectiveness, they do not focus on how to implement change, nor do they advocate and test actions designed to produce desired changes. In contrast, researchers in the following two sections have embraced this objective.

Organizations Increasing their Capacity for Change through
Intelligent Participation

Intervention research at the organization level of analysis explores questions of how to create organizations that act as flexible and responsive entities. Some researchers advocate human resources or manufacturing policies to improve organizational responsiveness. Others have noted organizational resistance to attempted changes, and proposed mechanisms to surmount that resistance.

Manufacturing experts Hayes et al. (1988) describe the implementation of just-in-time production systems to create learning organizations. Making critical information accessible and transparent by increasing the on-line interdependencies among workers is one element of increasing both the importance and chances of learning by individuals, who thereby contribute to creating learning organizations. Their pragmatic research primarily focuses on technical solutions to the problem of sustaining continuous organizational responsiveness; however, they devote a full chapter to the importance of human resources issues. Institutionalizing 'people first' assumptions, such as 'all employees are responsible, thinking adults who inherently want to do their best', and encouraging local experimentation are described as critical components of creating a learning organization (Hayes et al., 1988: 250). Fostering the participation and learning of all employees is described as essential for sustaining competitive advantage.

A growing number of executives, consultants, and scholars advocate the benefits of organizational learning. The potential for disillusionment among organizational decision makers, however, is great, as they discover that subtle beliefs and structures can sabotage well intentioned change processes. Studying efforts to implement new technologies in organizations, Ciborra and Schneider define organizational learning as 'the process from perception of a bad fit between the existing organizational design . . . and present contingencies to intervention to achieve a better match among the various components of the whole' (1992: 269).

Culture as learning and learning about culture   Schein (1993a) argues that organizational culture is a kind of learning. It is 'a learned product of group experience' and its strength is a function of the convictions of an organization's founders, the stability of the group or organization, and the intensity and nature of past learning experiences (Schein, 1990: 14–15). Secondly, the widely-shared, tacit assumptions which constitute an organization's culture can preclude organizational learning. Beliefs held by founders are extremely powerful, carrying on for years after the founders themselves have ceased to run the company (Schein, 1993a, 1993b). Thus a company's processes and structures reflect and are shaped by cultural assumptions (Schein, 1990), which must be uncovered, examined and often changed, to enable organizational learning.

Three kinds of learning occur naturally in organizations – knowledge acquisition, habit or skill learning and emotional conditioning (such as learned anxiety) (Schein, 1993b). The emotional component contributes to making cultural assumptions based on past mistakes rather than successes extremely difficult to unlearn; organization members can be paralyzed by a fear of making a mistake (Schein, 1993b).

Individuals Developing Interpersonal Skill or Awareness of Personal Causal Responsibility

Some theorists portray organizational learning as a phenomenon in which individuals in organizations develop and refine their cognitive maps – that is, their theories-in-use (Argyris and Schön, 1974) or 'mental models' (Senge, 1990) – and thus become more effective decision makers.

Cognition interacting with organizational complexity   The field of *system dynamics*, pioneered by Jay Forrester (1961) and expanded by his students John Sterman and Peter Senge, explores characteristics of organizations as complex systems, as well as how cognitive features of individuals interact with these characteristics to produce profound learning dilemmas. The dynamic behavior of systems like corporations is difficult to decipher, in part because human cognition is insensitive to the effects of feedback delays and nonlinearities (Sterman, 1989). A central premise of system dynamics is that *structures* determine results in organizations although managers tend to perceive these results as being caused by recent *events*. Thus, learning about the effects of one's actions or decisions in an organization is fraught with difficulty. Feedback is either missed – or misunderstood, as in Levitt and March's superstitious learning.

System dynamicists propose that for organizational learning to occur tools and training are required to facilitate diagnosis of the dynamics of the organizations in which actors find themselves (Isaacs and Senge, 1992). Sterman's work focuses on the cognitive features that lie behind the faulty organization designs observed by Forrester, and he advocates the use of computer models to incorporate more factors than allowed by limited mental models (Sterman, 1988). Senge, whose 1990 bestseller, *The Fifth Discipline*, introduces system dynamics models in accessible terms, emphasizes the role of *awareness of personal causal responsibility* in helping to create and sustain the systems in which we play a part, as a first step in creating a learning organization.

The subtle science of taking action   Learning in organizations is dependent upon being able to transmit relevant information without distortion – to enable high levels of understanding and productive decision making. However, interpersonal competence is generally so low and based on such flawed reasoning that communication about issues that are difficult or threatening rarely occurs without significant distortion (Argyris, 1962, 1982). Chris Argyris demonstrates in study after study that individuals' implicit theories, or 'theories-in-use', lead them to produce outcomes that are exactly contrary to what they hope to produce in interpersonal interactions. Moreover, these theories-in-use systematically preclude learning about ways to escape their counterproductive effects, and ultimately create organizational systems which reinforce anti-learning interpersonal dynamics (Argyris and Schön, 1974; Argyris, 1982). Analogous to competency traps, these are built-in impediments to learning at the micro-level of individual reasoning processes.

Individuals' theories-in-use influence organizational outcomes in the following way. There are two kinds of programs in people's heads; one is the espoused kind – if-then propositions we *think* lie behind our actions – that is, what we tell ourselves and others. The other kind of program is the theory-in-use – the 'if-then propositions an individual *actually* uses when he or she acts' (Argyris, 1982). The dilemma is that individuals, while acting, are unaware of the discrepancy between their *espoused theories* and their *theories-in-use*. The unawareness of this gap is partly due to the fact that we are largely unaware of our theories-in-use, having learned them so early in life. More insidiously, however, specific features of theories-in-use *keep* people unaware of the discrepancy.

Values of rationality, maintaining control, and maximizing winning shape the strategies people use in interpersonal interaction. Called 'Model I' by Argyris and Schön (1974), these strategies involve forming private attributions and evaluations about others and then crafting one's language so as to minimize the defensiveness one expects to be evoked in them. Overall, these strategies reduce sensitivity to feedback and inhibit the production of 'valid knowledge' (Argyris, 1993). Thus, the resulting ineffectiveness in managers' conversation is 'self-sealing'.

Argyris (1982) defines learning as detection and correction of error, and distinguishes between *single loop learning* (detecting mismatches without questioning underlying policies) and *double loop learning*, which *does* involve questioning and changing governing conditions or values. One of the central features of Model I theories-in-use is their reliance on abstractions and evaluations – inferences we have made that can be quite remote from 'directly observable data' but are treated by us as fact. Subsequent behavior is thus handicapped by piling error upon error. Model I is a system of well-learned interpersonal strategies that are not consciously employed, but are nonetheless highly skilled – much like riding a bicycle. Argyris calls this well-learned skillfulness, 'skilled incompetence' – a perplexing oxymoron that begins to suggest causes of intractability in social behavior in organizations.

Individuals using Model I will create Organizational I (O-I) systems, which are characterized by defensiveness, self-fulfilling prophecies, self-fueling processes and escalating error (Argyris, 1982). O-I systems are characterized by imbedded reinforcing dynamics, held in place by defensive reasoning strategies that actors are unaware of using. Thus, inter-dependent features of social systems (governing conditions, action strate-gies and consequences) feed back and reinforce each other and the status quo.

This creates a dilemma. Individuals 'cause' social systems to malfunction by virtue of their theories-in-use – yet at the same time O-I social systems 'cause' individuals to reason and act as they do! It is a vicious cycle of ineffectiveness which Argyris maintains can be altered through a kind of intervention called action science (Argyris et al., 1985). The process is long and requires considerable skill on the part of the interventionist and commitment on the part of the organization. However, as the source of dysfunction is the implicit theories of individuals, there is no way to avoid this investment if the vicious cycle is to be transcended.

Summary

A review of theories of organizational learning reveals considerable diversity. Some theorists describe how organizations learn whatever it is they learn, while others view learning as something that needs to be created. Those who have tackled the issue of usability of their theories and include intervention models in their thinking form a particular subset of the organizational learning literature. We propose that the *learning organization* rubric can be used to distinguish research aimed at creating organiza-tional learning from the larger body of work. This distinction serves to clarify terms for discussing the relationship between competitive advantage and learning processes in organizations. Given the variety of phenomena – both beneficial and detrimental to achieving organizational goals – that have been labeled organizational learning, we found that our own discussions about the effect of 'organizational learning' on 'competitive advantage' were hampered by this ambiguity. We thus re-framed our inquiry, to ask whether and how learning organizations gain competitive advantage, such as from the kinds of learning efforts proposed by the above researchers.

Learning How *and* Learning Why

The existence of different levels of learning is a central issue in intervention theories – that is, those related to creating learning organizations. Ex-amples include single versus double loop learning (Argyris, 1982) and incremental versus second-order learning (Ciborra and Schneider, 1992). Bateson (1972) previously articulated this distinction as Learning I (detect-ing errors, refining processes and selecting among known alternatives) and Learning II (changing the set of available alternatives, re-framing the situation and expanding the realm of activity). In all of these constructs, the lower level involves improving existing behaviors and making progress toward stated goals, while the higher level requires questioning the appropriateness of the goals, and recognizing the subjectivity of meaning. In developing theories for intervention purposes, an awareness of these differences as well as of a need to shift from one level to another to escape the self-sealing nature of frames or contexts, appears to be critical. However, despite these apparent commonalities in discerning two levels of learning, and despite the theoretical precision, operationalizing these different levels introduces some ambiguity. Distinctions between first- and second-order learning are often abstract and difficult to identify in real organizational settings.

We propose that organizational learning processes can be characterized as learning how or learning why, a distinction that is similar to those described above but with an advantage of more colloquial familiarity. These terms are inspired by educational philosopher Olivier Reboul (1980), who described three kinds of learning for individuals – learning that, learning how and learning to understand – but our meanings depart significantly from his. A recent article by Kim (1993) uses the terms operational learning and conceptual learning, which we believe capture the essence of the distinction between learning how and learning why. Our goal here is to elaborate further on this distinction, and to draw connections between these two kinds of learning processes and competitive advantage.

We define *learning how* as organizational members engaging in processes designed to transfer and/or improve existing skills and routines. Learning how involves acquiring a 'recipe' or process, in which a relevant instruction might be 'just tell me how to do it, not why it works'. When learning how, the learner is attentive to feedback, and, within the scope of the given context, develops both skill and valuable information about contingencies. Organizations can develop learning how as a strategic capability, such that they become expert at implementing new processes quickly and with a high degree of consistency throughout a large system. This kind of capability can be applied to and implemented in a variety of new situations. We define *learning why* as organizational members inquiring into causality using diagnostic skills. The objective in learning why is to discern underlying logic or causal factors. Organizations can develop these processes as a strategic capability, such that individual members develop the capacity to diagnose and identify underlying causes in a variety of new situations, including potentially difficult interpersonal situations such as Argyris describes.

These terms are not meant to suggest mutual exclusivity. Individuals engaged in learning why necessarily will incorporate elements of skill acquisition; Argyris's teaching of Model II skills, which are designed to help people diagnose causal factors in problematic interpersonal interaction, illustrates how one can be learning how to use new skills while engaged in an encompassing 'learning why' experience. Similarly, one may be actively inferring reasons for the effectiveness of a specific procedure (hence, diagnosing) while engaged in a process of learning how. Our purpose in identifying the two categories of learning how and learning why is two-fold. First, we want to point out that two distinct kinds of activities are both widely referred to as 'learning', which may cause some confusion in attempting to draw conclusions about outcomes of organizational learning. Second, we want to call attention to – and question – an implicit hierarchy of these two kinds of activities in the organizational learning literature.

Reflecting on the definitions given above, it is tempting to conclude that 'learning why' is better, and indeed much of the organizational learning literature does just that – by focusing on those situations in which problematic barriers cannot be surmounted otherwise. One of the purposes of this chapter is to propose that learning how and learning why are both important, and that each is appropriate in qualitatively different situations. This proposal is based on an observation that not all competitive advantage requires frame-breaking change. There are situations which call for effective mobilization to meet relatively clear criteria for competitiveness, such that by being better, faster, more thorough, or inclusive of more employees, an organization can derive considerable competitive advantage. This is competitive advantage from developing an organizational capability of learning how. In other situations, diagnosing the whole system, or evaluating opportunities to change governing values or contexts, may offer critical opportunities for success, such that learning why serves as a source of competitive advantage. These differences will be explored in the next section.

Another way in which some existing theories may be misleading lies in the implication that moving from learning how to learning why is not only a desirable shift but one that involves leaving mundane learning how processes behind. We propose that learning how and learning why are intertwined and interdependent, such that organizations may benefit from members engaging in both types of processes in an ongoing way, depending on the needs of different situations. In summary, rather than assuming the necessity of learning why and attempting to understand factors influencing its implementation, organizational researchers can step back to ask first when it is necessary.

Re-framing Organizational Learning Research

A general research question emerges from this integrative approach. This can be phrased as: under what conditions is it desirable for organizational actors to become aware of their own framing of a situation, to understand causal factors, and to experiment with a different way of seeing the same situation? Similarly, when is it helpful instead to focus more attention on correcting errors and refining existing processes?

Theoretical context   Structural theories of organizational behavior, such as contingency theories (Lawrence and Lorsch, 1986) or theories of work design and leadership (Hackman and Oldham, 1980; Hackman and Walton, 1986) propose that if the right conditions are put in place, the desired behaviors are more likely to occur. In contrast, cognitive theories, from social construction (see Weick, 1979) to the theory of action (Argyris, 1993), maintain that mental models of individual actors play the pivotal role in influencing organizational outcomes. Therefore, structuralists will focus on processes related to learning how as vital for organizational effectiveness. In this view, a well-designed organizational system is more dependent on its members learning how to do their jobs and actively engaging in self-regulation (both as individuals and as teams) to alleviate errors and deviations. Cognitivists, on the other hand, will require organizational members to learn why, because of the nature of their theories, in which ineffectiveness in organizations is seen as a matter of faulty mental models or self-sealing interpersonal processes. Individuals, in this view, must learn to confront, question, and rethink the frames that they themselves have imposed on reality.

An integrative approach maintains that both bodies of theory have a corner on part of the truth. These different theories may emerge out of experience in different kinds of organizational situations. There are situations in which, if the right structure is in place, participation and fine-tuning are all that is required for the foreseeable future. There are others in which organizations are stuck in interpersonal or business traps they themselves have created, and they must become aware of their active role in doing so before they can become un-stuck. Similarly, there are difficult, face-threatening interpersonal situations in which self-sealing dynamics make progress impossible without double loop learning.

A Strategic Perspective on Organizational Learning

Intangible resources such as organizational knowledge are a particularly viable source of competitive advantage because they can be causally ambiguous and difficult to imitate as Nanda and Collis show in their chapters in this volume. If intangible resources can be put to use to provide competitive advantage, those resources are considered 'strategic' and they constitute a kind of capital as described by Pierre Bourdieu (1993). We view both learning how and learning why as organizational capabilities, each of which involves the application of distinct intangible resources, and each of which can constitute a kind of capital in certain market environments. This means each capability can be a source of competitive advantage, and is then a 'strategic capability'. Learning how involves the application of a set of routines characterized by imitation and error-correction behaviors. It is thus a collective capability to mobilize human resources to new tasks, to replicate processes, and to organize systems and structures for widespread diffusion of routines. Learning how is a capability that resides in the organization and is difficult to imitate because it involves interweaving a complex array of administrative and human skills. Similarly, learning why is the application of a set of routines characterized

by asking questions about contexts and systems. It is a capability characterized by intelligent application of diagnostic tools, and can be similarly
difficult to imitate.

An organizational capability of learning how can facilitate implementing
a new production process, or providing a new service, to produce a
particular outcome valued by the market. The same basic capability thus
can be applied in different situations, for different activities. With changing
customer demands or changing technologies, a capability of learning how
can be applied again and again to different specific content. Similarly, an
organizational capability of learning why can be applied to understanding a
new customer need, or to surmounting behavioral barriers to change, or to
diagnosing a top management team problem, or to designing an innovative
corporate strategy. This is a capability of creating a new model – which
then facilitates taking action.

Illustrations of Competitive Advantage from Learning Capabilities

Operationalizing learning how   Learning how involves processes associated with the transfer and improvement of existing skills and routines.
Programs focused on reducing errors or increasing yields typically require
widespread learning how. Quality improvement activities, in which small
teams are assigned improvement goals also illustrate this construct.
Participants in these learning processes are working within a well-defined
scope of activities, even if facing and achieving ambitious targets. Activities supporting the implementation of new training programs or problem-
solving initiatives throughout an organization also exemplify learning how.
In such designs, a well-honed formula for success is being transferred as
accurately and across as many parts of the organization as possible. The
criteria for the US Government's Malcom Baldrige Award illustrate one
format for structuring such learning processes. An organization that uses
the Baldrige Award's elaborate set of guidelines and checklists for
improving quality as a blueprint for implementing widespread learning
initiatives is engaging in learning how.

An illustration of competitive advantage from learning how   Intel Corporation, a producer of computer components, maintains a leading position in
its industry in both revenues and profits, through a unique set of
organization capabilities. A combination of utilizing scientific expertise to
develop revolutionary technology, managing external relationships to
influence industry standards, and maintaining effective internal coordination has contributed to Intel's phenomenal growth for the past twenty years
(Nanda and Bartlett, 1994). One critical component to achieving exponential growth in revenues was developing the capability to continue to
produce rapidly increasing manufacturing volumes as needed in an expanding market. Both product quality and production yields are critical in the

microprocessor business, posing a particularly acute challenge given the frequent introduction of new generations of technologies.

As described by an Intel manager specializing in installing new fabrication plants, 'the rate of learning is the key to short and long term success of the fab'.[1] And, in reflecting on a decade of change, another Intel manager claims that their manufacturing abilities have evolved from hardly adequate ten years ago to become a source of competitive advantage today – not in terms of low cost, but in terms of speed of reaching full production runs. Intel's manufacturing costs are in fact higher than others in the industry; they have instead focused on bringing new technologies from design engineering to full-scale manufacturing faster than other companies. To do this, Intel developed a process of learning how, called 'Copy Exactly', to transfer new technology from research and development to a new or existing fabrication plant.

Copy Exactly is both a philosophy and a system for training all plant employees – both engineers and technicians – in copying exact procedures, as a way to transfer new technologies from one location to another and to enable the desired increases in production. It is a kind of institutionalized 'forced learning' – a phrase used by one of the managers interviewed – which involves acquiring skills and routines with phenomenal attention to detail. Thus, while other companies may be as advanced technically as Intel, Intel's speed in 'ramping up' production runs for new process and component technologies has allowed them to gain sizable market share in a still expanding market. This success can be traced to many factors, including technological expertise and a willingness to invest aggressively in new plants; however, the ability to bring several thousand employees up to speed in new manufacturing procedures plays a major role.

Intel is the leader in an industry that currently has clear customer preferences and clear rules for success. Both technological excellence and production volume are rewarded. The company has developed a unique set of capabilities for serving these customer needs, and successfully engaged a large number of employees in utilizing these capabilities. Further, they have successfully exploited a window of opportunity, during which the market has been able to absorb as many chips as they can make. We propose that having developed an organizational capability of learning how is a critical component of Intel's competitive advantage. Windows of opportunity, by definition, have limited time spans. The capability of learning how is less useful in situations with unclear criteria for success or fundamental changes in the market environment. In such ambiguous contexts, having the capability to learn why – that is, to diagnose causal factors and taken-for-granted sources of ineffectiveness – becomes critical.

Operationalizing learning why   Learning why is a first step in developing interpersonal competence as Argyris (1985, 1993) describes, which can be a source of competitive advantage in situations that require establishing and maintaining relationships. As discussed above, Argyris maintains that individuals must first become aware of how their own theories-in-use are causing communication problems – and limiting their own and others' abilities to learn – before modifying them to enable more productive interactions. Learning to engage in conversation about difficult or threatening issues without counterproductive dynamics involves extensive training, in which individuals learn to diagnose and change their theories-in-use. Similarly, management teams can engage in dialogue designed to uncover taken-for-granted assumptions (Isaacs, 1993). System dynamicists have initiated learning projects in which teams of managers create models of the dynamics of their organization and in so doing discover that they themselves have been contributing to the problems which they face (Kim, 1993; Senge, 1990). An automotive design team working with researchers at MIT has dramatically improved its design process in part due to learning to diagnose the whole system in which they work. In summary, an organizational capability of 'learning why' can be applied to understanding strategic, structural, or interpersonal problems.

An illustration of competitive advantage from learning why   Argyris describes a long-term research project in which he worked with a strategy consulting firm, Monitor Company, to help develop the inquiry skills of its directors and consultants. According to Argyris (1993) participants in the project increased their capacity for productive inquiry, especially in the diagnosis of interpersonal dynamics, and have been thus able to work through difficult problems with clients, as well as to improve the quality of internal interactions. To learn more about these results, we interviewed directors and consultants at Monitor to gather their observations about the reasons for, and results of, the learning process in which they engaged. Our goal was to understand how enhancing the capability to learn why might give them a competitive advantage over other consulting firms. Two themes emerged from these interviews: improved client relationships and improved efficiency through a reduction of internal interpersonal tensions. The former is a source of differentiation. The latter is a source of increased efficiency and hence cost and/or speed advantage.

One of the directors describes his own and others' enhanced ability to diagnose interpersonal dynamics, in particular to understand causes of dysfunction in interactions with clients. In his view, this capability serves two vital functions. The first is the ability to avoid counterproductive interpersonal interactions which lead clients ultimately to reject sound advice. The second is the ability to actively teach clients to learn why, themselves – that is, to learn to diagnose causal factors in their own business environments. This director was careful to point out that not all clients *value* learning why; some, in fact, are in search of a simple solution – and, in our terminology, want to *learn how* – that is, to implement a recipe. However, the director explains that having this interpersonal diagnostic capability 'allows us to get 'good' clients' – meaning 'CEO-level contacts' and firms facing interesting strategic challenges. Thus, client firms who are themselves interested in pursuing diagnostic capabilities – those who want to 'learn why' – are more likely to select Monitor over other companies. Moreover, the director believes that this capability will be extremely difficult to copy. Monitor has invested more than five years in developing the skills of its consultants, thus creating a lead that will make it difficult for others to catch up. More critically, however, the unique combination of developmental processes in which they have engaged would be difficult for others to discern and hence difficult to copy.

A consultant we interviewed focused on the internal efficiencies Monitor has gained from diagnosing behavioral dynamics and being able to avoid the unproductive internal competition 'that is typical of professional service firms'. 'We are better at working out problems internally because we can diagnose them and figure out ways to avoid them', he explains. This ability to examine 'unproductive frames', that is, to examine causes of interpersonal tension, as well as to experiment with implementing new behaviors, creates sizable savings in consultants' time. As he explains, 'being stuck in behavioral dynamics costs money'. Another director explains that 'several years ago, we found ourselves faced with classic professional-services-firm nastiness, and we decided to try to change it'. Through working with Argyris, 'we learned – and are still learning – how to diagnose and fix these dynamics, which are a significant source of ineffectiveness'.

A third director sheds light on both internal and external sources of advantage. In his view, 'we built this business out of teaching clients how to diagnose their own business issues. This was to be our source of differentiation – but we didn't have the interpersonal competence to implement this strategy. . . . Inept interpersonal styles of some of us high-powered consultants made it impossible for us to gain advantage from the analytical rigor we had on board.' He believes that it is possible to differentiate the firm with a unique combination of technical and behavioral skills, and that 'you can't implement good ideas without both'.

All of those interviewed believe that Monitor has developed a unique ability to cope with complex problems – those which combine intellectual rigor and behavioral dynamics – such as the 'defensive routines' identified by Argyris. Several cited client situations in which Monitor succeeded in maintaining contracts with clients that had rejected several previous consulting firms. In their view, Monitor's ability to diagnose and work to change clients' 'defensive routines' made these productive relationships possible. However, as the first director we interviewed explained, some clients do have 'routine problems', and, for them, *learning why* is not important. For these clients, a consulting approach which tells them what to do and how to do it is appropriate. These clients can 'be given a recipe and use it'. Monitor, in contrast, wants to work with clients who do not yet understand what their problem is, requiring a blend of causal diagnosis, design and action.

A Working Conclusion and Direction for Future Research

For situations in which technical success (including such features as speed, consistency, productivity, quality and product excellence) is the central determinant of market competitiveness, an organizational capability of *learning how* is likely to be an important source of competitive advantage. For situations in which relationship success is the critical determinant of market competitiveness or internal organizational effectiveness, *learning why* will be a source of competitive advantage. In selecting the second case described above, we have focused on learning to understand one's own and others theories-in-use in interpersonal interaction (and thereby learning to avoid the counterproductive, nonlearning dynamics Argyris has identified) as a particular kind of learning why; however, we see developing organization members' diagnostic skills in a more general sense as an important source of advantage in ambiguous and complex market environments. For example, situations requiring creative, frame-breaking solutions to problems also involve the capability of learning why.

Finally, we propose that most organizations can develop both capabilities – learning how *and* learning why – as potential sources of competitive advantage. Learning how is required for the many situations in which speed and quality matter; learning why is required for diagnosis and relationship building. Most organizations face both kinds of situations in an ongoing way. Thus, the meta-source of competitive advantage is knowing when to use which resource. Developing the organizational capability of judicious application of the right 'intangible resource' – whether the behavioral routines of learning how or the behavioral routines of learning why – is one aspect of becoming a learning organization. Thus analyzing when to learn how and when to learn why is itself a capability. To illustrate, in this chapter, we focused on Intel's ability to manufacture successive new generations of computer chips, an example of learning how. However, as these learning how processes are underway, others at Intel Corporation are actively learning why – diagnosing current and future market and technological developments in anticipation of making critical changes. Similarly, as an illustration of learning why, we showed Monitor consultants learning to diagnose and change counterproductive interpersonal dynamics with each other and with clients. Meanwhile, as part of day-to-day operations, others at Monitor are actively learning how; new recruits are being trained in sophisticated techniques of data analysis, as well as learning how to use the company's strategy models. In summary, we propose that at different points in an organization's history, competitive advantage may be more determined by learning how than by learning why, and vice versa, depending on the market environment; however, both capabilities will typically be in use in an organization at any given time, and both are sources of competitive advantage in different environments.

Conclusions

The organizational learning literature encompasses a range of phenomena, some of which involve learning as a source of business effectiveness. In this chapter, we have proposed that 'the learning organization' rubric be used to distinguish these normative approaches from the larger body of work. Second, to facilitate exploring the relationship between organizational learning processes and competitive advantage, we have proposed a new framework, which attempts to clarify a distinction between different kinds of learning processes in organizations. We have defined *learning how* as organizational members engaging in processes to transfer and improve existing skills or routines, and defined *learning why* as organizational members diagnosing causality. We argue that these represent two distinct organizational capabilities, which each can become strategic capabilities in different market environments. Where such factors as cost, quality and productivity are key determinants of market success, learning how is a strategic capability. Where relationship-building and thoughtful analysis matter, learning why becomes a strategic capability. Further empirical research must be undertaken to understand factors influencing the use and development of both of these learning capabilities, as well as to assess the effects of these processes on market success.

Notes

1 This section is based on interviews with manufacturing executives from Intel's computer components divisions, conducted by Amy Edmondson, as part of research with the Center for Organizational Learning at MIT.

References

Argyris, C. (1962) *Interpersonal Competence and Organizational Effectiveness*. Homewood, IL: Dorsey Press.
Argyris, C. (1982) *Reasoning, Learning and Action: Individual and Organizational*. San Francisco, CA: Jossey-Bass.
Argyris, C. (1985) *Strategy, Change and Defensive Routines*. Boston, MA: Pitman.
Argyris, C. (1993) *Knowledge for Action: A Guide for Overcoming Defensive Behaviors*. San Francisco, CA: Jossey-Bass.
Argyris, C. and Schön, D. (1974) *Theory in Practice*. San Francisco, CA: Jossey-Bass.
Argyris, C. and Schön, D. (1978) *Organizational Learning: A Theory of Action Perspective*. Reading, MA: Addison-Wesley.
Argyris, C., Putnam, R. and Smith, D.M. (1985) *Action Science*. San Francisco, CA: Jossey-Bass.
Bateson, G. (1972) *Steps to an Ecology of Mind*. San Francisco, CA: Chandler.
Bourdieu, P. (1993) *Sociology In Question*. London: Sage.
Brown, J.S. and Duguid, P. (1991) 'Organizational learning and communities of practice: Toward a unified view of working, learning, and innovation', *Organizational Science*, 2(1): 40–57.
Ciborra, C.U. and Schneider, L.S. (1992) 'Transforming the routines and contexts of management, work and technology', in P.S. Adler (ed.), *Technology and The Future of Work*. Cambridge, MA: MIT Press. pp. 269–291.

Cohen, M.D. (1991) 'Individual learning and organizational routine: Emerging connections', *Organizational Science*, 2(1): 135–139.

Cyert, R.M. and March, J.G. (1963) *A Behavioral Theory of the Firm*. Englewood Cliffs, NJ: Prentice Hall.

Daft, R.L. and Weick, K.E. (1984) 'Toward a model of organizations as interpretation systems', *Academy of Management Review*, 9: 284–295.

Duncan, R. and Weiss, A. (1979) 'Organizational learning: Implications for organizational design', in B. Staw (ed.), *Research in Organizational Behavior*, vol. 1. Greenwich, CT: JAI. pp. 75–123.

Epple, D., Argote, L. and Devadas, R. (1991) 'Organizational learning curves: A method for investigating intra-plant transfer of knowledge acquired through learning by doing', *Organizational Science*, 2(1): 58–70.

Fiol, C.M. and Lyles, M.A. (1985) 'Organizational learning', *Academy of Management Review*, 10(4): 803–813.

Forrester, J.W. (1961) *Industrial Dynamics*. Cambridge, MA: Productivity Press.

Hackman, J.R. and Oldham, G. (1980) *Work Redesign*. Reading, MA: Addison-Wesley.

Hackman, J.R. and Walton, R.E. (1986) 'Leading groups in organizations', in P. Goodman (ed.), *Designing Effective Work Groups*. San Francisco, CA: Jossey-Bass. pp. 73–119.

Hayes, R.H., Wheelwright, S.C. and Clark, K.B. (1988) *Dynamic Manufacturing: Creating the Learning Organization*. London: The Free Press.

Huber, G.P. (1991) 'Organizational learning: The contributing processes and the literature', *Organizational Science*, 2(1): 88–115.

Isaacs, W.N. (1993) 'Taking flight: Dialogue, collective thinking and organizational learning', *Organizational Dynamics*, 22(2): 24–39.

Isaacs, W.N. and Senge, P.M. (1992) 'Overcoming limits to learning in computer-based learning environments', *European Journal of Operational Research*, 59: 183–196

Jones, A.M. and Hendry, C. (1992) *The Learning Organization: A Review of Literature and Practice*. University of Warwick, Coventry, UK: The HRD Partnership.

Kim, D.H. (1993) 'The link between individual and organizational learning', *Sloan Management Review*, 35(1): 37–50.

Lawrence, P. and Lorsch, J. (1986 [1967]) *Organizations and Environment*, 2nd edn. Boston, MA: Harvard Business School Press.

Levitt, B. and March, J. (1988) 'Organizational learning', *Annual Review of Sociology*, 14: 319–340.

March, J. and Simon, H. (1958) *Organizations*. New York: John Wiley.

Nanda, A. and Bartlett, C.A. (1994) 'Intel Corporation – Leveraging capabilities for strategic renewal', Harvard Business School Case No. N9–394–141.

Nelson, R. and Winter, S. (1982) *An Evolutionary Theory of Economic Change*. Cambridge: Harvard University Press.

Pedler, M., Burgoyne, J. and Boydell, T. (eds) (1990) *Self-Development in Organizations*. London: McGraw-Hill.

Pettigrew, A.M. and Whipp, R. (1991) *Managing Change for Competitive Success*. Oxford: Blackwell.

Powell, W.W. and DiMaggio, P.J. (eds) (1991) *The New Institutionalism in Organizational Analysis*. Chicago, IL: University of Chicago Press.

Reboul, O. (1980) *Qu'est-ce qu'apprendre?* Paris: PUF.

Schein, E.H. (1990) 'Innovative cultures and adaptive organizations', *Sri Lanka Journal of Development Administration*, 7(2): 9–39.

Schein, E.H. (1993a) *Organizational Culture and Leadership*. San Francisco, CA: Jossey-Bass.

Schein, E.H. (1993b) 'How can organizations learn faster: The problem of entering the green room', *Sloan Management Review*, 34(2): 85–92.

Senge, P. (1990) *The Fifth Discipline: The Art and Practice of the Learning Organization*. New York: Doubleday.

Shrivastava, P. (1983) 'A typology of organizational learning', *Journal of Management Studies*, 20(1): 7–28.

Stata, R. (1989) 'Organizational learning: The key to management innovation', *Sloan Management Review*, 12(1): 63–74.

Sterman, J.D. (1988) 'A skeptic's guide to computer models', in L. Grant (ed.), *Foresight and National Decisions: The Horseman and the Bureaucrat*. Lanham, MD: University Press of America. pp. 133–169.

Sterman, J.D. (1989) 'Modeling managerial behavior: Misperceptions of feedback in dynamic decision-making', *Management Science*, 35(3): 321–339.

Weick, K. (1979) *The Social Psychology of Organizing*. New York: Random House.

Weick, K.E. (1991) 'The nontraditional quality of organizational learning', *Organizational Science*, 2(1): 116–124.

2

Organizational Learning Style as a Core Capability

Anthony J. DiBella, Edwin C. Nevis and Janet M. Gould

'Core capability' has become a popular concept in the literature on corporate strategy. Through the establishment of goals and the implementation of strategic action, firms may choose to create capabilities that give them a decided advantage in the marketplace. The key is that core capabilities and competencies differentiate a company so that it has a distinct advantage over its competitors (Hamel and Prahalad, 1994; Leonard-Barton, 1992; Collis, this volume; Nanda, this volume).

Organizational learning has been defined as the capability of an organization to adapt to its environment (Hedberg, 1981). As firms operate in an environment that appears to be increasingly more prone to change, organizational learning has been identified as a capability required of all firms (Garvin, 1993). But where are firms to find such capability and how is it to be strategically constructed? While there appears to be no shortage of theorists who can discuss how the learning organization is to be built, the notion of core capability as set forth by Prahalad and Hamel (1990) suggests that firms begin by looking at themselves. They define core competence as existing capability that represents collective learning. Thus the question is not how to build capability, but how to identify it and then strategically use it for competitive advantage.

The relationship between learning and capability has been considered in terms of frameworks for thinking about an organization's learning style. For example, Stata (1989) and McKee (1992) discuss the capability of organizations to learn from innovation as opposed to production. Bolton (1993) discusses the competitive advantage of learning through imitation versus innovation. Shrivastava (1983) used a matrix of two bipolar dimensions to develop a typology of six organizational learning styles, which represent different capabilities.

We have been engaged in field research to identify learning capabilities within a small set of firms and to develop a typology of organizational learning styles. Firms may alter their capabilities by improving on existing learning styles, developing complementary styles, or radically transforming their culture which is the key factor that determines what, why and how organizations learn. Through our research we have developed a framework to identify learning styles on the basis of seven orientations to learning. This chapter presents our model and describes its key elements.

Method

Our research was based on intensive field observations at four companies: Motorola Corporation, Mutual Investment Corporation (MIC), Electricité De France (EDF), and FIAT. Our data collection at Motorola involved observations of and interviews with fifty senior managers, site visits, and a review of about twenty-five internal documents. At MIC, we observed and interviewed managers in the Corporation Investment Funds Group and the Marketing Group.[1] AT EDF, we observed and interviewed staff in Nuclear Power Operations, and at FIAT we observed and interviewed managers in the Direzione Technica (Engineering Division) of FIAT Auto Company in Italy.

Several criteria were used in selecting these sites. We wanted to have both service and manufacturing settings and both US and European environments. We chose two sites where we had access to very senior management and two where we were able to study organization units at lower levels. Three firms were selected because of their association with our sponsor and, in the case of EDF, a base to start from because of another study done by us at EDF. Motorola was selected as an example of a company that has been identified as a good learning organization, and for providing an opportunity to observe organizational learning in their fourteen-year quality improvement effort. As an MIT Organizational Learning Center Sponsor, Motorola was also accessible. We did not attempt to study entire firms or to concentrate on individual work units.

Using the initial findings from the field observations, supplemented by our study of reports on other companies, we constructed a two-part model that embraces the critical factors required to describe organizations as learning systems. Then as our fieldwork continued, we focused our data collection on these specific dimensions of learning. The following section discusses this model together with our site findings.

Findings

All Organizations have Learning Capability

All the sites we studied have learning capability. There are formal and informal processes and structures in place for acquisition, sharing and utilization of knowledge and skills in all of these firms. Values, norms, procedures and outcome data are communicated broadly and assimilated by members, starting with early socialization and continuing through all kinds of group communications, both formal and informal. We have talked with staff in some firms who claim that their companies were not good learning organizations, but in each of these instances we were able to identify one or more core competencies that could only have come into existence if there were learning investments in those areas. There would have to be some type of structure and process to support the informed experience and formal educational interventions that are required for knowledge acquisition, knowledge sharing and knowledge utilization to take place.

And, indeed, that is what we found in both our field sites and other firms. For example, one firm that considers itself to be a poor learning organization because of its difficulty in changing some dysfunctional activities, has a reputation in its industry for having a superior field marketing function. In looking at this group it is clear that they have well-developed recruiting, socialization, training and development, and rotational assignment practices that support a continuously filled cadre of respected marketing people. Obviously, some learning has been assimilated at a fairly deep level.

Learning Conforms to Organizational Culture

The nature of the learning and the way in which it takes place are determined in large measure by the culture of the organization. For example, the entrepreneurial nature of MIC's Investment Funds Group results in a learning approach in which considerable amounts of information are made available to fund managers and analysts but the use of that information remains at the discretion of the managers. In addition, there is a good deal of leeway as to how the fund managers make their investment decisions; some are intuitive, some rely heavily on historic performance, and a few use computer programs of some sophistication. It follows from this that the utilization or application of learning among fund managers is largely an informal process and not one dictated by formal, firm-wide programs. By contrast, the Mutual Funds Marketing Groups strive to develop a more collaborative culture and base their learning more on the work of cross-functional work groups and improved communication.

The findings at Motorola are illuminating in a different way. There is no question that a great deal of organizational learning about quality has occurred in the firm, but the emphasis on engineering and technical concerns resulted in a much earlier and complete embrace of the total quality quest by discrete product manufacturing groups than by other functions. As a culture that heavily rewards discrete product group performance, total quality in products and processes that require integrated, inter-group action lags behind, particularly in the marketing of systems that cut across divisions.

There are Stylistic Variations in Organizational Learning Systems

From the above, it follows that there are a variety of ways in which organizations attempt to create and maximize their learning. Basic assumptions of the culture lead to learning values, and to select investments in different aspects of the business. This produces a learning style which will be different for one with another pattern of values and investments. These variations in style are based on a series of *learning orientations* (dimensions of learning) which may or may not be consciously perceived by members of the organization. We identified seven learning orientations, expressed as bipolar variables. These are discussed below.

As an example of these factors, each of two distinct groups at both Motorola and MIC Investments had a different approach to the way knowledge and skills were accrued and utilized. In one of the Motorola groups there was a great deal of concern for specifying the metrics that would be used to define and measure the targeted learning. In the other, there was much less concern with very specific measures. Instead, broad objectives were stressed. In the two groups at MIC, the methods for sharing and utilizing knowledge were very different. One was informal and the other was more formal and collaborative.

From these variations, we concluded that the pattern of the learning orientations is a large part of what makes up an organizational learning system. It may not tell us how *well* learning is promoted, but it does tell us a great deal about what is learned and where learning takes place. We identified three styles in our four sites, and two more in other organizations. These are discussed in detail below.

Learning is Facilitated by Several Generic Processes

How well an organization maximizes learning within its chosen style is not a haphazard matter. There is a normative aspect to our findings which suggests that to talk about 'the learning organization' is partially correct. Some policies, structures and processes do seem to make a difference. The difference is in how easy or hard it is for useful learning to occur, and in how effective the organization is in 'working its style'. While we did not see all of these factors in each of the four sites we studied intensively, we did see most of them, and we do see them in other sites. Thus, we are prepared to view them as generic factors, those which any organization can benefit from, regardless of its learning style. For example, scanning, in which benchmarking plays an important role, was so central to the learning at Motorola that it is now an integral, ongoing aspect of every important initiative in the company. Although MIC tends to create knowledge and skill internally, it maintains an ongoing vigilance with regard to its external environment. On the negative side, the absence of solid, ongoing external scanning in other organizations is considered to be an important factor in their economic difficulties. Others have commented on this in case analyses of mature firms. Altogether we identified ten such factors, which are discussed below.

A Model of Organizations as Learning Systems

Based on the above findings, we propose a two-part model of organizations as learning systems. One part is composed of *facilitating factors*, the

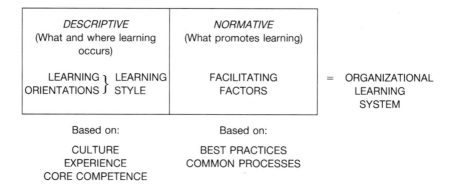

Figure 2.1   *A model of organizational learning*

structures and processes that affect how easy or hard it is for learning to occur and the amount of effective learning that takes place. These are normative factors based on the best practices in dealing with generic issues. The second part is composed of *learning orientations*, the values and attitudes that determine where learning will take place and the nature of what is learned. These orientations form a pattern that defines a given organization's 'learning style'. In this sense, they are descriptive factors which help us to understand without making value judgments.

The complete model is depicted in Figure 2.1. We show it as an additive model for convenience and for lack of sufficient knowledge at this time as to the relative importance of the two sets of factors (individually or as a group). The important thing is that both sets of factors are required for an understanding of an organization as a learning system; one without the other provides an incomplete picture. In addition, separating the factors in this way enables organizations to see that they do indeed function as learning systems of some kind, and that their task is to understand better what they do well and what they do poorly. The notion of assessment of what exists is more supportive to useful actions than is the pejorative notion that there is only one good way to be a learning organization. Finally, we believe that a more refined, detailed listing of factors related to organizational learning may be helpful in selecting entry points for learning improvement that do not demand drastic culture change but, rather, can lead to incremental culture change over time. These implications will be discussed further in a later section.

Facilitating factors

The facilitating factors are summarized in Table 2.1. In this section we expand on the definition of each of the ten factors and provide examples that support the importance of the factor.

1 Scanning imperative   By this we mean an ongoing effort backed by a well-assimilated acceptance of the importance of vigilance. Sound learning

Table 2.1 *Facilitating factors*

1 Scanning imperative	Interest in external happenings and in the nature of one's environment. Valuing the processes of awareness and data generation. Curious about what is 'out there' as opposed to 'in here'.
2 Performance gap	Shared perception of a gap between actual and desired state of performance. Disconfirming feedback interrupts a string of successes. Performance shortfalls are seen as opportunities for learning.
3 Concern for measurement	Spend considerable effort in defining and measuring key factors when venturing into new areas; strive for specific, quantifiable measures; discourse over metrics is seen as a learning activity.
4 Experimental mindset	Support for trying new things; curiosity about how things work; ability to 'play' with things. Small failures are encouraged, not punished. See changes in work processes, policies, and structures as a continuous series of graded tryouts.
5 Climate of openness	Accessibility of information; relatively open boundaries. Opportunities to observe others; problems/errors are shared, not hidden; debate and conflict are acceptable.
6 Continuous education	Ongoing commitment to education at all levels; support for growth and development of members.
7 Operational variety	Variety exists in response modes, procedures, systems; significant diversity in personnel. Pluralistic rather than monolithic definition of valued internal capabilities.
8 Multiple advocates	Top-down and bottom-up initiatives are possible; multiple advocates and gatekeepers exist.
9 Involved leadership	Leadership at significant levels articulates vision and is very actively engaged in its actualization; takes ongoing steps to implement vision; 'hands-on' involvement in educational and other implementation steps.
10 Systems perspective	Strong focus on how parts of the organization are interdependent; seek optimization of organizational goals at the highest levels; see problems and solutions in terms of systemic relationships.

cannot occur without a foundation of enhanced consciousness or apprehension of the environment in which one is functioning. In recent years much has been written about the importance of environmental scanning, with substantial agreement that many organizations got into trouble because of limited or poor efforts in this regard. In Motorola's quality effort, it was not until five years into the program that a significant scanning effort showed them what others, particularly the Japanese, were doing. As a reaction to this new awareness, Motorola substantially changed their approach and won the first Baldrige Award four years later. By contrast, it seems fair to say that mainframe computer manufacturers (Cray, Unisys,

IBM) got into trouble by failing to respond to changes that sound investigative work would have made painfully visible.

2 Performance gap   There are two aspects of this factor. One has to do with the kind of variance analysis that managers are familiar with in looking at the differences between targeted outcomes and actual performance. When feedback shows a gap, particularly if it implies failure, analysis often leads to correction or the development of new insights and skills. One of the reasons that well-established organizations often are not good learning systems is that they experience lengthy periods in which feedback is almost entirely positive. The lack of *disconfirming evidence* is a barrier to learning. The second aspect of this factor is related to vision and the possibilities for generative learning. In this variation, there is a potentially new outcome that is not simply a quantitative extension of the old or goes well beyond the level of performance that has been seen as achievable in the old vision. The process here is one in which one or more members of the firm visualize something which previously has not been noted. Once articulated, this helps to create a performance gap of a different kind. One of the reasons why awareness of a performance gap is so important for learning to occur is that it often leads to awareness that something needs to be learned or that something believed to be known may not be operable. Even if a group cannot articulate exactly what the needed knowledge might be, awareness of ignorance can be a powerful motivator of learning initiative.

3 Concern for measurement   This refers to the importance given to developing and using metrics that support learning in a given area. It includes such issues as whether the measures are internally or externally focused, the degree of specificity sought, the use of custom built or standard measures, and so on. The importance of metrics in total quality programs has been well documented (for example, by Schmidt and Finnigan, 1992), and in target setting programs such as management by objectives. Here, the interest is in how the discourse about metrics, and the search for the most appropriate ones, is a critical aspect of the learning, almost as much as the learning that comes about from responding to the feedback that the metrics provide.

Motorola executives believe that concern for measurement was one of the most critical reasons for their success in the quality program. At three or four critical junctions in this program, re-examination of measurement issues help propel movement to a new level of learning. This factor is being applied to new initiatives, and was a major concern of the executive groups we observed in this study. The value of metrics is clearly associated with 'performance gap' at EDF. Its nuclear power plants are authorized to operate at certain specifications which, if not met, may suggest or predict an unplanned event leading to shutdown. Each occasion becomes an opportunity for learning to take place.

4 Experimental mindset This factor overlaps somewhat with that of 'climate of openness', but it emphasizes encouragement to try out things on an ongoing basis. If learning comes through experience, it follows that the more one can plan guided experiences, the more one will learn. Until organizing for production at any stage of the value chain is seen as a learning experiment as well as a production activity, learning will come slowly. Managers need to learn to act like applied research scientists at the same time as they deliver goods and services. This point of view is supported by Leonard-Barton (1992) who considers the next production frontier to be organization of the factory as a learning laboratory. Sitkin (1992) has written eloquently on the importance of 'small failures' in promoting organizational learning, and these can only occur if one ventures into uncharted waters. Following Sitkin's lead, we suggest that organizations who wish to improve their experimentation find the organizational equivalent of Vygotsky's 'zone of proximal [potential] development' (Wertsch, 1985), which he defined at the individual level as the very next learning task that a child can attempt while remaining supported by a teacher.

5 Climate of openness This factor is related to the permeability of boundaries around information flow and the degree to which observation opportunity is available to people. Much informal learning that takes place is a function of daily, often unplanned interactions among people. In addition, the opportunity to be part of meetings with other groups and to see higher levels of management in operation promotes learning. This has been referred to as 'legitimate peripheral participation' by Lave and Wenger (1990). The factor includes the freedom with which people can express their views and the degree of disagreement and debate that is legitimate. Another very critical aspect is the extent to which errors are shared and not hidden. Argyris (1985) has made a very cogent argument that organizational learning is severely hampered by the widespread habit of managers to cover over or hide errors in order to avoid organizational punishment.

6 Continuous education By this we mean internalization of a commitment to lifelong education at all levels of the organization. This includes the existence of formal educational programs but goes well beyond that to more pervasive support of any kind of developmental experience for members of the organization. Mere presence of traditional training and development activities is not considered sufficient; it must be accompanied by a palpable sense that one is never finished learning and practicing (something akin to the tradition of the Samurai). In many ways, this factor is another way of expressing what Peter Senge (1990) called 'personal mastery' in his model.

MIC does an excellent job of exposing its young analysts to powerful developmental experiences. Its chairman is also known to be a seeker for new knowledge in many areas, not just direct financial matters. Motorola appears to have embraced this concept vigorously. This includes a policy that every employee receives some educational experience every year, joint ventures with several community colleges around the US, joint programs with the State of Illinois for software competence development and training of school superintendents, and on-the-job as well as classroom experiences for managers up to senior executives. Motorola spends 3.6 percent of its revenues on education (Reese, 1993).

7 Operational variety   This factor is a companion to 'experimental mindset' in that it implies that there are more ways than one to accomplish work goals. It states that an organization that supports variation in strategy, policy, process, structure and personnel is more adaptable when unforeseen problems arise. It provides more options from which to choose and, perhaps even more importantly, it allows for richer stimulation and interpretation in the consciousness of all organizational members. This should help to enhance future learning in a way that a singular approach does not make possible. We did not see a great deal of operational variety at our sites except at MIC Investment Funds Group where we identified three different methods used by fund managers in making investment decisions.

8 Multiple advocates   While involved leadership sets the stage for learning, robust organizational learning requires more than one 'champion' if it is to succeed. This is particularly true in the case of learning that is related to changing a basic value or a long-cherished method. The greater the number of gatekeepers who bring knowledge into the system, and the greater the number of advocates who promote a new idea, the more rapidly and extensively will the learning take place. Moreover, in an effective learning system it ought to be possible for any member to be an awareness-enhancing agent or an advocate for new competence development. In this way, both top-down and bottom-up initiatives are made possible.

9 Involved leadership   Much has been said about the importance of leadership in setting vision that mobilizes enhanced performance. Our findings suggest that merely creating vision is not enough. For assimilated learning to occur, leadership at any organizational level must engage in hands-on implementation of the vision. This includes eliminating the layers of management, being visible in the 'bowels' of the organization, and being an active early participant in any learning effort. Only through direct involvement that reflects coordination, vision and integration can leadership obtain important data, as well as provide a powerful role model. At Motorola, CEO Bob Galvin not only drove the quality vision, he was a student in the first seminars designed to learn about it, and he made it the first item to be reported to him by his division executives in their monthly meetings.

Table 2.2 *Learning orientations*

1 Knowledge source	Preference for developing knowledge internally versus seeking inspiration in ideas developed externally.
2 Product-process focus	Emphasize accumulation of product knowledge versus expanding competencies in basic processes.
3 Documentation mode	Knowledge seen in personal, tacit terms, as something possessed by individuals versus being seen as explicit statements of publicly available know-how.
4 Dissemination mode	Emphasize informal methods of sharing learning, such as role modeling and communities of practice, versus formal, prescribed organization-wide programs.
5 Learning focus	Emphasize incremental, single loop learning versus transformational, double loop learning.
6 Value-chain focus	Center learning investments on 'design and make' side of the value chain versus the 'deliver' side.
7 Skill development	Stress development of individuals versus development of teams or groups. Emphasize individual skills versus skills in learning and working collectively.

10 Systems perspective   This factor deals with the ability of key actors to keep a broad perspective and to think in terms of the interdependency of organizational variables. Involved here is the degree to which organizations can look to their internal systems as a source of their difficulties, as opposed to blaming external factors. Studies at the MIT System Dynamics Group and elsewhere have demonstrated how managers elicit unintended consequences by taking actions in one area without seeing the dynamic relationship of that action to its effects. Senge (1990) considers this 'discipline' as the one that integrates all the others in his five-factor model of organizational learning.

Despite its importance, this factor is relatively lacking in our sites. MIC and Motorola are structured so that the boundaries between groups and functions tend to be strong. Both have heightened their perspective in recent years, MIC as a consequence of unexpected internal problems related to the October 1987, drop in the stock market, and Motorola after experiencing difficulties in selling large-scale systems (as opposed to discrete products).

Learning Orientations

The learning orientations are summarized in Table 2.2. In the next section of the chapter we expand on the definition of the seven orientations and provide examples that support the existence of each.

1 Knowledge source   This orientation is defined as the extent to which the organization prefers to develop new knowledge internally versus the extent to which it is more likely to seek inspiration in the ideas developed by external sources. This distinction is often thought of as being the difference between innovation and adaptation, or imitation. In the United States there has been a tendency to value the innovative approach more highly and to look down on those who seem to be 'copiers'. American critiques of Japanese businesses often mention the Japanese as being good imitators but not good innovators. We see both of these approaches as having great merit, and we propose that they be seen as stylistic opposing choices rather than as normative or pejorative behaviors. In a recent, well-argued paper, Bolton (1993) makes a distinction between learning by doing (innovation) and learning by watching (imitation). She breaks imitation into two varieties: *pure* imitation and *reflective* imitation. Pure imitation is the 'unchewed' introjection of an idea and results in a low level of learning because there is not an enriched ground upon which to build new knowledge. Reflective imitation requires active adaptation, comprehension, or interpretation of the knowledge to a new setting and requires real work to assimilate a new possibility. Bolton shows the competitive advantages of both innovation and reflective imitations, indicating Japanese successes that have come from reflective imitation. To see that this difference is not a phenomenon of national culture, one need only look at how IBM used reflective imitation some forty-five years ago to take what Univac had innovated and to gain domination of the field by better implementation of the concept. Our findings show a tendency for organizations to prefer one mode over the other, though the distinction is not clear-cut. While MIC does scan its environment, it prefers to innovate in responding to customer needs and problems and has been a leader in coming up with new financial products and services. EDF modeled its nuclear power plants on American technology. Motorola is interesting in that the firm appears to be equally vigorous in innovation and in reflective imitation.

2 Product-process focus This orientation refers to a preference for accumulation of knowledge related to product and service outcomes, versus a preference to invest in knowledge about basic processes that might underlie or support various products. Many observers have stated that one of the reasons the Japanese are so competitive is that they make considerable investment in process technologies compared with American lack of investment in this area. The difference here is between interest in 'getting product out the door' and curiosity about the steps in the processes involved at each state of the endeavor. We propose that both interests are necessary but that organizations place more value on one side than the other. All organizations give some attention to both sides; the question is one of organizing for learning in these two domains.

3 Documentation mode This refers to variations in attitude as to what constitutes knowledge, and as to the repositories of knowledge that are supported. At one pole, knowledge is seen in very personal terms, as something that an individual possesses by virtue of education and experience. This is the kind of knowledge that is lost when an old hand leaves an organization; processes and insights evaporate because they were not made a part of a collective memory. This approach legitimizes highly subjective ways of knowing. At the other pole, the emphasis is on defining knowledge in more objective, social terms, as being a consensually supported result of information processing. It emphasizes organizational memory or a publicly documented body of known things. Nonaka (1991), borrowing from M. Polanyi's distinction between tacit and explicit knowledge, has shown how both of these approaches exist in a dynamic relationship in a knowledge-creating setting.

4 Dissemination mode Though related to documentation mode, this has to do with the difference between establishing an atmosphere in which learning evolves, and one in which a more structured, controlled approach is taken to induce learning. In the more structured approach, a decision is made that a valuable insight or method should be shared and used by others on a broad, institutionalized basis. Various forms of written communication and formal educational methods are generally employed for this purpose. Another approach is the certification of learning through the writing of procedures. In the more informal approach, learning is spread through encounters with role models and gatekeepers who actualize the insight or method by behaving in a compelling way. Another version of the informal approach is the kind of learning that occurs when members of an occupational group or work team share their experiences in ongoing dialogue. Brown and Duguid (1991) have referred to this as learning through 'communities of practice', and suggest that it will take place as a result of the social nature of most work. Organizational policies and rules can act to enhance this learning or they can act as barriers to its fulfillment.

5 Learning focus The distinction we make here is another one that has been seen in value terms, rather than as stylistic differences. It has to do with whether learning is concentrated on methods and tools to improve what is already being done, versus concentration on testing the assumptions underlying what is being done. Argyris and Schön (1978) call the former 'single loop learning' and the latter 'double loop learning'. They rightfully have argued that organizational performance problems are more likely related to a lack of awareness and ability to articulate and check underlying assumptions, than are they a function of poor efficiency in what they do. We see these learning capabilities as reinforcing each other. Organizations may have a preference for one mode over the other, but a sound learning system can benefit from good work at both modes.

6 Value-chain focus This orientation indicates which core competencies and learning investments are valued and supported. By learning investment we mean all personnel and money allocations to develop knowledge and skill over time. This includes training and education, pilot projects, developmental assignments, slack in overall budget, and so on. Thus, when we say that a particular organization is 'engineering-focused' or 'marketing-driven', it is safe to assume that they are biased in favor of substantial learning investments in that area over time. Prahalad and Hamel (1990), in their seminal paper on core competencies, observed that a decision to exit a function or stage in the value chain and to have an alliance with another firm that performed that service, is a decision to de-invest in ongoing learning in that area. In defining the value chain for present purposes, we have taken some liberties and divided it into two categories: those activities of an internally directed, 'design and make' nature, and those of a more externally focused 'sell and deliver' nature. At MIC's Investment Funds Group the focus is clearly on the 'design and make' side and on the nature of the products. While this is balanced by learning investments on the 'deliver' side in the MIC Marketing Groups, there is a strong boundary between these groups, and fund management is regarded as the core of the organization. Motorola's total quality effort clearly recognizes the importance of value-added at both sides of the chain, but the 'design and make' side is significantly ahead in learning investments around quality than is the 'deliver' side. FIAT's Direzione Technica is oriented toward the 'design and make' side, although its new system of simultaneous engineering is giving them a more balanced approach with increased sensitivity to the 'deliver' side. EDF Nuclear Operations focuses squarely on efficient production.

7 Skill development   The area of team or group learning has received much attention in recent literature on organizational learning (Kasl et al., 1992; Marsick et al., 1991; Senge, 1990). These authors have argued that collaborative learning is better for organizational purposes than is individual learning, and that team skills are sorely needed in today's interdependent, networked world. Others have shown how American product development and production are hampered by a lack of cooperation among interdependent groups (Dertouzos et al., 1989). We support the need for team skills but believe that both individual and group development are necessary, and that it might help to look at them as stylistic choices, as opposed to seeing them in normative terms. In this way, organizations can assess how they are doing on both sides and take action for improvement in either one. MIC's Investment Funds Group is designed to promote individual learning, which seems to fit with its individualistic culture and its reward system. On the other hand, MIC's Marketing Groups are more supportive of collective learning, and are now investing in team development as one way to improve their effectiveness as a total unit. FIAT's Direzione Technica has been more oriented toward individual development. However, with its new reliance on cross-functional work teams, group development is increasingly more important. Motorola has become more team-oriented in recent years and is making heavy invest-

Table 2.3   *A typology of learning styles*

PATTERN OF LEARNING ORIENTATIONS:	
Rugged individualism	Create knowledge internally Emphasize product knowledge Individual development Knowledge as 'personal property' Informal dissemination mode
Techno-analytic	Emphasize incremental learning Focus on 'design/make' side Individual development Emphasize process knowledge Knowledge as 'personal property' Formal, firm-wide dissemination
Communal	Seek internal and external knowledge Emphasize incremental learning Emphasize team development Knowledge is collectively available
Traditional	Create knowledge internally Emphasize incremental learning Focus on 'design/make' side Individual development Formal, firm-wide dissemination
Evangelical	Create knowledge internally Transformational learning Emphasize process knowledge Individual development Informal dessemination

ments in collaborative learning. As Motorola is using more and more teams, documented cases of team development in the firm have now appeared (Katzenbach and Smith, 1993). At EDF both individual and group development are employed, especially with respect to control room teams. All EDF employees follow individual training programs to be certified in their craft or to prepare them for promotion. Control room teams also learn together, in groups, through the use of plant simulators.

Toward a Typology of Organizational Learning Styles

The above learning orientations can be arranged in a matrix. An organizational unit may be described in terms of the pattern of its orientations in this matrix. This provides a way of describing its *learning style*. Based on the data from the sites in this study, and other sites with which we are familiar, we believe that it may be possible to identify patterns, or styles.

As a starting point for further exploration, we have identified five styles. The first three of these can be seen in our sites; the last two appear in other settings. Table 2.3 lists the five styles, together with the pattern of their major learning orientations. In looking at these styles, the reader will note that some orientations appear in more than one style. The important consideration here is the *pattern* of the orientations taken as a whole. Subsequent field research will explore the validity of these and other styles.

Rugged Individualism

This pattern reflects some of the basic values in individualistic cultures. It assumes that people learn best when they have a great deal of freedom and when they are allowed to 'stand on their own two feet'. The style assumes that the best development is self-development, and that if you staff your organization with highly intelligent, well-motivated, ambitious people, their individual actions will aggregate into a high-performing unit. We can think of this as an heroic learning style for which John Wayne's movie roles might serve as a metaphor. MIC's Investment Funds Group fits this style. A nonsite firm with this pattern is Digital Equipment Corporation; MIT belongs in the category with regard to its style of learning (as opposed to styles of teaching).

Techno-analytic

This assumes that rational, detailed approaches, backed by well-organized plans and programs, are the best way to ensure learning. The style is interesting in that it embraces knowledge from without and develops knowledge internally. A major element is the need to define, understand and measure any process that is considered of value. The style tends to be supported by engineering cultures and companies based on well-defined technologies that favor analytic modes. It appears also to be an accompaniment to values of fairness, conflict avoidance and the importance of the 'best' process. Model-building is also valued as an activity in this style. Motorola and EDF show this as a predominant style. Organizations that have well-developed competency models are likely to show this learning style. Royal Dutch Shell has a strong component here, but also displays signs of a Communal Learning Style.

Communal

The key assumption here is that the most critical organizational learning is around skills for binding people into a collective identity. Valued norms and response modes should be possessed by all unit members. Although this may be stated as an attempt to achieve a high level of efficiency and effectiveness, there is an implicit, but very strongly experienced, assumption that loyalty to the firm is essential. In our study, FIAT's Direzione Technica appears to fit this style. MIC's Marketing Group is moving in this direction, as part of a growing belief that they could do more for their customers if they functioned as a communal learning system. Others that appear to fit this style are some organized religious groups and military units such as the US Marines.

Traditional

This style is somewhat similar to the techno-analytic style, but has some other characteristics that lead us to propose it as a separate pattern. The major assumption is that the best learning is that which adds to what is already known. Learning from past experience is critical to understanding the present, and, if a system has worked well over time, learning investments should focus on its maintenance and improvement. Discontinuous, radical approaches should be viewed with caution; conservatism is the byword. When it works well this style builds on solid foundations and passes on that which has enduring utility. We saw some elements of this in our sites, but none of them truly fit this category. Since the style was constructed as an additional pattern of our learning orientations, we believe that research with additional organizational units will strengthen or refute its legitimacy. It appears that many large, old-line firms, such as General Motors, have had this as a learning style. EDF has some qualities that suggest it might be placed in this category.

Evangelical

We did not see evidence to support the existence of this style at any of our sites, but we have formulated it as one which may exist elsewhere, and which well might be included in further studies. The emphasis in this style is on change and transformation, on attempts to go beyond what currently exists, and on challenges to current dogma. It derives much energy from a vision or from some new knowledge that is generated internal to the unit, with a few people acting as catalysts for truly discontinuous learning. Missionary zeal appears to be an important aspect of the style. We do see individuals attempting to move their organizations in this direction. Moreover, it seems that a significant number of new, knowledge-based firms start out with this style (for instance, the early Apple Computer was based on and utilized numerous contrarian ideas), but we have no detailed knowledge of any units that function this way. We hope to locate some in the next phase of this research.

Implications

Our results suggest that it is possible to study organizational units as though they have learning capabilities. Guided by our list of the qualities of a good learning organization, we were able to make on-site observations of aspects of learning and to develop a revised list of factors that appear to have more focus and more breadth. Although we did not see all of our factors in any of our sites, there was enough data for each in either the sites or other settings to warrant including all of them in the model we will use in further research.

If one accepts the potential of the two-part model of normative (facilitating factors) and descriptive (learning orientations) variables, it follows that two general directions are indicated for enhancing learning in an organizational unit. One direction is to embrace the style that exists and to try to improve the effectiveness of this style. This is the strategy of actualizing a fundamental part of the culture to the fullest extent possible. For example, a firm that is more of a reflective imitator than an innovator could accept this with heightened awareness of its value. One that has benefited from heavy learning investments in the 'make' side of the value chain would see the value of this and decide to build further on it. This approach builds on the notion that full acceptance of what has been accomplished is very validating and energizing for those involved. It is similar to the appreciative inquiry being advocated by numerous organization change consultants (Srivastva and Cooperrider, 1990). The work would then be that of looking at the facilitating factors and selecting two or three to improve upon.

The second direction is to change the learning style by addressing the learning orientations so as to move toward the opposite pole of what exists currently. In this approach, an organization would look at its pattern and attempt to move to the opposite pole on each of the orientations. This group would strive to make more learning investments at a different part of the value chain, try to be an innovator if it is now more of an imitator, and so on. These are different changes than those involved in enhancing the facilitating factors, and the change tactics will be different; some will be seen as an attack upon the organization's basic values. It may be possible to get around this by advocating a move toward more balance between the two poles; the existing style would be supported and the 'new look' would be advocated as a supplementary measure.

Learning style represents an organization's acquired capability. To use that capability for competitive advantage, organizations must first be able to recognize what that capability consists of. Identifying one's learning style provides a starting point for strategic action to change, augment, or enhance one's style. Rather than presuming no existing competence and the need to build it from the bottom up, managers are advised to heed the dynamics of organization change and to work with and from what is. Strategic interventions can then be designed to ensure the success of strategy implementation.

Notes

Support for this research was provided by a grant from the International Consortium for Executive Development Research and by the MIT Organizational Learning Center.

1 Mutual Investment Corporation is the pseudonym for a large financial services company located on the East Coast of the United States.

References

Argyris, C. (1985) *Strategy, Change and Defensive Routines*. Boston, MA: Pitman.
Argyris, C. and Schön, D.A. (1978) *Organizational Learning*. Reading, MA: Addison-Wesley.
Bolton, M.K. (1993) 'Imitation versus innovation', *Organization Dynamics*, 30–45.
Brown, J.S. and Duguid, P. (1991) 'Organizational learning and communities of practice', *Organization Science*, 2(1): 40–57.
Dertouzos, M., Lester, R. and Solow, R. (1989) *Made in America*. Cambridge, MA: MIT Press.
Garvin, D.A. (1993) 'Building a learning organization', *Harvard Business Review*, 78–91.
Hamel, G. and Prahalad, C.K. (1994) *Competing for the Future*. Boston, MA: Harvard Business School Press.
Hedberg, R. (1981) 'How organizations learn and unlearn', in N.C. Nystrom and W.H. Starbuck (eds), *Handbook of Organizational Design*. Oxford: Oxford University Press.
Kasl, E., Marsick, V. and Dechant, K. (1992) 'A conceptual model for group learning', *Proceedings, Adult Education Research Conference*, College of Education, Saskatoon, Canada, 131–138.
Katzenbach, J.R. and Smith, D.K. (1993) *The Wisdom of Teams*. Boston, MA: Harvard Business School Press.
Lave, J. and Wenger, E. (1990) *Situated Learning: Legitimate Peripheral Participation*, IRL Report 90–0013, Palo Alto, CA, Institute for Research on Learning.
Leonard-Barton, D. (1992) 'The factory as a learning laboratory', *Sloan Management Review*, 39–52.
McKee, D. (1992) 'An organizational learning approach to product innovation', *Journal of Product Innovation Management*, 9: 232–245.
Marsick, V.J., Dechant, K. and Kasl, E. (1991) 'Professional ways of knowing', *Proceedings: Commission for Continuing Education of the AAACE*, Montreal, Canada.
Nonaka, I. (1991) 'The knowledge-creating company', *Harvard Business Review*, 96–104.
Prahalad, C.K. and Hamel, G. (1990) 'The core competencies of the corporation', *Harvard Business Review*, 79–91.
Reese, Jennifer (1993) 'America's most admired corporations', *Fortune*, 44–88.
Schmidt, W.H. and Finnigan, J.P. (1992) *The Race Without a Finish Line: America's Quest for Total Quality*. San Francisco, CA: Jossey-Bass.
Senge, P.M. (1990) *The Fifth Discipline*. New York: Doubleday.
Shrivastava, P. (1983) 'A typology of organizational learning systems', *Journal of Management Studies*, 20: 7–28.
Sitkin, S.B. (1992) 'Learning through failure: The strategy of small losses', *Research in Organizational Behavior*, 14: 231–266.
Srivastva, S., Cooperrider, D.L. and Associates (1990) *Appreciative Management and Leadership*. San Francisco, CA: Jossey-Bass.
Stata, R. (1989) 'Organizational learning – the key to management innovation', *Sloan Management Review*, 63–74.
Wertsch, J.D. (ed.) (1985) *Culture, Communication and Cognition: Vigotskian Perspectives*. New York: Cambridge University Press.

3

Competitive Advantage from Tacit Knowledge?
Unpacking the Concept and its Strategic Implications

J.-C. Spender

Knowledge as the Basis of Competitive Advantage

It is now widely accepted that the firm's competitive advantage flows from its unique knowledge (Prahalad and Hamel, 1990; Rumelt et al., 1991). This idea has been in our literature for many years, from the traditional SWOT analysis (strengths, weaknesses, opportunities and threats) to Selznick's (1957) 'distinctive competence'. But it has been repackaged recently as the rent-oriented 'resource-based' theory of the firm (Conner, 1991; Wernerfelt, 1984). Strategic interest is focused on idiosyncratic knowledge that is rare, sustainable and immobile (Barney, 1991). This, it is argued, leads to economic rents (see Collis, this volume).

There are no fewer than three types of economic rent: Ricardian, monopolistic and entrepreneurial (Mahoney and Pandian, 1992; Rumelt, 1987). The sources of the first two are exogenous and therefore typically beyond management's control. The third type of rent is different in that its source is endogenous. One concept of entrepreneurial rent is that it derives from the particular knowledge which the entrepreneur brings to the firm. Here it is the firm that is being entrepreneurial rather than the entrepreneur. The implicit model of the firm is that it not only transforms inputs into outputs, employing knowledge in the process, but also generates unique knowledge about new combinations and processes. This leads to renewed interest in organizational learning (for example, Attewell, 1992; Brown and Duguid, 1991; Van de Ven and Polley, 1992). These writers assume that the learning is under management's control and that a theory about managing learning is also a theory of rent generation. At the same time theorists have begun to try to analyze the knowledge which is the result of the learning process (for example, Hirschhorn, 1984; Kagono et al., 1985; Kogut and Zander, 1992; Nelson and Winter, 1982; Nonaka, 1991; Nonaka and Takeuchi, 1995; Senker, 1995; Winter, 1987).

One approach to integrating knowledge into strategy theory is to see rents as accruing directly from information asymmetry, the heterogeneous distribution of knowledge among economic actors. This assumes that the knowledge itself, or what these actors know, is unproblematic. One example is the owner's 'inside' knowledge about whether the second-hand auto being offered for sale is a 'lemon' (Akerlof, 1970).

Moving away from a classification based on the simple presence or absence of common knowledge to one based on experience is fraught with difficulties. Writers such as Winter, Teece or Nonaka have sought other ways of classifying the organization's knowledge as a precursor to developing theories which relate strategic management to knowledge management. It turns out that neither knowledge nor learning are straightforward concepts. For instance, it is not enough just to talk about learning, we must identify ways of retaining and benefiting from learning. There are also questions about how the resulting knowledge is stored. Is it 'of the organization' or is it 'of those participating in the organization's activities'? What are the agency implications of individuals being central to the organization's learning process? Does the organization's knowledge 'go home in the evening'? How is it to be protected or moved around? How is it to be transferred from the times when, and places where, it is generated to when and where it is applied? How are we to value unapplied or 'slack' knowledge?

Organizational Knowledge

With the term 'knowledge' most theorists allude to what they have learned of the positivist model of science. This treats knowledge as a model of a reality 'out there', empirically tested and validated. It is objective in that it is independent of the knower. All admissible knowledge, positivists believe, is of this one 'scientific' type. Knowledge is unproblematic except for in its absence, which is called uncertainty. This leads some theorists to focus on uncertainty (or ambiguity) and on the firm's ability to deal with it, as the basis for its competitive advantage. Others suggest that scientific knowledge is only problematic because it needs to be transformed into technology before it can be of use, that it is the presence of technology rather than of scientific knowledge that leads to advantage. In this view, the winning firm is the one best organized to absorb and apply scientific knowledge through its innovation processes (Cohen and Levinthal, 1990).

Quite different possibilities open up as soon as we go beyond the narrow positivist notion of science and suggest that organizational knowledge may be of several types. For instance, some analysts suggest a distinction between technological and administrative knowledge (Daft, 1982; Ettlie, 1988). Others see differences between core skills (competencies) and those which are peripheral or complementary (Prahalad and Hamel, 1990; Teece, 1987). Differences in the accessibility and mobility of knowledge obviously matter. Some knowledge can be protected and immobilized, some cannot and is readily appropriated by others. If the firm itself is not aware of its rent sources, they may be inappropriable on that score (Lippman and Rumelt, 1982). Since the firm has to deal with environmental uncertainty as well as with its internal production, some knowledge will fit its core technology, some will be more relevant to its boundary-spanning activities (Thompson, 1967).

While these categories are interesting, none of them challenge the epistemological limits of scientific knowledge. Nor do they seem adequate to a theory of knowledge management. They merely indicate preferred types of scientific knowledge without helping us understand the relationship between knowledge and strategy. Thus a number of theorists (Nelson and Winter, 1982; Teece, 1987; Winter, 1987) have recently turned to Polanyi's (1962) distinction between objective and tacit knowledge. This challenges the positivist definition of knowledge directly. While objective knowledge is similar to science – abstract and independent of the knower – tacit knowledge is subjective and intimately tied up with the knower's experience. Thus, Hirschhorn (1984) has suggested that the engineer's way of knowing an industrial plant can be distinguished from the skill of the craftsman who made it, for this knowledge is too limited, and from the operator's, for his tacit understanding lacks theoretical depth.

Polanyi argued that tacit knowledge is the underlying fertile intellectual ground for all scientific work (Gelwick, 1977). Yet he illustrated tacit knowledge with kinetic examples, such as that which bicycle riders can demonstrate but cannot explain (Polanyi, 1962). The incommunicability of the firm's craft-like tacit knowledge seems an appropriate way to point to its idiosyncratic experience-based knowledge. Indeed, it may be that the essential difference between science and technology lies in their tacit components. But, given Polanyi's sketchy analysis, much about the notion of tacit knowledge remains unclear, and it is obviously a long leap from bike riding to a theory of the creation of competitive advantage based on some kind of epistemological entrepreneurship. One of the aims of this chapter is to point out that the term tacit is underspecified, and means too many things to be a useful analytic term, in spite of its seeming appeal. First of all, tacit does not mean knowledge that *cannot* be codified (see Nonaka's treatment); it is best defined as 'not yet explicated'. This chapter presents three different reasons why knowledge remains uncodified, or not explicated.

The Categories of Tacit Knowledge

In this section we unpack Polanyi's concept of tacit knowledge by considering some recent empirical research.

Polanyi tended to define the tacit in terms of its incommunicability. Although this seems clarifying at first, it makes it difficult to see how we can relate incommunicable personal knowledge to a useful and communicable theory of organizational strategy. Several other lines of research, such as that on 'bias' by Tversky and Kahneman, explore the difference between the universal rationality of science and the restricted nature of human reasoning. Here the argument is that much human knowledge is personal, restricted and 'biased' while science is public. The scientific method is about eliminating such experientially grounded 'bias' so as to generate the universal objective models of reality which belong to Popper's (1973) 'third world'. Different again is the argument that all knowledge is socially constructed, that there can be neither truly value-free objective knowledge, nor can there be private knowledge. All knowledge is in the social domain, there is none in the privacy of personal experience. Knowledge becomes evident in the collective language and practices that are understood and communicated to other members of the society, but it never captures the immediacy of individual experience.

These essentially epistemological questions about whether knowledge is objective, personal or social, have recently become the subject of empirical research by cultural ethnographers such as Kusterer (1978) and Scribner. Scribner and her associates (Scribner et al., 1991) researched the activities of various workers in a commercial dairy – warehouse order packers, delivery drivers, inventory takers, and clerks from the offices – and observed a kind of effortless expertise with which many of these workers performed complex calculations in their jobs.

Scribner's theorizing was based on Vygotsky's activity theory, which stresses the centrality of workplace activity in analyzing the thinking applied in practices such as those she observed in the dairy. While Polanyi presumed activity yielded tacit knowledge that remained private, Vygotsky argued that activity shaped consciousness in ways that were social and were eventually reflected in language and social structure (Vygotsky, 1962; Wertsch, 1985). Thus practical knowledge is not only integrated with practice, as Polanyi suggests, it is also integrated with the consciousness of the community of practitioners. In this sense the expert workers were not simply using heuristics, which are purely intellectual tools; rather they were using practical knowledge intimately bound up with the products involved and with the social and physical context in which the products were handled. Importantly, these experts lost their expertise when they were presented with identical problems in a new context – in this case a classroom. When their task was decontextualized and rendered unfamiliar – and they were forced into the different practices of abstract analysis – they were suddenly far from expert, becoming both unproductive and error prone. Simon (1987) has also commented that becoming an expert may have more to do with accumulating a large number of recallable instances of appropriately contextualized problems (around 10^5) than with the development of powerful intellectual heuristics or proto-theories.

Scribner's research suggested that much of workplace expertise lies in being able to formulate problems in ways that successfully reflect the context and its possibilities. Knowing the problem cannot be separated from knowing the environment in which the problem occurs. Her research demonstrated the gulf between scientific and workplace knowledge. It established the boundedness and complex specificity of workplace knowledge. Explicit individual knowledge can be tacit when it is bound to the context in which it is used.

The Automatic Element of Tacit Knowledge

Effortlessness seems to be one of the characteristics of tacit knowledge. It suggests that the user is unaware of the tacit knowledge being applied, for example, in the case of Scribner's dairy workers. This lack of awareness makes research into workplace knowledge doubly difficult, but also more important. Being unaware of their taken-for-granted knowledge, workers are often unable to tell management about the costs and consequences of actions which force them to change their knowledge-base (Hirschhorn, 1984). Ethnographers are trained to discover what people take for granted in their activities. As they research the modern workplace they reveal more of the vast store of complex knowledge which actually makes up the firm's technological and competitive capabilities. The metaphor of the iceberg may apply, what is known explicitly by individuals is little indication of the vast mass of knowledge that lies beneath the surface of everyday organizational activity.

Simon (1987) has denied the automatic or unconscious element of organizational knowledge, and has argued that intuition (the automatic) is simply analysis (the conscious) 'frozen into habit'. We can re-express this by saying that intuition is analysis habituated or sedimented into the taken-for-granted. Polanyi, on the other hand, struggled to distinguish the automatic with his distinction between 'focal' (conscious) and 'subsidiary' (unconscious) awareness. Again he illustrated this kinetically, arguing that an expert carpenter focuses on the nail and remains unaware of the hammer's shaft in his or her hand. This relates consciousness to attention, while allowing that we can do certain things automatically, despite not attending to them. Tools are especially important in the way they direct our focal attention away from the irrelevant (the way the tool works) toward the task that we wish to perform, thus separating the subsidiary and focal awareness. Well-designed tools offer 'affordances' which make them 'user-friendly' so that they leave our attention free to attend to the task at hand (Norman, 1989).

The tool's affordances are not detachable from the tool's use; they are the aspects that call forth the user's non-conscious automatic knowledge. They are meaningless without this knowledge, for without such affordances they call forth nothing. This may be because the user has no relevant knowledge. No amount of effort to create user friendliness at the design stage can make up for the user's ignorance of skilled performance. In this sense a tool is always an aid to skilled performance, not a substitute. Even if the user's automatic knowledge is present, acquired through considerable practice, it may still be inaccessible at the purely conscious level. For example, Norman (1989) reported that expert typists are seldom able to arrange key caps correctly in the pattern of the QWERTY keyboard that they use all day. Similarly experienced drivers maintain several fields of subsidiary attention, on the sound of the auto's engine and transmission, on the rear-view mirror that shows the traffic coming up behind, on the feel of the road through the steering wheel, on the radio, and so forth. The skilled musician is completely focused on the work being played and on the nuances of its interpretation, unaware of the mechanics of his or her performance. Indeed a switch of attention, reversing the focal and the subsidiary, will interrupt the expert performance, the auto weaves, the pianist stumbles, the carpenter bends the nail.

Bargh, an experimental psychologist, has unpacked some of the complexities of the automatic mode of knowing (1989). He argued that 'automaticity' is a notion with several dimensions: (1) awareness, (2) attention, (3) intention and (4) control. These terms can be illustrated in the following ways. First, an actor is often unaware of his or her activity when it is effortless. Thus high-intensity activity seems effortless when one is in a state of 'flow' and one's entire attention is focused outwards on the objective of the activity rather than on its process (Csikszentmihalyi, 1988). Second, some actions are automatic because they do not require one's conscious attention. Reacting to sudden noises or avoiding near accidents like tripping or catching a falling object, involve skilled performance, but without the actor's attention being focused. Third, activity is also automatic when it cannot be associated with a goal and is thus without intention. One example of this is 'side-effect encoding', when people remember patterns which are unrelated to their task. Another is the 'action slip', for instance, William James's oft-repeated story of the man who, on going upstairs to dress for dinner, 'finds' himself in bed. Fourth, automaticity also implies loss of conscious control. Habits are not only effortless and beyond one's attention, they are frequently uncontrollable even when one is aware of them. They refuse to remain in one's focal awareness, sliding uncontrollably to the subsidiary level. While the automaticity is clearly psychologically complex, research underlines that automatic behavior is both prevalent and researchable. It is also clear that one way to build up automatic knowledge is via conscious practice. This 'sediments' the incommunicable aspects of practice into the nonconscious domain while it adds to the inventory of contextualized practice that Simon noted.

In the sections above we suggest that workplace knowledge is (1) likely to be practical rather than scientific, and (2) can be either conscious or automatic. We can also suggest that the conscious and the automatic complement each other in an actor's practice. It follows that an actor might be able to switch attention between the conscious and automatic modes according to whether the practice is succeeding or failing (Louis and Sutton, 1991). However this implies a problematic meta-rationality capable of monitoring performance in the nonconscious automatic mode. It also presupposes the priority of the conscious mode of knowing, which is the opposite of what Polanyi believed.

The Collective Component of Tacit Knowledge

In this section we recall Vygotsky's action theory and extend our typology in a different way by suggesting that practical knowledge may be more of a social or collective feature than an individual property. We distinguish between the knowledge that has been developed by the individual and shared with others, and that which is part and parcel of the social system. Without positing a collective mind, it seems difficult to argue for collective knowledge. But we have just argued that much practical knowledge is 'automatic' and inaccessible to the individual. In Polanyi's oft-quoted phrase, 'we know more than we can say'. Cultural anthropologists recognize that much of what people do is the result of the taken-for-granted knowledge which they have acquired during their upbringing. In this sense, they are agents of a collective body of knowledge. People are often unaware of how much they know about their society's norms and collective knowledge until they are confronted with morally questionable actions. Then they learn something about the character they have acquired from their social context. They have that immediate 'gut-reaction' which enables them to distinguish right from wrong and reveals the extent and power of their taken-for-granted acculturation. This is collective rather than universal knowledge and it only becomes conscious to the individual through such character-shaping events or through disciplined study, introspection or psychoanalysis.

Much of the culture of the modern workplace is about collective knowledge. Often lumped together with organizational culture, this goes well beyond affect or the constraints of individual cognition. The Hawthorne experiments made us aware of the power of the work-group and the way knowledge is wrapped up in processes which no one worker can articulate. Similarly Nelson and Winter argue that organizations retain their knowledge in 'organizational routines' which no one person understands (1982).

Orr (1990) uncovered some of the processes which generated and stored practical knowledge as his fellow repairmen fixed photocopier machines at customer sites and later socialized together. First he showed that their work process was social and involved the customers as well as the machines. The real service problems occurred in the relationship between the customer and the copier, so knowing how to 'fix the customer' was as important as knowing how to fix the machine. Second he showed that the knowledge which the repairmen required was contextualized in the user's practice rather than in the practice of the machine's designers. The faults would generally be beyond those imagined by the designers, so they were not covered in the machine manuals. Nor could the problems be traced to faulty manufacture. Third, by paying attention to the stories which the repairmen swapped, Orr found the technicians operated as a cohesive community of practice (Brown and Duguid, 1991). The story-telling connected them with their collective memory. Faced with a new breakdown, the repairmen would swap stories, drawing on this collective memory and proposing tentative diagnoses of the fault. As they converged on a common diagnosis their story-telling would cease. When they rejoined their colleagues, they would tell new stories of the latest repair, so adding to the collective memory.

There is more to this than sharing data. Science is not only a body of knowledge, it is also the methodology of a community of practice, a socially legitimized way of gathering and communicating evidence. Scientific knowledge is structured as objective causal relationships, models and theories. But those who generate and exchange these models form a community of scientific thought and analysis. Scientific discourse is designed to be objective, free from ambiguity, and to be an appropriate means for communicating this community's abstractions. But it is still embedded within the community's less structured conversation. Orr's repairmen were engaged in an overtly narrative form of discourse, much closer to the ballads that carry forward our social knowledge and ancient myths. Both Hunter (1991) and Schön (1983) have argued that narrative enables practitioners to bridge between the abstractions of principles, and scientific knowledge, and the particulars of a situation. The implication is that narrative is an essential part of the acquisition of practical knowledge. It is an ambiguous medium, able to capture more of the profession's technical, social and moral context (Daft and Wiginton, 1979; Weick, 1987). Narrative is obviously social, for it uses language. Thus it both reflects and reconstitutes the community of practice. Its ambiguity lets individuals adopt any of the many legitimate social roles within the community, to be a listener or a participant, a supporter or a detractor within the ongoing conversation.

The spoken word is not the only form of collective memory. Ethnography teaches us much about signs and symbols as keys or pointers to a society's collective database. Professionals, especially technical professionals, make great use of drawings to key into elements of their collective knowledge. Vincenti (1990) and Ferguson (1992) have argued that much of engineering's collective knowledge is retained as visual images. Sometimes these are formalized in reference books, but more often the images are acquired through years of study, careful observation and design experience as engineers move through their careers. As Simon implied, the experienced designer starts with a vast body of taken-for-granted practical images, whether they be of airplanes, bridges, or electronic circuits.

The previous sections suggest four types of organizational knowledge, one scientific and familiar, three tacit and less easily understood. These are the conscious, the automatic, and the collective. We can show their relationship in a matrix; see Figure 3.1.

The individual types of knowledge (the conscious and the automatic) derive from the two ways in which we can know as isolated individuals. The social types of knowledge suggest other inventories of knowledge. Indivi-

	Individual	Social
Explicit	Conscious	Objectified
Implicit	Automatic	Collective

Figure 3.1   *Types of organizational knowledge*

duals may draw on these to add to or complement their own knowledge. We suggest that actors can only draw on scientific knowledge explicitly. However, as cultural anthropology demonstrates, individuals often draw on collective knowledge without being aware of doing so.

Strategic Relationships with the Types of Knowledge

Each of the four types of organizational knowledge could provide the basis for a theory of competitive advantage. Thus one firm might have more 'individual automatic' knowledge (which we might call skill) than another firm. Alternatively there might be differences in the degree to which firms are able to absorb and apply 'collective' knowledge. Although advantage might accrue from any of these types of knowledge, the strategic implications of each, and the approach that the executives should take to the management of each, are clearly quite different.

If the firm's advantage is based on scientific knowledge, then its strategy must recognize that such knowledge tends to be professionally accessible, abstract and mobile. Appropriability is likely to be a key issue, and patents, contracts, nondisclosure agreements and similar appeals to legal or institutional structures may or may not protect the advantage (Teece, 1987). The knowledge itself, and the ability to create similar knowledge through re-engineering or parallel research, is likely to be widely held outside the firm. By contrast, if the advantage is based narrowly on automatic knowledge, such as that of a high-performing fund manager or industrial designer, then appropriability may be less of an issue, possibly quite the opposite. Now the real difficulty may be to find ways of integrating this individual's special knowledge with the complementary assets necessary to generate the rent stream and into the rest of the organization. On the other hand, if the crucial knowledge is practical, local and conscious, then secrecy, bonding or behavioral incentives may be required.

In the last two instances, where the knowledge is knowingly held by a single individual or small group, the dominant strategic issue for the firm may be the moral hazard, the temptation for the knowledge holders to 'hold up' the organization in an attempt to capture the rent for themselves (Kotowitz, 1989; Williamson, 1975). However, if the advantage is based on collective knowledge, the strategic problems will be reduced because individuals, such as a star copywriter or performer, cannot so readily hold the firm to ransom. Nor is it easy for another firm to imitate and put together a similar high performing team. One way to deal with the moral hazard mentioned above is to ensure that the firm has secure possession of one or more of the complementary assets which the star entertainer or copywriter needs to develop the rent-stream. For instance, recording artists need a distribution network as well as talent. John D. Rockefeller was able to dominate the oil industry by controlling its means of distribution. Only later did he translate this power into control over the means of production.

We can suspect that the firm's competitive advantage generally arises from the interaction of different types of knowledge, or of different types of people (Alchian and Demsetz, 1972). The simplistic model, which attributes advantage to a single source such as a core competence, is almost certainly inadequate. Teece's (1987) notion of complementarity adds a second dimension of complexity, but it also throws doubt onto the underlying soundness of the idea of core competencies. If possession of the complementary assets becomes the explanation of success (Teece, 1987) then these assets have surely become the core assets. Thus the notion core competence may be little more than a tautology. Seeing competitive advantage we presume competence. But until we identify the substance or nature of a core competence we have only a substitute for the idea of competitive advantage, not an explanation.

The CT Scan Story

To get a sense of how these different types of knowledge might interact in practice we can consider the example of computed axial tomography (sometimes called CAT scanning, though now generally known as computed tomography or CT scanning). a great deal has been written about this technology and the strategic shifts it occasioned within the medical imaging industry. At first sight EMI's experience in this industry was a classic case of the weakness of a strategy based upon some scientific knowledge that could be readily appropriated by others (Teece, 1987). But the reality that the innovating firm's strategists confronted was really quite different.

The popular version of the story is simple. Hounsfield, the inventor of CT scanning, won the Nobel Prize in 1979. However, EMI, his British employer, had by then lost their leadership in the medical imaging business. In 1980 they exited after first making good profits but then making losses as they came into competition with a number of international majors, including GE, who eventually bought the remains of EMI's patent and market position. Teece suggests that had EMI been able to secure legal control of the CT technology, they could have leveraged that into control of the complementary assets and so assured themselves a long-term dominant position. Their failure to do this was 'a strategic error'

(1987: 207). Teece's analysis, which relies heavily on Martin's (1984) brief history, was a substantial improvement over the lay view that EMI was yet another research company that was badly managed by scientists and engineers who failed to pay proper attention to market forces. Teece (1987) leaves open some questions about whether EMI lacked the necessary training, support and service facilities which, he suggests, could have been supplied by Siemens, or whether it was their inadequate defense of their patent position that was at the heart of their strategic error.

Teece's story is written with one kind of knowledge in mind, scientific, or maybe technological. Our fourfold typology above suggests that other types of knowledge may have played an important part in the CT story. We must note a general criticism of such stories of the development of technology whenever they are extracted from their social and historical context. Bijker and Law (1992) argue that history shows that technologies do not develop along 'trajectories' determined by their inner scientific momentum. They suggest instead that technologies are developed and applied in a social world which also develops, or stagnates, at the same time. This is clearly the case in CT scanning, and the case also reinforces the significance of the individual and collective tacit knowledge that complemented the objectified scientific knowledge to which Teece refers.

In fact, the CT story cannot be told properly without paying attention to the collective knowledge and the communities of practice which interacted as a result of the innovation (Mitchell, 1995). Blume's (1992) analysis shows that Hounsfield had little understanding of the potential of CT scanning when he built the first prototype. He was a senior researcher in EMI's computer research laboratory. His primary interest was in computers and, in this particular application, exploring the potential of computers to capture more meaning from X-ray images. He knew virtually nothing of the medical field. In particular he lacked the appropriate tacit understanding of medical imaging equipment, or of the radiological community by whom it would be used. Webb (1990) and others have shown that computed tomography was well established before Hounsfield became interested in the subject. Indeed radioisotope scanning, especially Kuhl's CT-scanner-like apparatus, was widely adopted in the 1950s (Webb, 1990). By the late 1960s a large number of researchers were working on CT, and a large number of radiologists had both objective knowledge or practical experience of a variety of head and body scanning techniques and ideas. The most significant inventors were Oldenburg and Kuhl in America and Cormack in South Africa, though there was also a Russian group at the Kiev Polytechnic Institute. A number of mathematicians were also struggling with the special problem of the mathematical reconstruction of the linear emission data which, ironically, had already been solved in 1917 by the Austrian mathematician Johann Radon.

The EMI division in which Hounsfield worked was primarily a military electronics R and D and subcontract manufacturing facility. They knew little of the medical imaging business and had no wish to develop a revolutionary apparatus for an unfamiliar market. But, seeing the possibilities after some desk research, they thought to tempt an arm of the UK government, the Department of Health and Social Services (DHSS), into providing research funding. The DHSS, which was initially interested in mass-screening for political reasons, eventually rose to the bait and supported the work. Hounsfield was able to work with Ambrose, a senior neuro-radiologist based at the Atkinson Morley Hospital, who began to work out the practical implications of the new apparatus for the radiological community. It was the DHSS funding, rather than either Hounsfield or EMI's management, that set the strategic agenda. EMI only embraced the agenda after Powell, their new technical director, championed it and because, at that time, they were anxious to increase the nonmilitary portion of their business.

As the first prototype was being hand-built in EMI's Hayes workshop, it became obvious that the capital commitments involved were far beyond EMI's normal levels, especially as Hounsfield's patent was seen to be vulnerable and the company had determined that they should build a defensible position through aggressive manufacturing and marketing. They discovered that there were many previous US patents as well as other manufacturers, such as Kuhl, already active in the field. Hounsfield eventually shared the Nobel Prize with Cormack, with Oldenburg, Goetlin and many other significant contributors feeling distinctly put out. The point is less the scientific one of who could lay the best claim to the invention, than the broader one that many radiologists, many engineers and most of the medical imaging companies had contributed to the body of collective knowledge and immediately understood what the EMI scanner was able to do. It combined new computer analysis of the X-ray data with more powerful X-ray sources. But it was nevertheless only an incremental innovation for the radiological community. Thus EMI had almost no chance of developing a long-term winning strategy. Powell saw that EMI's opportunity was dependent on securing and exploiting a first mover advantage. Through happenstance (the meeting with Bull, the surgeon, which led Hounsfield to apply his imaging ideas to the medical field) they had stumbled upon a widely understood technology which was of sufficient interest to the DHSS, who would fund their research, but which had tremendous overseas potential, especially in the US market. EMI started out without knowledge of these markets. Had they known, they probably would have realized that they did not have the funds or manufacturing skills necessary to compete in them. Yet this ignorance led them to proceed and succeed.

Blume's analysis showed that CT scanning, as the DHSS had defined it for EMI, was a radiological procedure which would extend current radiological practice. In this sense it was strategically located in the center of an existing and powerful community of practice. CT scanning was not like ultra-sound, a radically new technology that foretold of a new community of sonic imaging practitioners among gynecologists (Blume,

1992). The X-ray community existed already. EMI, for its part, was not a member of this community, so their immediate strategic objective was to gain entrance. They chose to show off their technology, so falling into a classic trap for owners of intellectual property rights. When they made their first clinical scan in October 1971, successfully diagnosing a brain tumor in a forty-one year old woman, the entire project was still a closely guarded medical and technological secret. Only those involved at the EMI Hayes laboratories and in the special department set up at the Atkinson Morley Hospital knew what was going on.

In April 1972, with the working prototype and initial clinical tests behind them, they plunged ahead and announced their work to the world's press at the British Institute of Radiology Conference. They issued complete technical specifications. In the following October they demonstrated the machine in Chicago at the annual conference of the Radiological Society of North America. The response to the machine and to Ambrose's paper was overwhelming, not only from the international radiological community but also from every major imaging equipment supplier (except Siemens, which merely noted this increase of activity from a distance). EMI, whose initial market estimate was for ten machines, were eventually backlogged with orders for 250 machines. Much to their own surprise (like IBM's surprise at the market's response to the PC) they inadvertently triggered a major response within a community of practice dominated by a small number of substantially larger and more aggressive competitors. Of course this community included the radiologists who determined the equipment's purchase and use. But it also included the few large and powerful suppliers who dominated the international X-ray imaging and supplies business. These oligopolists saw immediately that the new CT scanner threatened their livelihood and hurried to develop a strategic response. They had a substantial understanding of how their industry worked and were able to bring new machines to market in short order, often by buying the small specialist firms which had been working on similar equipment for years (such as Pfizer's support of Digital Information Systems, the result of Ledley's collaboration with Oldenburg and Cormack, Technicare's acquisition of Ohio Nuclear, and GE's work with Neuroscan).

EMI's lack of understanding of the tacit components of radiological practice put them at a substantial disadvantage to the established suppliers because the purchase decisions were shaped by the radiologists. Barley (1986) has shown how these radiologists protected their power base as the new CT scanning equipment was introduced, for they had to teach themselves how to integrate the equipment into their practice. The practice of radiology, especially the interpretation of X-ray images, depends on tacit knowledge and is still relatively uncodified. Had CT scanning been a radical innovation, one which destroyed rather than enhanced the radiologists' existing competencies (Tushman and Anderson, 1986), the interaction between EMI and the radiologists' collective knowledge would have been very different. As it was, there was an immediate but short-lived premium on radiologists who had recently graduated from the teaching hospitals where CT scanners were installed since they could assist the radiologists in the field as they struggled to upgrade their practical knowledge. The radiologists also had to realign their relationships with the radiology department technicians who were often relatively more knowledgeable about both the CT machine and the interpretation of its images. From a strategic point of view, we can see that EMI's decision to let the radiologists teach themselves and so extend their existing collective knowledge made EMI extremely vulnerable to competitive suppliers, such as Siemens, Philips and GE, who had long-established relationships with both the radiologists and the hospital financial executives. The 'strategic error' was that they failed to take control of this body of knowledge. Clearly EMI never had an opportunity to do this, nor did they think otherwise. It would have required a new technology which effectively rendered obsolete the existing body of collective radiological knowledge. Teece's charge, therefore, arises from a misunderstanding of the relationship between objectified knowledge, such as might be patented or built into a machine, and the collective knowledge which is embedded in practice.

But the CT interaction was not solely between EMI and the radiological community of practice. In the late 1970s and early 1980s the US market made up well over fifty percent of the entire world market for CT scanners, and within the United States the hospitals the Federal government and the medical insurers were also involved. Between 1972 and 1983 the market was significantly shaped by the third party reimbursement system. Though, as we argue above, the CT scanner was an extension of existing practice, it nonetheless provided hospitals an opportunity to offer a completely new service which could be charged separately and this gave them a new profit center. The possession of a scanner was also a useful way for gaining prestige in the community, for competing against neighboring hospitals, and for attracting the leading surgeons and physicians (Trajtenberg, 1990). The US market for scanners developed extremely rapidly even though the scanner's actual diagnostic value remained in some doubt. The equipment played to the competitive business practices of both the radiologists and the kinds of hospitals in which they were located. By 1982 virtually every US hospital with more than 400 beds had its own scanner, while only three percent of the hospitals with less than 100 beds were so equipped.

The pace of the market attracted the attention of the Federal government which worried that the third-party reimbursement system might be combining with the hospitals' competitive practices in ways which were socially dysfunctional. They were especially concerned at the amount of money being spent, and made, on CT scanning (Iglehart, 1982). As a result, they attempted to slow the introduction by establishing Certificates of Need (CON) under Section 1122 of the Social Security Act. To a certain extent, this institutional pressure dampened the market. But with Reagan's election and the decay of many types of Federal regulation, the radiologists began to take matters into their own hands, setting up private CT clinics and circumventing the CON system. The CT market peaked for a second time. However, by now it was beginning to be saturated, with all the large hospitals and specialist clinics adequately equipped. In addition, an even more expensive competing technology appeared, magnetic resonance imaging (MRI). By 1985 the CT market in the US was becoming severely saturated and the boom was finishing as quickly as it had begun. The future growth areas would be down-market in low cost scanners for the rest of the world. Here the US firms would lock horns with Siemens, Philips, and especially the Japanese manufacturers such as Toshiba. The distribution and manufacturing problems would be radically different. Thorn, which had bought EMI for reasons unconnected with this imaging business, had no intention of entering this escalating global market.

Without going further into the details of the CT industry's dynamics we can see that EMI's strategic problems were very much tied up in the varieties of knowledge which they needed to master the X-ray imaging business. They certainly had some crucial scientific expertise, but their proprietary knowledge was neither complete nor inimitable. Pfizer's second generation whole body scanner, with its Automatic Computerized Transverse Axial (ACTA) technology, was successfully patented as a significant advance on Hounsfield's technology and came onto the market in 1975. The third and fourth generation systems, with first rotating and then a fixed 360° ring of multiple detectors, followed quickly (Trajtenberg, 1990).

EMI also needed new manufacturing expertise which had significant tacit content (Collins, 1974). In the event they had few manufacturing problems and did surprisingly well given where they started. But they also committed themselves strategically to the US market. Powell, short on time and resources, gambled on a single strategy, choosing to enter the major and most competitive market with force and speed, but also with complete technological exposure. Without an international presence or a place in the radiological community of practice, they were more or less forced to create and depend on market pull by exposing their technology to radiologists, inventors, researchers and competitive manufacturers alike. They legitimized themselves by significant contributions to the community's knowledge via publications in the leading medical journals and appearances at trade shows. Powell's strategy succeeded in drawing the attention of the radiologists who would be their eventual customers, and they made a substantial amount of money. Nevertheless, they also triggered competitive responses with which they were relatively ill-equipped to deal. Even though the EMI patents still dominated the CT field in 1980 (Trajtenberg, 1990), the combination of financial troubles in the parent company and the saturation of the US market made withdrawal an intelligent strategic choice. With the financial stakes rising rapidly, Thorn chose a dignified retreat over a Pyrrhic war against the entrenched oligopolists that Hounsfield had stirred into action. Ironically, the collective knowledge EMI had built up, and their understanding of the tacit aspects of radiological and hospital practice, were of little value to GE, who sought only their scientific assets.

Conclusions

In this chapter we explore the strategic implications of the proposition that tacit knowledge is at the root of competitive advantage. We turn to recent empirical research into workplace activity to help us sort out the various types of knowledge which are applied in organizations. We suggest a four-fold typology that distinguishes three types of tacit knowledge from the objective or scientific knowledge with which organizational theorists are most comfortable. The three types of tacit knowledge are (1) conscious practical knowledge, (2) automatic practical knowledge, and (3) collective practical knowledge. Each of these types of knowledge can provide the basis for a competitive advantage. But their strategic implications are radically different. The problems or threats which each pose, and the ways in which firms can deal with these, are also different. It follows that there will be a set of strategic contingencies relating the different kinds of knowledge to particular market, institutional and technological circumstances.

Our types are also 'ideal types' of knowledge. Real organizations contain all types of knowledge. But our principal argument is that we cannot perform effective strategic analysis, especially of knowledge intensive activities, without paying attention to all these types of knowledge. In our discussion of the CT story we add to Teece's, and Bijker and Law's, arguments, and suggest that an analysis of the strategic process or competitive advantage must consider the interplay of knowledge types. Using this story we are able to go beyond strategy's current typologies and consider briefly the interplay of scientific, individual and collective knowledge.

References

Akerlof, G. (1970) 'The market for lemons', *Quarterly Journal of Economics*, 84: 488–500.
Alchian, A. and Demsetz, H. (1972) 'Production, information costs and economic organization', *American Economic Review*, 62: 777–795.
Attewell, P. (1992) 'Technology diffusion and organizational learning: The case of business computing', *Organization Science*, 3: 1–19.
Bargh, J.A. (1989) 'Conditional automaticity: Varieties of automatic influence in cognition', in J.S. Uleman and J.A. Bargh (eds), *Unintended Thought*. New York: Guilford Press. pp. 3–51.
Barley, S.R. (1986) 'Technology as an occasion for structuring: Evidence from observations of CT scanners and the social order of radiology departments', *Administrative Science Quarterly*, 31: 78–108.
Barney, J. (1991) 'Firm resources and sustained competitive advantage', *Journal of Management*, 17: 99–120.

Bijker, W.E. and Law, J. (eds) (1992) *Shaping Technology/Building Society*. Cambridge, MA: MIT Press.

Blume, S.S. (1992) *Insight and Industry: On the Dynamics of Technological Change in Medicine*. Cambridge, MA: MIT Press.

Brown, J.S. and Duguid, P. (1991) 'Organizational learning and communities-of-practice: Towards a unified view of working, learning, and innovation', *Organization Science*, 2: 40–57.

Cohen, W.M. and Levinthal, D.A. (1990) 'Absorptive capacity: A new perspective on learning and innovation', *Administrative Science Quarterly*, 35: 128–152.

Collins, H.M. (1974) 'The TEA set: Tacit knowledge and scientific networks', *Science Studies*, 4: 165.

Conner, K.R. (1991) 'A historical comparison of resource-based theory and five schools of thought within industrial organization economics: Do we have a new theory of the firm?' *Journal of Management*, 17: 121–154.

Csikszentmihalyi, M. (1988) 'The flow experience and its significance for human psychology', in M. Csikszentmihalyi and I.S. Csikszentmihalyi (eds), *Optimal Experience: Psychological Studies of Flow in Consciousness*. Cambridge: Cambridge University Press. pp. 15–35.

Daft, R.L. (1982) 'Bureaucratic versus nonbureaucratic structure and the process of innovation and change', in S.B. Bacharach (ed.), *Research in the Sociology of Organizations*, vol. 1. Greenwich, CT: JAI Press. pp. 129–166.

Daft, R.L. and Wiginton, J. (1979) 'Language and organization', *Academy of Management Review*, 4: 179–191.

Ettlie, J.E. (1988) *Taking Charge of Manufacturing: How Companies are Combining Technological and Organizational Innovations to Compete Successfully*. San Francisco, CA: Jossey-Bass.

Ferguson, E.S. (1992) *Engineering and the Mind's Eye*. Cambridge, MA: MIT Press.

Gelwick, R. (1977) *The Way of Discovery: An Introduction to the Thought of Michael Polanyi*. New York: Oxford University Press.

Hirschhorn, L. (1984) *Beyond Mechanization: Work and Technology in a Postindustrial Age*. Cambridge, MA: MIT Press.

Hunter, M.K. (1991) *Doctor's Stories: The Narrative Structure of Medical Knowledge*. Princeton, NJ: Princeton University Press.

Iglehart, J.K. (1982) 'The cost and regulation of medical technology', in J.B. McKinlay (ed.), *Technology and the Future of Healthcare*. Cambridge, MA: MIT Press. pp. 69–103.

Kagono, T., Nonaka, I., Sakakibara, K. and Omura, A. (1985) *Strategic vs. Evolutionary Management: A US–Japan Comparison of Strategy and Organization*. Amsterdam: North-Holland.

Kogut, B. and Zander, U. (1992) 'Knowledge of the firm, combinative capabilities, and the replication of technology', *Organization Science*, 3: 383–397.

Kotowitz, Y. (1989) 'Moral hazard', in J. Eatwell, M. Millgate and P. Newman (eds), *The New Palgrave: Allocation, Information, and Markets*. New York: W.W. Norton. pp. 207–213.

Kusterer, K.C. (1978) *Knowhow on the Job: The Important Working Knowledge of 'Unskilled' Workers*. Boulder, CO: Westview Press.

Lippman, S. and Rumelt, R.P. (1982) 'Uncertain imitability: An analysis of interfirm differences in efficiency under competition', *Bell Journal of Economics*, 12: 413–438.

Louis, M.R. and Sutton, R.I. (1991) 'Switching cognitive gears: From habits of mind to active thinking', *Human Relations*, 44: 55–76.

Mahoney, J.T. and Pandian, J.R. (1992) 'The resource-based view within the conversation of strategic management', *Strategic Management Journal*, 13: 363–380.

Martin, M. (1984) *Managing Technical Innovation and Entrepreneurship*. Reston, VA: Reston Publishing.

Mitchell, W. (1995) 'Medical diagnostic imaging manufacturers', in G.R. Carroll and M.T. Hannan (eds), *Organizations in Industry: Strategy, Structure and Selection*. New York: Oxford University Press. pp. 244–272.

Nelson, R.R. and Winter, S.G. (1982) *An Evolutionary Theory of Economic Change*. Cambridge, MA: Belknap Press.

Nonaka, I. (1991) 'The knowledge-creating company', *Harvard Business Review*, 96–104.

Nonaka, I. and Takeuchi, H. (1995) *The Knowledge-Creating Company: How Japanese Companies Create the Dynamics of Innovation*. New York: Oxford University Press.

Norman, D.A. (1989) *The Design of Everyday Things*. New York: Doubleday.

Orr, J.E. (1990) 'Sharing knowledge, celebrating identity', in D.S. Middleton and D. Edwards (eds), *Collective Remembering*. Newbury Park, CA: Sage. pp. 169–189.

Polanyi, M. (1962) *Personal Knowledge: Towards a Post-Critical Philosophy*, corrected edn. Chicago, IL: University of Chicago Press.

Popper, K.R. (1973) *Objective Knowledge: An Evolutionary Approach*, revised edn. Oxford: Clarendon Press.

Prahalad, C.K. and Hamel, G. (1990) 'The core competence of the corporation', *Harvard Business Review*, 68(3): 79–91.

Rumelt, R.P. (1987) 'Theory, strategy and entrepreneurship', in D.J. Teece (ed.), *The Competitive Challenge: Strategies For Industrial Innovation and Renewal*. Cambridge, MA: Ballinger. pp. 137–158.

Rumelt, R.P., Schendel, D. and Teece, D.J. (1991) 'Strategic management and economics', *Strategic Management Journal*, 12: 5–29.

Schön, D.A. (1983) *The Reflective Practitioner: How Professionals Think in Action*. New York: Basic Books.

Scribner, S., Di Bello, L., Kindred, J. and Zazanis, E. (1991) *Coordinating Two Knowledge Systems: A Case Study*. New York: Laboratory for Cognitive Studies of Work, CUNY.

Selznick, P. (1957) *Leadership in Administration: A Sociological Interpretation*. New York: Harper and Row.

Senker, J. (1995) 'Tacit knowledge and models of innovation', *Industrial and Corporate Change*, 4: 425–447.

Simon, H.A. (1987) 'Making management decisions: The role of intuition and emotion', *Academy of Management Executive*, 1: 57–64.

Teece, D.J. (1987) 'Profiting from technological innovation', in D.J. Teece (ed.), *The Competitive Challenge*. Cambridge, MA: Ballinger. pp. 185–219.

Thompson, J.D. (1967) *Organizations in Action: Social Science Bases of Administrative Theory*. New York: McGraw-Hill.

Trajtenberg, M. (1990) *Economic Analysis of Product Innovation: The Case of CT Scanning*. Cambridge, MA: Harvard University Press.

Tushman, M.L. and Anderson, P. (1986) 'Technological discontinuities and organizational environments', *Administrative Science Quarterly*, 31: 439–465.

Van de Ven, A.H. and Polley, D. (1992) 'Learning while innovating', *Organization Science*, 3: 92–116.

Vincenti, W.G. (1990) *What Engineers Know and How They Know It: Analytical Studies from Aeronautical History*. Baltimore, MD: Johns Hopkins University Press.

Vygotsky, L.S. (1962) *Thought and Language*. Cambridge, MA: MIT Press.

Webb, S. (1990) *From the Watching of Shadows: The Origins of Radiological Tomography*. New York: Adam Hilger.

Weick, K.E. (1987) 'Organizational culture as a source of high reliability', *California Management Review*, 29: 112–127.

Wernerfelt, B. (1984) 'A resource-based view of the firm', *Strategic Management Journal*, 5: 171–181.

Wertsch, J.V. (1985) *Vygotsky and the Social Formation of Mind*. Cambridge, MA: Harvard University Press.

Williamson, O.E. (1975) *Markets and Hierarchies: Analysis and Antitrust Implications*. New York: Free Press.

Winter, S.G. (1987) 'Knowledge and competence as strategic assets', in D.J. Teece (ed.), *The Competitive Challenge*. Cambridge, MA: Ballinger. pp. 159–184.

4

Organizations in the Fog:
An Investigation into the Dynamics of Knowledge

Philippe Baumard

The idea that today's competitive organizations are those that can be described as innovative, intelligent, or flexible is increasingly widespread. However, what is meant by these words is not completely straightforward. This chapter focuses on organizations that derive their competitive advantage from their 'effectiveness in ambiguity', borrowing an expression used by Herzberg (1987) to define intelligence. Thus the focus of this chapter is on organizations that remain competitive in the worst conditions. This chapter examines situations in which firms lose their way, and executives' vision becomes fogged. The strategic task is then to restore *clarity* – as opposed to *ambiguity* – by generating new knowledge or by transforming the existing knowledge to 'get out of the fog'.

This chapter discusses the dialectics between ambiguity and knowledge. The conventional view is that relevant knowledge in organizations comes from explicit situational analysis, and is thus objective knowledge. In contrast to a positivist notion that views knowledge merely as 'information enriched with meaning and experience', we argue that cognitive and organizational issues should not be approached separately. By identifying the roles played by particular types of knowledge in resolving ambiguous situations, we shall try to illuminate the role played by richness, density and versatility of knowledge.

To analyze the different ways knowledge can shift within organizations facing an ambiguous situation, a two-by-two matrix inspired by Spender (in this volume) and Nonaka (1991, 1994) is elaborated. Two distinctions are made. One is *explicit* versus *tacit*, from Polanyi's work (1958, 1966), and the other is *individual* versus *social* from Durkheimian sociology. To avoid misinterpretation, we use instead an *individual* versus *collective* dimension (following Nonaka, 1991).

In seeking the basis of a 'grounded theory' (Glaser and Strauss, 1967) of organizational knowledge dynamics, we investigated managers' behaviors and knowledge mutations facing ambiguous and unpredictable situations. Case study research was conducted in France, Australia and in the United States. In this chapter, we unpack the role played by four types of knowledge (explicit/individual; explicit/collective; tacit/individual; tacit/collective) as organizations try to deal with ambiguous situations. In so doing, tacit knowledge is discovered as a source of competitive advantage.

Defining Ambiguity

Ambiguity is a concept that is frequently used inaccurately in the management literature; it is often confused with uncertainty, from which it differs in important ways. The word's etymology comes from the Latin *ambo* (two). It expresses the inability to see one definite *meaning* of a situation, sentence, word, thought, action, or person. Oracles, for example, are traditionally ambiguous. They offer many interpretations, and cannot be trapped in one definite meaning.

Uncertainty is a different concept. While ambiguity is concerned with meaning, uncertainty is defined as the characteristics of an event that cannot be determined. Uncertainty can apply to a situation that is known, clear and identifiable. In contrast, an ambiguous situation requires dealing with a reality in which nothing is permanent, or definitely true or definitely false. This was the situation of the organizations we studied; it was not possible to determine the actual degree of uncertainty of the choices they faced.

Struggling with Ambiguity

Organizations are neither systematically deterministic, nor spontaneously voluntaristic, but work under sets of *minima* (minimal consistency, minimal faith, minimal contentment, etc.), such that they are typically 'weathering the storm', and 'unlearning yesterday' to continue to 'fly without flying apart' (Hedberg et al., 1976). In maintaining these minima, managers try to make sense of the stimuli they perceive. Subsequently, 'those interpretations are generated within the organization in the face of considerable perceptual ambiguity' (March and Olsen, 1976: 19). First, managers do not notice everything. Moreover, they must struggle with contradictory stimuli, which carry many antithetical meanings. This is a permanent struggle with ambiguity.

Freaking Out in the Fog: Ambiguity as an Obstacle to Decision Making

'Struggling with ambiguity' (Alvesson, 1993) can determine the fate of an organization. For example, tolerance for ambiguity has been identified as a critical factor of success when dealing with foreign countries and cultures (Marquardt and Engel, 1993). While decision theorists idealize and rationalize the 'human thinking system', in actuality, 'people do not know all of the sources of stimuli, nor do they necessarily know how to distinguish relevant from irrelevant information' (Starbuck and Miliken,

1988: 41). People act according to 'criteria' that they view as important, sometimes quite unable to define why these criteria are important, for they tend 'to deal with a limited set of problems and a limited set of goals' (Cyert and March, 1963: 117). 'Bounded rationality' in which actors search for answers close to the problem represents another struggle with ambiguity. 'Perceptual filtering' (Starbuck and Miliken, 1988) is a cognitive 'mechanism' by which people cope with ambiguity. Because we have 'to live with complexity' (Starbuck and Miliken, 1988: 58), we must learn and 'unlearn' (Hedberg, 1981). However, organizational scholars are pessimistic about the ability of organizations to 'unlearn old behaviors and world views' in facing new situations (Hedberg, 1981).

Thriving in the Fog: The Tactical Use of Ambiguity

The preceding section reviewed how ambiguity is viewed as an obstacle to decision making in the current literature. This section shows that ambiguity can be actively sought and enacted for tactical purposes.

One of the domains where ambiguity might be sought is language. To protect their personal space, managers are often imprecise about their objectives in bureaucratic environments. By using loose role definitions or avoiding direct confrontation, they maintain a 'blur zone' (Crozier and Hedberg, 1977). Imprecise role definition, using ambiguous language, serves a tactical purpose when role conflicts arise (Shenkar and Zeira, 1992). Thus, ambiguous language can be a means of gaining competitive advantage. Détienne and Vernant (1974), in their study of cunning intelligence in ancient Greece, show how politicians used 'oblique knowledge' to deal with 'ambiguous, shifting and disconcerting situations'. Today, ambiguous language can be used to manipulate voters (Dacey, 1976).

Research Method

The goal of our empirical research was to identify the existence of specific modes of knowing in 'ambiguous, mutable and unpredictable' situations in the workplace, and thus to answer the following questions: As organizations struggle with ambiguity, is there a type of knowledge from the 2 × 2 matrix which is dominant at particular times? If so, how can moving around the matrix help organizations to succeed in their struggle with ambiguity? Can organizations derive a competitive advantage from such a dynamic handling of their organizational knowledge?

Revelatory Situations and Purposeful Sampling

We used multiple case study research (Glaser and Strauss, 1967; Lincoln and Guba, 1985) to investigate the phenomenon of organizational ambiguity within its real context. To justify multiple case study research, we first needed to produce evidence that the different cases involved the same syndrome (Yin, 1984). Each case had to be carefully selected to be certain that the organization was really facing an ambiguous, unpredictable and mutable situation. Organizations were selected on the basis of situations they faced (involving unexpected ruptures in the course of events, such as sudden political turbulence).

With such criteria, four organizations were selected for their commonality in certain attributes of interest (task complexity, situation ambiguity) and divergence in other attributes (different countries, different products and services, different purposes). The four organizations are Pechiney (France, Guinea), Indosuez (USA), Qantas (Australia) and Indigo (France). Two of these organizations (Pechiney and Indigo) will be described below, as case studies illustrating different ways firms deal with ambiguity.

Engaging Interviewees in 'Reflective Practice'

'Reflective practice' is thinking about and critically analyzing one's actions with the goal of improving one's professional practice (Osterman, 1990; Peters, 1991; Schön, 1988). Reflective practice involves taking on the perspective of an external observer in considering one's own work; and to identify underlying assumptions and feelings that may affect one's practice (Imel, 1992). This tradition finds its roots in the works of Dewey, Lewin and Piaget, 'each of whom advocated that learning is dependent upon the integration of experience with reflection and of theory with practice' (Imel, 1992: 1). We were interested in reflective practice as a research method because it fits with a naturalistic and empirical inquiry of tacit knowledge as a competitive advantage in ambiguous situations. First, 'reflective practice' is a process of making sense of one's own practice, during or after the action has taken place (Osterman, 1990). This is a central activity of a person or group facing ambiguity. Second, reflective practice is one's own investigation into his or her own 'knowledge system'. Thus, reflective practice is an excellent tool to identify which part is tacit or explicit, and individual or collective. Lastly, 'reflective practice' provides a research tool that is versatile, allowing in-process analysis along with ad-hoc and post-data gathering analysis ('reflection in action' versus 'reflection on action'). To conduct interviews and play the role of 'catalyst', we followed the rules that Peters (1991) proposed, using a process called DATA: 'describe, analyze, theorize and act'.

Completing 'Reflective Practice' with Direct Observation

However, as Schön judiciously noticed, 'skillful action reveals a knowing more than we can say' (1983: 51), or a 'knowing more than we can tell' (Polanyi, 1966). Thus, we cannot entirely rely on what managers have to tell us about their 'way' of managing knowledge. For this reason, we also use a second method, *direct observation*. This, however, implies that the researcher must be present when (1) the person discovers the ambiguous situation (emergence), (2) when this person deals with ambiguity by using different types of knowledge (explicit, tacit, individual, collective) and, finally, (3) when this person escapes, avoids, or thrives in this ambiguity to achieve his or her purpose.

Reaching 'Triangulation' by using Different Sources of Data

Multiple sources of evidence were gathered to triangulate observation methods and to create a chain of evidence (Yin, 1984). Letters, memoranda, agendas, announcements, administrative documents (proposals, mission reports), news clippings and articles from the mass media were major sources of secondary data. In the Pechiney case – the studied events having occurred in the late 1920s and 1950s – complementary archival records were used (organizational records, organization notes, CEOs' diaries). *Direct observation* was intensively used with an average visit of six months in each organization. Direct observations were made throughout the field visit, 'including those occasions during which other evidence, such as that of interviews, was being collected' (Yin, 1984: 91). *In-depth interviews* were used to obtain 'the facts of a matter as well as . . . the respondents' opinions about the events' (Yin, 1984: 89). Interviews were *open-ended*, with considerable opportunity for feedback from respondents. Interviews were conducted with people both involved and not involved in the studied processes, to measure the awareness of these processes in the organization and to understand the articulation of the different types of knowledge. The research involved seventy interviews (with ten to twenty-five per organization, based on size).

Data Analysis

Reliability of theory construction is dependent on a 'process that must be designed to highlight relationships, connections, and interdependencies in the phenomenon of interest' because 'researchers cannot make deductions from concepts alone' (Weick, 1989: 517). Unlike positivistic research, inductive research 'lacks a generally accepted model for its central creative process' (Eisenhardt and Bourgeois, 1988). Lacking a model, data analysis for this research focused on the chronology of events, trying to identify for each phase what kind of knowledge plays what role (that is, individual/collective and explicit/tacit), based on a categorization inspired by previous findings (Nonaka and Hedlund, 1991). The purpose was to identify and to test the validity of a particular knowledge process which handles mutability and unpredictability.

Case descriptions were developed by combining the accounts of each respondent and by direct observation of events whenever possible (except for Pechiney). Opinions about actions and events that were not observable were included in data sets for further investigation. We used cross-case analysis and continuous feedback to respondents to improve both construct validity and adjustments (Eisenhardt, 1989). All data (from reflective practice, interviews, direct observations and archives) were compiled for analysis in tables (as suggested by Miles and Huberman, 1984). The goal was to identify, for each step of the organizational struggle with ambiguity, what type of knowledge (for instance, tacit/collective) was most often used. The outputs were tables relating the frequencies and the purposes of the use of one specific type of knowledge at one particular time. What emerged were propositions shedding light on the conditions surrounding the use of different types/modes of knowledge in the various steps of the organizations' struggles with ambiguity.

Elaboration of the Matrix

Explicit and Collective Knowledge

Explicit and collective knowledge is the knowledge a community can explain. Spender (this volume) uses the term 'objectified knowledge' to suggest that this knowledge is considered 'objective' by the community that shares it. In an organization, patents, written rules and procedures, organizational charts, and management decisions that are known by the whole organization (such as those disseminated through formal memoranda) are all part of the explicit and collective body of knowledge. Patents, for instance, are the written articulation of the technical know-how of the firm (Teece, 1987). The purpose of making knowledge explicit and collective can be to disseminate this knowledge to others, to inform people about recent management decisions, to implement new programs and procedures within the organization, or to signal to the 'external environment' the organizational purpose and positions. For example, prices are signals to the competitors and partners of the organization. All explicit and collective knowledge is not systematically explicit or collective in the first place. Rules that are informal and ephemeral can become permanent and explicit through 'institutionalization' (DiMaggio and Powell, 1983).

Explicit and Individual Knowledge

We can approach individual, explicit knowledge from two perspectives, the sociological and the technological. From an elementary sociological view, everything that becomes conscious to us, becomes part of our individual explicit knowledge. The other side of individual explicit knowledge is what we will call our 'known-expertise', which does not contradict previous findings on expertise which state that the essence of expertise lies in the tacit understanding of rules that are unknown to the beginner or non-expert. The example of the chess masters used by de Groot (1965) or Newell and Simon (1972) illustrates this point.

Tacit and Collective Knowledge

We all have some 'truths' that we hold collectively but do not state. The secret location for 'D-Day' was tacitly known by thousands of people without being expressed explicitly ('tacit' being understood as 'to know more than one is willing to tell'). Thus, people knew tacitly that D-Day was planned. The tacit circulation of knowledge helps organizations to solve problems that they cannot make explicit. Managers elaborate informal task forces that work on critical issues in parallel with – not exclusive of – formal structures. People gather to deal with a specific problem, and gather again when a similar problem arises. This 'web of complicities' allows organizations to deal 'obliquely' with delicate tasks when formal and explicit processes seem to fail (Baumard, 1994).

Knowledge is socially constructed (Berger and Luckmann, 1966). In life, we learn to assimilate and articulate the stimuli around us to formulate language. In organizations, people belong to 'communities of practice' (Lave and Wenger, 1991; Vygotsky, 1962) where they share a practical knowledge that is both a 'signature' of their belonging to this community and a source of change for this community. Similarly, many trades are learned tacitly and collectively.

Tacit and collective knowledge can also be a guarantee of organizational operational safety. The 'collective mind' of flight deck operators (Weick and Roberts, 1993) permits highly complex organizational tasks to be achieved with very few accidents. This 'organizational mentality' or 'organization mind' (Sandelands and Stablein, 1987) relies upon a tacit understanding that does not necessitate explication. Thus, technical knowledge is often acquired through repetitive tasks, for which know-how is difficult to communicate. Scribner (1986) explains how tacit knowledge is held collectively by workers in a commercial dairy (the warehouse order packers, delivery drivers, and inventory takers). This tacit and collective know-how is difficult to imitate, and can procure a valuable technological rent, allowing the firm to develop an 'appropriability regime' (Teece, 1987; Winter, 1987).

Tacit and Individual Knowledge

As Polanyi (1966) put it, 'We know more than we can tell'. First, there are many stimuli that we notice without being aware of noticing them. We learn without awareness of what is being learned (Thorndike and Rock, 1934). We cannot communicate what we learn, thus, we are the only ones to be the receivers of this 'knowledge'. Second, we do not always learn systematically or intentionally. There are many things that we have learned 'incidentally' (Jenkins, 1933) because we had the luck to encounter an unexpected learning experience, or because we were focusing on another task, and something 'else' was to be learned in this task that we did not expect. In the routine of repetitive tasks, we may also acquire a tacit knowledge concerning the improvement of our task. This 'procedural knowledge' (Anderson, 1976; Scribner, 1986) is difficult to share, and when somebody replaces us at our task, the 'know-how' is difficult to transmit. Implementing TQM in the United States has been seen as difficult because of difference in attitudes towards learning and knowledge

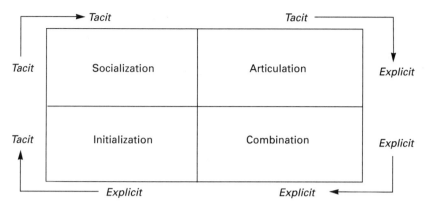

Figure 4.1   *Transitions from tacit to explicit and vice versa (Nonaka, 1990)*

between the United States and Japan (Nonaka and Hedlund, 1991). As termed by Spender (this volume), a large part of our knowledge is 'automatic knowledge'. We do not know where it comes from, and we cannot tell that we know, though 'it's here' and 'it works'. We encode without awareness of encoding (Hasher and Zacks, 1984). We act mindlessly (Langer, 1978), and instinctively, relying on 'animal knowledge', based on feelings, smells, guts, like animals do (Griffin, 1982; Morin, 1986). We often rely on 'practical knowledge' (Nyíri and Smith, 1988), that we are not able to isolate, define or describe, for we acquired it through mindless and automatic practice. This heterogeneous, and often mysterious, body of knowledge is our 'tacit and individual knowledge'.

Moving Around the Matrix

It would be misleading to state that the above four types of knowledge are independent of each other and constitute separate and idiosyncratic bodies of knowledge. The dynamics of knowledge involve continuous movements, exchanges and transformations of one type of knowledge into another, whether deliberate or not. We know that these transformations and shifts are fast and effortless; however, we know little about how the human brain processes these four types of knowledge.

Researching the epistemological and ontological dimensions of knowledge, Nonaka (1990) synthesized the four kinds of transitions between explicit and tacit dimensions of knowledge (see Figure 4.1). A specific mode of transition exists for each transformation. For instance, tacit knowledge circulates through *socialization*, that is, we learn tacit behaviors, or rules, by interacting and observing other people. This tacit knowledge can be *articulated* in more explicit rules (that is, by using different sets of measures in all various conditions of the process in order to identify the rules that are used tacitly by the baker), and then becomes

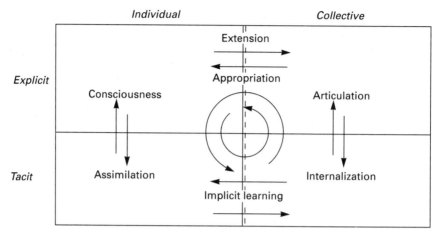

Figure 4.2   *An integrative framework to analyze transitions of knowledge types*

explicit knowledge. This explicit knowledge can then be combined with other elements of explicit knowledge. For example, two software programs can be merged together. The new set of instructions is a combination of formerly separate sets of instructions. When we face an explicit set of knowledge, we then have to integrate it into our behavior and practice. We achieve this task through practice of the explicit rules, techniques, scientific findings, etc. We *internalize* these elements of explicit knowledge in our tacit knowledge and make them ours.

Using previous findings (Nonaka, 1991, 1994; Polanyi, 1966; Spender, this volume; Teece, 1987; Winter, 1987), the above matrix was developed by integrating the individual and collective dimensions. Eight forms of transitions were thus identified in this integrative framework to analyze the different shifts between knowledge types (see Figure 4.2). These eight transitions are compiled in analytic tables (Miles and Huberman, 1984) to identify, describe and explain when and how they occur in the organizations studied.

Case Studies

Pechiney: A Collective Tacit Agreement

Organizations simultaneously generate processes that tend to change their characteristics and antithetical processes that affect these characteristics in the opposite direction (Starbuck, 1988). At Pechiney, three major 'disconcerting and ambiguous' situations, respectively in 1931, in the early 1950s, and between 1955 and 1960, were investigated through archival data (letters, internal memos, general and specialized press, agendas) and in-depth interviews with key witnesses (former CEOs and managers).

Persistent rumors (1931–1932)   In a letter from Gabriel Cordier to the president, on 24 November 1931, events unfold as follows:

> Dear President, since yesterday, events precipitate: we have been hastily attacked on Lyon stock exchange. Attacks were based on following facts: 1) We lost 600 millions in Russia, 2) We lost 100 millions with the B.N.C., 3) We still have considerable amounts held in Italy, 4) To pay the succession rights (due on April 15, 1932), the Gillet family, completely drained of ready money, sells all its shares, 5) We harass our subsidiaries to such an extent that we appear as a disordered cavalry. (Pechiney, Historical Archives)

In response, speculators spread rumors about the possibility of a bankruptcy. These rumors stated that two administrators of the company were silent because of their recent suicides, and four others resigned. None of this was true, and so Pechiney brought the case to Court. In an internal memo, a senior executive acknowledged: 'We didn't deny and didn't publicly refute any rumors . . . Such a communiqué would probably give consistency to noises.' Ambiguity thus remained, and the company's stock price lost twenty-five percent in ten days. A second conventional attempt to run down rumors was then made. The President of the Executive Board wrote a letter to shareholders to reassure them about the company finances. Here, the changeable situation was finally handled by changeable means. This illustrates how executives can build up clandestine and informal networks to counter rumors on a local basis (stock exchange traders, bankers, key share holders, influential personalities of the business community). Adopting the same mutable form as the disturbing rumors, these communication strategies act as antithetical processes.

The 3C^3 process (1950s)   In the early 1950s, Vachet and Lamourdedieu visited the Saint-Gobain glass factory, and came to the following conclusion: 'Why don't we flow our aluminum like Saint Gobain is flowing its glass?' (Lamourdedieu, 1990: 60). This suggestion was easier said than done. Under the name of 'flowing process 3C^3', a first, unsatisfactory, sketch is drawn. There was, however, an inventor by the name of Hazelett who successfully developed a similar process in Cleveland. The factory was soon visited by Lamourdedieu, but not much was learnt from unsuccessful trials presented that day. No viable technical answer was foreseen by Lamourdedieu. The choice was then to come back to Paris empty-handed, or to find an oblique way through the enigma. A dinner at Lamourdedieu's hotel followed the visit to the factory. Hazelett and four engineers were invited. 'Reserving a seat for myself near the flower pot, I profited from the opportunity of getting rid of my whisky as my colleagues' attention was becoming more and more fuzzy' (Lamourdedieu, 1990: 83). The day after, Lamourdedieu was welcomed as the hero who resisted this memorable drunken meal. The distrustful atmosphere faded away, and Lamourdedieu came back with valuable insights on the 3C^3 process cooling system. With few improvements, the insights were adopted into the final flowing process. As Lamourdedieu later noted (Lamourdedieu, 1990), official and organizational memories provided a different rationale for the discovery of the $3C^3$ process (Barrand and Gadeau, 1964).

The Guinean Revolution (1955–1960)   Pechiney's presence in Guinea followed the discovery of important bauxite deposits 200 miles from Konakry: 'The latter has a mediocre quality and has to be transformed on site, which is feasible thanks to the Koukouré river, that would provide energy' (Gignoux, 1955: 226). Such restricted geological conditions would later play a critical role, as there would be no other technical solution to transform the bauxite on site. The Koukouré river, however, was unpredictable, known to run at 1000 cubic meters in the rainy season and at ten cubic meters in the dry season. As there were no maps of Guinea and Pechiney, geologists were assigned to that task from 1942 to 1945. Pechiney was trapped in a technical escalade of commitments, and the engineers' agenda remained in the background of events until the final resolution. The geological and technical study was completed in 1951, and Pechiney management was 'seduced by the outcome' (Marchandise, 1990: 84). In 1957, the aluminum production site was almost operational, and the Company of Fria was founded.

However, in September 1958, the government of Guinea declared independence. A transient, shifting, disconcerting and ambiguous situation followed: 'All happened just as if the whole operation would have escaped the hands of its initiators, leaving people "on the ground" with the difficult task of reconciling the business imperative with the unpredictability of the Guinea government and society being in permanent revolution' (Larrue, 1990: 37). Then, an interesting tacit handling of the situation was initiated by Pierre Jouven, representing Paris management, Raoul de Vitry, President of the Company of Fria on site, and a few others. (Raoul de Vitry had obtained a tacit agreement from the new 'Revolutionary' government of Guinea related to the company's pursuit of the technical agenda.) Pierre Jouven's role was critical. In comparing all memos and internal letters of the company during the period, Jouven's reporting style stands apart. He carefully described all the relationships and connections of people he met, using a rich, vivid and detailed style. Every single personality was analyzed: 'This person was obliging, but I noticed an embarrassed meddling', 'the two Parliamentarians were most active in our discussions. They congratulated our position and our project' (Pechiney, Historical Archives). The gap between Jouven's 'soft' knowledge of subtleties and the technical reports about the industrial agenda is tremendous. The result was that Pechiney avoided the worst in the Guinea case, and kept the aluminum production running.

Process analysis   A process analysis on the Guinean case unfolds as follows: A disconcerting, ambiguous and unpredictable situation emerged when the Guinean government decided to nationalize plants and energy sources. Engineers stuck to the technical agenda and tried to tolerate the

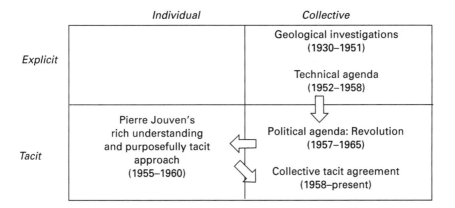

Figure 4.3   *Dominant knowledge modes in Pechiney's struggle with ambiguity*

ambiguity of the situation. But ambiguity persisted, and so management from both Paris headquarters and Konakry decided to take action. Pierre Jouven, along with others, played the role of mediator. Pierre Jouven's rich understanding served as a basis to develop a tacit understanding between different parties. A tacit collective agreement was finally reached.

When compiling data tables, the kinds of knowledge used show three successive shifts around the matrix (see Figure 4.3). From 1930 to 1951, the dominant mode of knowledge was one of engineers searching for energy sources and technical possibilities. When the technical agenda was set up, and operations first started (1952–1958), they were still in a collective and explicit knowledge mode. With the Guinean revolution, a new situation arose in which the worst outcome suddenly became possible. At this point, the positions of different parties became ambiguous, although there was an effort to clarify intentions and commitments. Here, the tacit and individual knowledge of a few key managers of Pechiney, especially Pierre Jouven, played a major role in improving understanding of the situation and creating dialogue. Thus, managers learned implicitly a way for dealing with a new ambiguous situation. A final shift to a collective and tacit knowledge mode occurred, as a tacit agreement on the continuity of Pechiney's operations in Guinea was reached.

Indigo: Thriving in the Fog

Founded in 1981, Indigo, Incorporated is a small publishing company specializing in the editing and printing of confidential letters. Publications include *Africa Energy and Mining*, *The Indian Ocean Newsletter*, *East Asian Affairs*, *Maghreb Confidential*. Access to publications is exclusively through direct subscriptions, and clients include governments and multi-nationals on five continents. Indigo has experienced rapid growth in its activities, and its publications are highly regarded by executives and government officials. This case was selected due to the assumption that accessing sensitive information requires abilities particular to handling disconcerting and ambiguous situations, as part of unveiling hidden realities to readers. Attention was focused on the work of the small staff of twelve who produce the letters and thus gain access to valuable insights.

Indigo's current mode of operations involves constantly shifting from 'an exhaustive and rational approach of events to a more intuitive approach' (CEO, interview). The first phase – made the shortest – consists in reading what is publicly known on the event:

> It gives us directions to search for the unpublished. We know the editorial habits, ideologies, and policies of the press that we scan. For example, in certain African countries, ethnic issues are never addressed directly. Instead, to suggest the role played by an ethnic group, journalists are mentioning the villages involved in the event. The African reader is aware of which ethnic group is involved.

Indigo editors never assume facts immediately: 'Results are lying in wait', the editor says. Thus, direct observation reveals 'a state of vigilant premeditation, of continuous concentration on activity that is in progress' (Détienne and Vernant, 1974: 14). As the Indigo founder put it in an interview with the author, 'Our job is to read the implicit like an open book, to navigate in the unsaid, eventually preparing the ground for the unsaid to be unveiled'. Unfortunately, the implicit is never revealed in any objective forms. The CEO continues, 'We maneuver in a tacit field, eventually reaching steadily a grip that we won't release until the situation makes sense'. All editors are boundary-spanners (Daft and Weick, 1984). Problems are tackled at their source, involving intense traveling: 'We constantly navigate backward and forward from the background to the foreground of knowledge' (founder, interview). When a French Deputy is known to be on an official visit in Africa (foreground), editors search for informal and tacit links between this deputy and a corporation that might be involved in a contract negotiation in the area (background): 'We imagine a rationale that would fit the events, and keep the succession of events in memory. And we wait for the illumination, helping it out by accessing informed sources.' Thus, knowledge is never exhaustively formalized until final publication. 'We incubate', as the CEO put it. That was Indigo's consistent routine until a day in which events did not turn out as expected.

That day, one of the editors discovered the picture of a new ambassador of Malte in the Seychelles: 'I found the whole thing awkward. Why is there a Malte Order in the Seychelles?' This started the process of navigating between the implicit and the explicit; as one of the editors explains, 'We avoid being too straightforward in our understanding of events'. The first search was disconcerting. Apparent ambiguity led to nothing more than further ambiguity. Nothing seemed rational or sustainable for publication. The enigma unfolded as follows: 'An ambassador who was not an ambassador, did and didn't own hotels, had and hadn't a questionable past'. Finally, creative induction provided a way out, and accurate meaning

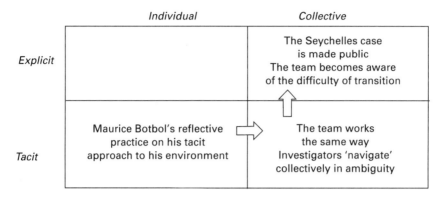

Figure 4.4 *Dominant knowledge modes in Indigo's struggle with ambiguity*

could be given to the dispersed and ambiguous events. Editors deliberately made their search highly mutable, letting their investigation be even more twisted than the reality it has to handle. 'There were no awaited immediate returns. The only thing awaited was the precise moment when an interesting line to pull would show up', the editor recalls.

One editor summarized their conclusions following the Seychelles case in an interview, maintaining that Indigo relies on 'tight resources' and 'artisanal means'. Yet, even at this small scale, the company 'manages to achieve tasks that foster envy in larger and more organized institutions'. The editor concluded that Indigo is 'dependent upon its ability to foresee interesting situations in advance' and then to follow them through.

Process analysis The chronology of events unfolds as follows: With a predilection to tacitness, Maurice Botbol undertakes the routine of investigating the environment for rare knowledge for his newsletters. Through serendipity, he discovers unusual links between a few elements of knowledge. Through creative induction, he builds a scenario that makes sense on the basis of the tacit knowledge he possesses of various involved elements. A disconcerting, ambiguous and unpredictable situation emerges in the Seychelles case as events go faster that he expected and unveil connections he did not suspect. Ambiguity persists, and Botbol tries to imagine a path that would fit the situation. With the help of others, trying to articulate their knowledge, Indigo members steadily grasp the situation, and make explicit what they believe to be an accurate understanding of it.

In compiling data tables, three successive shifts around the matrix are revealed (see Figure 4.4). With the dominant knowledge mode being *tacit individual*, Maurice Botbol detects incongruities in a sequence of events (for example, the Seychelles case) through means of serendipity and creative induction. He then tries to make sense of the contradictory stimuli, but ambiguity persists. Shifting to collective and tacit knowledge,

Indigo 'navigates' within ambiguity by socializing and exchanging undetermined, mutable elements of knowledge. Indigo finally has to formulate an explicit vision of the events for the newsletter, a difficult transition.

Findings

When trying to escape ambiguity, senior managers often neglect local and conjectural knowledge. This neglect seems stronger in large firms (Pechiney). When trying to escape ambiguity, senior managers tend to over-manage. Success in escaping ambiguity depends on an ability to switch promptly between appropriate modes of knowledge. However, these shifts are painful. They require organizational flexibility and a certain reflective thinking on the organizational knowledge.

Tacit knowledge plays a critical role in developing a rich understanding of ambiguous situations. Organizations (Indigo) or people (Maurice Botbol, Jean Claude Gruffat, Pierre Jouven) with greater skill in handling tacit knowledge show greater efficiency in handling such situations. Thus, tacit knowledge, when managed adequately, can constitute a source of competitive advantage for organizations or people. Tacitness (unsaid, incommunicable, transitory, mutable knowledge) leaves more margin for maneuvering. Finally, the Indigo case shows that organizations can even *create* ambiguity for the purpose of exploiting it, as Indigo's managers tended to *create* fog to *thrive in the fog*.

Conclusion

Specific recommendations for enhancing and systematizing a way of managing knowledge that would give tacit knowledge its deserved place in management have yet to be revealed. However, results of the research described in this chapter show that organizations often neglect the tacit dimension of knowledge both in their day-to-day operations and in their long-term thinking.

Large organizations are more institutionalized, hierarchical and resistant to change, and show a lower performance in developing competitive advantage from tacit knowledge. A smaller organization like Indigo, which is more democratic and flexible, can show better performance both in struggling with ambiguity and in adapting to ambiguous situations. Thus, one direction for further exploration is whether downsizing may facilitate better management of knowledge.

More generally, these research results show that there is more to knowledge than the conventional, positivistic perception of knowledge-as-information. Studying organizational knowledge creation not only illuminates many traditional organizational issues such as organizational learning and crisis management, it also opens the door for a new interpretation of organizations as *interrelated dynamic systems* of knowledge and issues.

Acknowledgments

Many thanks to the members of my dissertation committee, Professors Gérard Kœnig and Raymond-Alain Thiétart, University of Paris-Dauphine, and Professor William H. Starbuck, New York University, for contributing helpful comments and suggestions. I am also grateful to Professor J.C. Spender, Rutgers University, for challenging discussions and useful insights.

References

Alvesson, Mats (1993) 'Organizations as rhetoric: Knowledge-intensive firms and the struggle with ambiguity', *Journal of Management Studies*, 30(6): 997–1015.

Anderson, J.R. (1976) *Language, Memory and Thought*. Hillsdale, NJ: Erlbaum.

Barrand, P., Gadeau, R. et al. (1964) *L'Aluminium*, vols 1 and 2. Paris: Eyrolles.

Baumard, P. (1994) 'Oblique knowledge: The clandestine work of organizations', *Cahiers de Recherche DMSP* 228.

Berger, Peter L. and Luckmann, Thomas (1966) *The Social Construction of Reality*. Garden City, NY: Doubleday.

Crozier, Michel and Hedberg, E. (1977) *L'acteur et le système*. Paris: Editions du Seuil.

Cyert, Richard M. and March, James G. (1963) *A Behavioral Theory of the Firm*. Englewood Cliffs, NJ: Prentice Hall.

Dacey, Raymond (1976) 'The role of ambiguity in the manipulation of voters', *Norman: Center for Economic and Management Research*, College of Business Administration, Working Paper Series, 18 pp.

Daft, Richard L. and Weick, Karl E. (1984) 'Toward a model of organizations as interpretation systems', *Academy of Management Review*, 9(2): 284–295.

de Groot, A.D. (1965) *Thought and Choice in Chess*. The Hague: Mouton.

Détienne, Marcel and Vernant, Jean Pierre (1974) *Les ruses de l'intelligence: La mètis des Grecs*. Paris: Flammarion.

DiMaggio, Paul J. and Powell, Walter W. (1983) 'The iron cage revisited: Institutional isomorphism and collective rationality in organizational fields', *American Sociological Review*, 48: 147–160.

Eisenhardt, Kathleen M., (1989) 'Building theories from case study research', *Academy of Management Review*, 14(4): 532–550.

Eisenhardt, K.M. and Bourgeois, L.J. (1988) 'Politics of strategic decision making in high-velocity environments: Toward a midrange theory', *Academy of Management Journal*, 31(4): 737–770.

Gignoux, Charles J. (1955) *Histoire d'une entreprise française*. Paris: Hachette.

Glaser, Barney G. and Strauss, Anselm L. (1967) *The Discovery of Grounded Theory: Strategies for Qualitative Research*. Chicago, IL: Aldine.

Griffin, D.R. (1982) *Animal Mind, Human Mind*. New York: Springer-Verlag.

Hasher, L. and Zacks, R.T. (1984) 'Automatic processing of fundamental information', *American Psychologist*, 48: 1372–1388.

Hedberg, Bo (1981) 'How organizations learn and unlearn', in P. Nystrom and W. Starbuck (eds), *Handbook of Organizational Design*. New York: Oxford University Press. pp. 1–27.

Hedberg, Bo, Nystrom, Paul C. and Starbuck, William H. (1976) 'Camping on seesaws: Prescriptions for a self-designing organization', *Administrative Science Quarterly*, 21: 41–65.

Herzberg, Frederick (1987) 'Innovation: Where is the relish?', *Journal of Creative Behavior*, 21(3): 179–192.

Imel, Susan (1992) 'Reflective practice in adult education', *ERIC Digest No. 122*. ERIC Clearinghouse on Adult Career and Vocational Education, Columbus, OH; sponsored by the Office of Educational Research and Improvement, Washington, DC. Report No. EDO–CE–92–122.

Jenkins, J.G. (1933) 'Instruction as a factor of "incidental" learning', *American Journal of Psychology*, 45: 471–477.

Lamourdedieu, Marcel (1990) 'Carnet de Route', *Cahiers d'Histoire de l'Aluminium*, 6: 60–84.

Langer, E. (1978) 'Rethinking the role of thought in social interaction', in J. Harvey, W. Ickes and R. Kidd (eds), *New Directions in Attribution Theory*, vol. II. Hillsdale, NJ: Erlbaum. pp. 35–58.

Larrue, Jacques (1990) 'Fria en Guinée: Des aspects humains d'une industrialisation différente', *Cahiers d'Histoire de l'Aluminium*, 7: 37–48.

Lave, J. and Wenger, E. (1991) *Situated Learning: Legitimate Peripheral Participation*. New York: Cambridge Unvier.

Lincoln, Yvonna S. and Guba, Egon G. (1985) *Naturalistic Inquiry*. Beverly Hills, CA: Sage.

March, James G. and Olsen, Johan P. (eds) (1976) *Ambiguity and Choice in Organizations*. Bergen: Universitets-forlaget.

Marchandise, Jacques (1990) 'Extra muros: Histoire de Fria', *Cahiers d'Histoire de l'Aluminium*, 7: 84–86.

Marquardt, Michael J. and Engel, Dean W. (1993) 'HRD Competencies in a shrinking world', *Training and Development*, 47(5): 59–65.

Miles, Matthew B. and Huberman, A. Michael (1984) *Qualitative Data Analysis*. Beverly Hills, CA: Sage.

Morin, Edgard (1986) *La Méthode III: La Connaissance de la Connaissance*. Paris: Editions du Seuil.

Newell, A. and Simon, H.A. (1972) *Human Problem Solving*. Englewood Cliffs, NJ: Prentice Hall.

Nonaka, Ikujiro (1990) 'Managing innovation as a knowledge creating process', paper presented at New York University, Stern School of Business, International Business Colloquium.

Nonaka, Ikujiro (1991) 'The knowledge-creating company', *Harvard Business Review*, 69: 96–104.

Nonaka, Ikujiro (1994) 'A dynamic theory of organizational knowledge creation', *Organization Science*, 5(1): 14–37.

Nonaka, Ikujiro and Hedlund, Gunar (1991) 'Models of knowledge management in the West and Japan', Institute of International Business at the Stockholm School of Economics, Research Paper.

Nyíri, János Kristóf and Smith, Barry (eds) (1988) *Practical Knowledge: Outlines of a Theory of Traditions and Skills*. New York: Croom Helm.

Osterman, K.F. (1990) 'Reflective practice: A new agenda for education', *Education and Urban Society*, 22(2): 133–152.

Peters, J. (1991) 'Strategies for reflective practice', in R. Brockett (ed.), *Professional Development for Educators of Adults*. San Francisco, CA: Jossey-Bass.

Polanyi, Michael (1958) *Personal Knowledge: Toward a Post-Critical Philosophy*. Chicago, IL: University of Chicago Press.

Polanyi, Michael (1966) *The Tacit Dimension*. Garden City, NY: Doubleday.

Sandelands, L.E. and Stablein, R.E. (1987) 'The concept of organization mind', *Research in the Sociology of Organizations*, 5: 135–161.

Schön, D. (1983) *The Reflective Practitioner*. New York: Basic Books.

Schön, D. (1988) *Educating the Reflective Practitioner*. San Francisco, CA: Jossey-Bass.

Scribner, S. (1986) 'Thinking in action: Some characteristics of practical thought', in R. Sternberg and R.K.Wagner (eds), *Practical Intelligence: Nature and Origins of Competence in the Everyday World*. Cambridge: Cambridge University Press. pp. 13–30.

Shenkar, Oded and Zeira, Yoram (1992) 'Role conflict and role ambiguity of chief executive officers in international joint ventures', *Journal of International Business Studies*, 23(1): 55–75.

Starbuck, W.H. (1988) 'Surmounting our human limitations', in R. Quinn and K. Cameron (eds), *Paradox and Transformation: Toward a Theory of Change in Organization and Management*. Cambridge, MA: Ballinger.

Starbuck, W.H. and Miliken, F.J. (1988) 'Executives' perceptual filters: What they notice and how they make sense', in D. Hambrick (ed.), *The Executive Effect: Concepts and Methods for Studying Top Managers*. Greenwich, CT: JAI Press. pp. 35–65.

Teece, Donald J. (1987) 'Profiting from technological innovation', in D.J. Teece (ed.), *The Competitive Challenge*. Cambridge, MA: Ballinger. pp. 185–219.

Thorndike, E.L. and Rock, R.T., Jr. (1934) 'Learning without awareness of what is being learned or intent to learn it', *Journal of Experimental Psychology*, 1–19.

Vygotsky, L.S. (1962) *Thought and Language*. Cambridge, MA: MIT Press.

Weick, Karl E. (1989) 'Theory construction as disciplined imagination', *Academy of Management Review*, 14(4): 516–531.

Weick, Karl. E. and Roberts, Karlene H. (1993) 'Collective mind in organizations: Heedful interrelating on flight decks', *Administrative Science Quarterly*, 38(3): 357–381.

Winter, Sydney G. (1987) 'Knowledge and competence as strategic assets', in D.J. Teece (ed.), *The Competitive Challenge*. Cambridge, MA: Ballinger. pp. 159–184.

Yin, Robert (1984) *Applied Social Research Method Series*, vol. 5, *Case Study Research: Design and Methods*. Beverly Hills, CA: Sage.

Part 2
ORGANIZATIONAL LEARNING AND STRATEGIC CAPABILITY

What an organization is capable of doing in its various markets determines its success in attracting and maintaining customers. *Organizational capabilities* that are both valued by customers and difficult for other organizations to imitate are thus critical sources of competitive advantage. The next three chapters argue that such capabilities are products of learning processes. This section examines the emerging role of resources, capabilities and competencies in strategic management, as well as the resulting implications for organizational learning.

Nanda reviews core concepts and definitions from the resource-based view of the firm, and discusses the interrelationships among these concepts. He then characterizes *strategic resources* and draws implications for business practice (and for organizational learning). The next chapter, by Andreu and Ciborra, focuses squarely on the learning aspects of capability development, and explores how information technology (IT) contributes to developing an organization's capabilities. Specific organizational examples illustrate how IT can be embedded in an organization's core capabilities and can function as *strategic information systems*. Guidelines for how IT can contribute to improving the effectiveness of an organization's learning processes are also offered.

The final chapter in this section synthesizes the economic theory of commitment with the newer resource-based perspective in strategic management. Collis shows that organization capability, defined as a firm's dynamic routines that continuously and locally advance the production frontier, can be a source of economic profit. To do this, he outlines a theory of profit, in which profit accrues to a firm that possesses a singular product market position immune to the threats of imitation, substitution, appropriation and dissipation. He shows how these conditions relate to the tacit collective knowledge that underlies organizational capability.

5

Resources, Capabilities and Competencies

Ashish Nanda

A review of current resource-based literature suggests that, while considerable work has been done towards linking firm resources with competitive strategy, the field is in a state of considerable flux and confusion. Mutually contradictory definitions abound, researchers draw widely divergent normative prescriptions, and there is a paucity of work linking the resource paradigm with intraorganizational processes. This chapter attempts to address these needs, by defining resources, capabilities and competencies, and discussing how these concepts are interrelated. It then proceeds to characterize strategic resources, and draws implications for strategy.

The Resource-based View of the Firm

The last few years have seen an outpouring of literature on the *resource-based* view of the firm, coming from several directions. A common basic concern of these approaches has been to understand how organizations configure and manage their resources, especially human resources. Different disciplines have tried to describe this phenomenon from their perspectives.

Economics

In looking at the firm, economists have addressed three related issues: why do firms exist,[1] what determines optimal firm size, and what determines firm growth rate? Organizational economists hypothesized that certain fixed factors of production are organized within the firm, rather than transacted for in the market, since these factors are specific to the transaction, susceptible to moral hazard and adverse selection risks. A market solution involving a *transaction-specific asset* involves the risk of ex-post opportunism through holdup or slack (Williamson, 1975). Besides, if the value of an asset is verifiable only through experience, there is a risk of adverse selection in the asset-market (Akerlof, 1970). To overcome such problems, the parties to a transaction can resort ex-ante to a long-term contract with severe penalties for breach of contract. The firm may be viewed as a nexus of such contracts (Williamson, 1975).

A related argument is that high *transaction costs* (Coase, 1952; Williamson, 1975) may necessitate that a long-term contract remain incomplete.[2] Given *bounded rationality* of economic agents (Simon, 1945), they have limited ability to account for all possible future states of nature, and incur increasing cost of writing a more complete, more complex contract which takes more contingencies into account. Hence, the contracting parties choose to leave the contract incomplete. Arranging such *incomplete long-term contracts* internally within an organization may reduce transaction costs in comparison with market contracts (Grossman and Hart, 1986; Williamson, 1975).

In order to explain firm size, economists, who identify firm resources with factors of production, maintain that a firm initially faces increasing returns to scale owing to scale and scope economies, and hence, efficiency dictates that firm size is not too small (Baumol et al., 1982). However, optimal firm size may be limited by eventually decreasing returns to scale, since fixed factors may not be duplicable as the firm expands (Prescott and Visscher, 1980).

Another perspective has concentrated on the nature of the growth of a firm. Penrose described the firm as 'a collection of the productive resources it employs' (1981: 24). Rubin (1973) remarked that at any point in time, a firm possesses a set of resources and carries out a group of activities. The firm expands in order to utilize available resource capacity. Resource capacity is released over time as a firm's activities get routinized and it uses its resources more efficiently (Penrose), or existing resources may be used by the firm to create new resources (Rubin).

Labor economists have also studied the impact of firm-specific human capital, although their focus has been on the operation of the labor market rather than the firm. (See Parsons (1986) for a survey.) Their stylized results are:

- Quit-rate from a firm will decline over time, due to job-shopping and screening out of highly mobile workers at the initial stage of employment, and by increasing valuation of the job as human capital grows (Jovanovic, 1979).
- Optimal compensation mechanism in such a circumstance may involve fixed wages and a separation bond to cover relationship-specific investment, or sharing of the relationship-specific investment (Becker, 1975).

The economists have offered rigorous and generalized conclusions, but they have been tentative in moving into studying intraorganizational phenomena. Besides, their focus has been descriptive rather than prescriptive.

Sociology

Sociologists have also long been concerned with the development and utilization of human capital resources through organizational learning and institutionalization. Selznick (1957) studied the conversion of an organization – an expendable tool, a rational instrument engineered to do a job – into an institution – a long-lived, responsive, adaptive organism. Argyris (1985) inquired into organizational inertia which resists new learning. Argyris and Schön (1978) distinguished *single loop learning* in which behavior is adjusted to fixed goals, norms, and assumptions, from *double looped learning* in which goals, norms, and assumptions are also changeable.

Research focusing on knowledge-intensive organizations and professionals observed that these individuals bring unique and heterogeneous skills to their firms, and a major task of the organizations is developing, sustaining, coordinating and leveraging these skills. Freidson (1986) studied the role of professionals within organizations and the workings of professional organizations. Eccles and Crane (1988) explored the operation of investment banks as flexible, self-designing network organizations.

In the last few years, studies of traditional manufacturing organizations have also been stressing the importance of managing these *strategic capabilities*. Nohria and Eccles (1991) described corporate capabilities of five conglomerates, and asserted that corporate capability underlies superior performance. Nohria and Garcia-Pont (1991) studied interorganizational links in the global automobile industry during the 1980s as attempts to share capabilities.

Overall, sociologists have offered rich descriptions of complex organizations, but their insights have usually lacked generalizability and performance-hypotheses.

Organizational Theory

In organizational theory, the tendency has been to look either at the vertical structure or at the lateral interactions within the firm. The vertical-relations perspective has a long history dating back to the *scientific management* school, which attempted to provide managers with time and motion study methods to optimally allocate tasks to workers (Taylor, 1911), and the administrative theorists, who attempted to determine general administrative principles (such as span of control, line and staff distinction, and balance between responsibility and authority) underlying the optimal structuring of organizations (Fayol, 1949; Gulick and Urwick, 1937). In their current manifestation, vertical-relations theorists look on the firm as a sequence of principal-agent relationships (Jensen and Meckling, 1976; Pratt and Zeckhauser, 1985). Their focus has been on the *moral-hazard* issue: how the principal can achieve his or her goals, given lack of complete observability of the agent's actions.

An alternate approach, also with old intellectual roots, has been to look at an organization as a cooperative system with a collective purpose binding it together (Barnard, 1938). The *Carnegie tradition*, which evolved on the interface between economics and behavioral science, focused on organizational decision processes and lateral intraorganizational linkages.

Simon (1945), the progenitor of the Carnegie school, asserted that since human beings are *boundedly rational*, economic action is *satisficing* rather than optimizing in nature. Based on Simon's behavioral assumptions, Cyert and March (1963) developed their model of a firm as comprising coalitions of disparate interests, taking satisficing decisions to achieve quasi-resolutions of conflicts, within the context of bounded rationality. The *evolutionary view* of the firm was also rooted in the Carnegie tradition. It described an organization as possessing a repertoire of *organizational routines*, which evolve through organizational learning (Nelson and Winter, 1982).

Organizational theorists have offered an attractive mixture of sparse theory and rich descriptions, general rules and specific circumstances, but they are divided between the competing paradigms of agency theory and the Carnegie perspective.

General Management Viewpoint

Building on these discipline-bases, the applied field of general management has been trying to develop a *resource-based* perspective, which informs the practitioners. Its principal goal has been to develop a business-normative theory. It has moved along two related directions – the business policy and the strategy perspectives.

The business policy perspective   Business policy case studies of successful American organizations, Japanese businesses and multinational enterprises recognized that successful strategies involved not only environmental analysis, but also preservation and development of firm resources. Itami (1987) remarked that successful strategy involves optimally utilizing the firm's *invisible assets* – its 'information-based resources'. Bartlett and Ghoshal (1988) recognized that the challenge for converting a multinational into a successful *transnational* is to institute multidirectional flow of capabilities within the organization. Prahalad and Hamel (1990) highlighted the importance of *core competencies* – collective organizational learning – for firm performance. Essentially, these researchers were revisiting the traditional business policy prescription of an integrated analysis of environmental opportunities and internal resources (Andrews, 1971).

A related stream of empirical research in technology management has also stressed the importance of harnessing organizational resources. Research on quality (Garvin, 1988), speed (Stalk, 1988), flexible manufacturing (Jaikumar, 1989), technological changes – both incremental and radical (Hayes and Garvin, 1982; Henderson and Clark, 1990; Jaikumar, 1990), and new product development (Leonard-Barton, 1992) have all directly or implicitly traced the source of competitive advantage to *organizational capabilities*.

Business policy researchers have tried to be simultaneously descriptive of practices among the outlier companies they have studied intensively, and normative in projecting their practices as what best practices ought to be. Since most of their analysis is case-study driven and deductive, their insights have tended to be rich, but they have been challenged as being nonrobust, nongeneralizable, subject to sampling and observer biases, and not grounded in theory.

Strategy perspective The *resource-based* view emerged in the 1980s partly in reaction to the perceived external environment-bias of the dominant competitive strategy paradigm. Porter's (1980) work was the standard-bearer for this paradigm. Drawn from industrial organization, this approach offered an elegant and robust framework for competitive strategy analysis. In subsequent work, Porter (1985) related corporate resources with the external environment by linking the *value-chain* in the production process with the competitive strategy of the firm. However, the external environment remained the driver of corporate strategy in Porter's framework.

This approach was criticized as being oriented to the product-market to an extent that it ignores the strategic relevance of firm resources (Barney, 1986c; Teece et al., 1990). Building on Penrose's (1981) seminal contribution, theorists began to look inward again at organizational resources as a basis of competitive advantage. Wernerfelt and Rumelt were among the first to explicitly focus on strategic management of firm resources. While Wernerfelt (1984) looked at multi-use resources as the drivers of successful diversifications, Rumelt (1984) proposed that a single-business strategy be formulated by first looking at firm-resources, and then seeking the suitable product-market where they could be applied. Considerable theoretical work has since been done to develop the resource-based view (Barney, 1986c, 1991; Dierickx and Cool, 1989; Peteraf, 1993). Empirical studies have comparatively lagged behind. One of the few such inquiries was Collis' (1991) case study of the global strategies of three international bearings manufacturers from a resource perspective.

Thus, strategy researchers have been almost entirely normative in their attempts to develop theoretical insights into the linkage between resources and strategy. While the analysis has been sophisticated at macrotheoretic level, it stands relatively unsupported by microtheoretic foundations on the one side and empirical verifications on the other.

It seems there is scope in the general management field to integrate the administrative focus of business policy with the business-normative focus of strategy. It may be useful for the theory to proceed apace with empirical validation, which may further offer theory-building insights. The theory-building stage may be too primitive to allow definitive large-sample validations, and the appropriate empirical vehicle at this stage may be careful case analyses. But the two – case studies and theory building – should proceed together. Armchair theorizing is conjectural fantasy at best, case studies which are not grounded in theory may not aggregate beyond interesting stories.

Distinguishing Features of the Resource-based View

Learning Organization

The resource perspective views firms as learning organizations, improving their existing capabilities through experience. A firm is viewed as a social institution whose knowledge is stored in its behavior rules, which are constantly being shaped, preserved and modified (Nelson and Winter, 1982). Knowledge-based competencies are enhanced even as they are applied (Prahalad and Hamel, 1990), since they are firm-specific assets, which are subject to learning and change through their very application to actual problem-solving (Dosi and Marengo, 1992).

Path-dependence

There is an irreversibility in organizational decisions, and firm resources evolve in a path-dependent manner – past resource acquisitions determine and constrain future opportunities. A firm has only a limited range of repertoires, and these ingrained repertoires limit its future choices (Nelson and Winter, 1982). Hence, *history matters* (Teece, 1984), and a firm's strategy is shaped by its *administrative heritage* (Bartlett and Ghoshal, 1989).[3]

Thus, the resource perspective stresses the bidirectional linkage between strategy and structure; not only may a strategic change lead to the need for a change in organizational structure (Chandler, 1962), but the past, embedded in the current organizational structure and systems, itself determines the strategic opportunities of the present (Bower, 1970; Burgelman, 1983, 1991).

Causal ambiguity

The resource view acknowledges that the entire process of resource acquisition may be so complex that even the firm, which comes to possess the resource eventually, may not know the exact process by which it came to be acquired. *Causal ambiguity* may arise because of technological uncertainty (Lippman and Rumelt, 1982) or because the entire process of resource acquisition is a socially complex phenomenon (Barney, 1989; Dierickx and Cool, 1989).[4] As a result, the resource-acquisition process may be inimitable, across firms, and even within the same firm, over time.

Sustainable Competitive Advantage

Once acquired, durable firm specific resources generate rent-streams. However, competitive imitation, substitution and resource mobility, imperfect though they are, slowly reduce these rents. In addition, the assets generating the rent-streams depreciate over time, and the technology and the market change (Barney, 1986c).[5]

Characteristics of Strategic Resources

The general management field has been deeply involved with identifying those resources which yield *sustainable competitive advantage*. This concern is understandable from the practitioners' perspective, since, if a manager knows which of the several organizational resources are strategic, he or she can focus attention on them.

Prahalad and Hamel (1990) determined that *core competencies* are *multi-use*, *valuable* and *inimitable*. Barney (1986b, 1991) identified the conditions for a resource to offer *sustained competitive advantage* as *value*, *rarity*, *inimitability* and *non-substitutability*. In a practitioner-oriented article, Grant (1991) recognized that for a profit-generating *sustainable capability* to emerge, it must be *durable*, *non-transparent* (inimitable), *non-transferable* (immobile), *nonreplicable* and *appropriable*. Peteraf (1993) described the conditions underlying sustainable competitive advantage as *resource heterogeneity*, *ex-post limits to competition*, *imperfect resource mobility*, and *ex-ante limits to competition*.

Some of these factors are not independent; the value of a resource will decline if it becomes less scarce; a resource is less valuable and less scarce if it is easily imitable. Similarly, a transparent resource is replicable; nontransferability leads to appropriability. Theorists other than Peteraf also don't address the issue of ex-ante racing for the assets.

Some of the stated conditions help drive rents up, but they are not necessary conditions for rent generation. Peteraf's resource heterogeneity condition is essentially the dual of the product market assumption of asymmetric product differentiation (Tirole, 1988). The resources may be asymmetrically horizontally differentiated, leading to differential rents. Alternately, the resources are vertically differentiated with asymmetric expectations about their benefits. As a result, access to superior resources will yield *Ricardian rents* to firms (Rumelt, 1987). However, what drives superior rents is not resource heterogeneity per se, but the *scarcity* of the superior resources. Heterogeneity does help raise rents, since substitutability becomes costly. But it is not a necessary condition; it is possible to contemplate homogeneous resources yielding rents, because they are scarce (for instance, control over oil reserves, or diamond mines).

Hence, the various strategic resource characteristics listed above do not seem to be mutually exclusive and collectively exhaustive.

An Appraisal

Promising though the possibilities of the resource-based approach are, it is in a state of considerable flux. There are three broad areas in which confusion currently exists.

Definition

The confusion begins with definitions. There is an embarrassing profusion of riches – phrases such as *firm resources*, *organizational capabilities* and *core competencies* have been used loosely and interchangeably. Beginning with *distinctive competence* (Andrews, 1971; Hofer and Schendel, 1978; Selznick, 1957), several competing terms have arisen: *strategic firm resources* (Barney, 1986a), *invisible assets* (Itami, 1987), *strategic firm-specific assets* (Dierickx and Cool, 1989), *core competencies* (Dosi et al., 1991; Prahalad and Hamel, 1990), *corporate culture* (Crémer, 1989), *corporate capabilities* (Nohria and Eccles, 1991), *organizational capabilities* (Baldwin and Clark, 1991), *dynamic capabilities* (Teece et al., 1990), and so on.

The definitions are sometimes tautological; resources are defined as firm strengths, and firm strengths are then defined as strategic resources; capability is defined in terms of competence, and competence is then defined in terms of capability. Moreover, the definitions range from extremely broad interpretations to very specific descriptions.

Selznick (1957) introduced the term *distinctive competence*, but he did not formally define it. He described it as a constituent element of organizational character. Andrews identified distinctive competence very broadly with 'what it [an organization] can do particularly well' (1971: 46–47). In the same spirit, Hofer and Schendel defined competencies broadly as 'the pattern of . . . resource and skill deployment that will help it [the firm] achieve its goals and objectives' (1978: 25–26). Snow and Hrebiniak described distinctive competence as 'those things that an organization does especially well in connection to its competitors' (1980: 317). Dosi et al. (1991) also defined core competencies inclusively as a set of differentiated skills, complementary assets, and the organizational routines and capacities that provide the basis for a firm's competitive capacities in a particular business. Prahalad and Hamel (1990) interpreted core competencies more narrowly, principally in human resource terms.

In these characterizations, competencies are, by definition, those resources which yield competitive advantage to the firm. Once they are so defined, it becomes tautological to then search for those competencies which will yield competitive advantage to the firm. In a manner similar to the above tradition, Wernerfelt identified resources as 'anything which could be thought of as a strength or weakness of a given firm' (1984: 172). Barney (1991: 101) quoted Daft (1983) in stating that firm resources 'include all assets, capabilities, organizational processes, firm attributes, information, knowledge, etc. controlled by a firm that enable the firm to conceive of and implement strategies that improve its efficiency and effectiveness', and referred to Learned et al. (1969) in describing 'firm resources are strengths that firms can use to conceive and implement their strategies'. But then, what are firm strengths but such resources as will yield competitive advantage to the firm?

While Wernerfelt (1984) and Barney (1991) relied on broad interpretations of *resources*, Itami (1987) focused on *invisible assets* as the basis of competitive advantage, and Crémer (1989) concentrated on *corporate culture*.

Nohria and Eccles defined corporate capability as 'an activity performed by a company in which it has a distinctive competence relative to its competitors' (1991: 2). This definition of corporate capability basically passed the question on to the need to define 'distinctive competence', but elsewhere they equated the two terms: 'The science of switchable molecules and the technology for performing this activity, which involves producing media based on the layering of these molecules, are *a distinctive competence of Polaroid or what we call Polaroid's "corporate capability"* ' (Nohria and Eccles, 1991: 1; emphasis added). Once again, we face a circularity in these definitions.

It seems that the problem arises from the choice of most researchers to define these concepts as productive services that are supplied ('a distinctive competence is that which yields a competitive advantage'). Once so defined, it becomes impossible then to analyze why they are productive. If resources are defined in terms of what they *do* rather than what they *are*, it becomes impossible to distinguish among them the strategic and the nonstrategic resources. An alternate route could be to start with a general definition of resources as inputs to the organizational production function, and then to analyze the circumstances under which these resources are useful.[6]

Application

The resource-based perspective posits that if all firms are symmetric ex-ante, rents will emerge only due to luck (Barney, 1986a). As Peteraf (1993) explained, insights from resource-based models, freely available to all comers, would lead to ex-ante races for the resources, which would eliminate potential rewards from superior knowledge. Thus, given ex-ante symmetry, the resource-based view offers a perspective on organizations; it does not offer strategic insights per se.

Where this approach may be useful in formulating strategy is that, given ex-ante asymmetry, firms may be in a position to take strategic actions in acquisition and utilization of resources. Given asymmetry, strategy formulation in the factor-market becomes the dual of product-market strategy. Wernerfelt exposed this duality by stating that firms should aspire for 'first-mover advantage in attractive resources' using the Porter-five forces model for analyzing resource-markets (1984: 175).

The resource-based approach is sought to simultaneously address issues of both diversification and single business unit strategy. There is a stream of empirical research done by Wernerfelt and his colleagues to test Penrose's (1981) and Rubin's (1973) theoretical assertion that multimarket expansion is triggered by the available (excess) capacity of a firm-specific multi-use resource. Montgomery and Wernerfelt (1988), Wernerfelt and Montgomery (1988), Montgomery and Hariharan (1989), and Chatterjee and Wernerfelt (1991) related successful product-market diversification to the effective utilization of multi-use assets. Prahalad and Hamel (1990) posited that core competence should be applicable to multiple markets. Nohria and Eccles (1991) ascribed sustained superior performance of conglomerates to the possession of corporate capability. Essentially, the attempt is to link characteristics of an intrinsically multi-use resource with successful product-market diversification.

On the other hand, Rumelt (1984) and Barney (1991), for instance, used the resource-based perspective in studying sustainable competitive advantage within a single product market as an alternate paradigm to the Porter perspective on corporate strategy – strategy within a single business unit may be driven by the analysis of available resources rather than environmental opportunities.

The two approaches are related, but are subtly different. The resource underlying multimarket expansion need must be a multi-use resource, but the strategic resource for a single market need not possess this multi-use property. Ghemawat (1991b) addressed this difference, perhaps too strongly, since he asserted that multi-use assets are generic, and hence, cannot be strategic. An asset is strategic if investment in the asset is irreversible. Only a durable, idiosyncratic asset represents a sunk cost. Since a generic factor can shift costlessly to alternate uses, it doesn't represent a sunk cost. While the distinction between multi-use and single-use resources is worthwhile, it is not necessary that an immobile, multi-use resource will always be generic. There may be non-generic multi-use assets, investment in which is sunk for a limited number of product markets, and which can move only inefficiently from one industry to another (Collis, this volume). As Montgomery and Wernerfelt (1988) theorized and verified, the wider a firm diversifies, the less specific its asset base is and/or the more its asset base will tend to lose value in transferring across markets, and hence, the lower the rents generated.

Proponents of the resource-based perspective also claim that the basis of sustained competitive advantage is efficiency advantages, and hence, strategic management concerns at the firm-level are consistent with social welfare concerns at the economy-level. This is really a throwback to the traditional debate between the Chicago and the Cambridge schools. While the Cambridge school attributed rents to market power (Bain, 1956), the Chicago school attributed them to superior efficiency (Demsetz, 1974). Neither of the two schools has been proven entirely correct or been entirely discredited (although, it is interesting to note that the US Department of Justice merger guidelines still pay considerable attention to the potential effects of market power, in the Cambridge tradition). Peteraf (1993), Barney (1991) and Conner (1991) referred to the Chicago argument in asserting that firm-rent maximization is consonant with social welfare optimization. The resource-based perspective by itself does not provide any new evidence to show that efficiency benefits outweigh, or replace, pecuniary benefits.[7]

Further, while ex-post efficiency rents may not cause allocative inefficiency, ex-ante racing for superior resources may lead to socially wasteful rent-seeking behavior (Posner, 1975). Peteraf (1993) and Barney (1991) ignore the welfare consequences of this racing for resources. Thus, the social welfare implications of the resource perspective are rather limited.

An error of omission that the resource-based perspective seems to be making is the obverse of some of the same mistakes it accuses the competitive strategy approach of making – it seems to be ascribing preeminence to the inside-out perspective of strategy. Barney (1986c), for instance, asserted that the analysis of a firm's skills and capabilities will be of greater strategic value than the analysis of its competitive environment. However, as Wernerfelt (1984), Collis (1991) and Ghemawat (1991b) pointed out, strategic analysis must recognize the duality between the resource-based and the product-based perspectives of the firm.

Level of analysis

Some proponents of the resource-based view claim that the paradigm implies that strategy insights are most feasible if the unit of analysis is the firm rather than the industry.[8] However, the resource-based theory also predicts that rents can be generated from asymmetries in the resource market. If asymmetries have to be generated, and exploited, a broader, industry-level analysis is necessary.[9] On the other hand, a simple modelling of the firm as a production function, as industry-level studies are wont to do, risks missing out on firm-specific variables such as *invisible assets* and firm-specific human capital. Thus, what is needed is a careful multi-level analysis, both at the level of the industry, to understand asymmetries, and at the level of the firm, to catch firm-specific capabilities.

Perhaps, what really lies at the core of some of the existing confusion is that while the focus of the resource-based view has been on developing the paradigm at a macro-level (Barney, 1991; Peteraf, 1993), and on translating its implications into a practitioner-oriented framework to implement corporate strategy (Grant, 1991; Wernerfelt, 1984), the approach has not studied the issue of effectively configuring resources in any significant detail. Besides, very little work has been done on establishing microfoundations of tractable models, which carefully explore the interlinkages among various variables and parameters.

Defining Resources, Capabilities and Competencies

Resources

These are the fixed, firm-specific input factors of production. Our definition of resources follows Rubin (1973) who distinguished fixed inputs from variable inputs, and Caves who defined resources as the tangible and intangible assets 'semi-permanently tied to the firm' (1980: 65). The definition is in the spirit of Dierickx and Cool's (1989) differentiation between stocks and flows.

However, we differ from Amit and Schoemaker (1993), who defined resources as transferable input factors of production, and capabilities as the fixed firm-specific input factors of production. Their capabilities are our resources, and their resources are our factor-inputs.

Resources may be physical or intangible. *Intangible resources* are identical to Itami's (1987) *invisible assets* – 'information based resources' such as consumer trust, brand image, distribution control, corporate culture, and management skill. An intangible asset is durable, contributes as a production input, and depreciates over time (Dierickx and Cool, 1989). An intangible asset differs from a physical asset in two ways:

- It has no physical existence.
- It is the accumulation of a by-product of the firm-production process.

Examples of intangible assets include:

- By-product flow:[10] employee learning; product quality; organizational learning; and societal spill-overs.
- Intangible asset: worker human capital; brand capital; organizational knowledge; and public goodwill.

A firm may erroneously look on several of these flows as externalities. However, these flows accumulate as intangible assets, which contribute to the production function.

Intangible resources may further be classified into two groups: *organizational knowledge* and *boundary resources*.

Organizational knowledge This is an intraorganizational intangible resource, which is accumulated from organizational learning, a by-product of the production process.[11]

A plethora of terms have been used to describe organizational knowledge, which is internally generated, and evolves through the process of learning: Nelson and Winter's (1982) description of organizational routines which evolve through learning, Prahalad and Hamel's interpretation of *core competencies* as 'the collective learning in the organization' (1990: 82), Dosi and Marengo's (1992) description of organizational knowledge as a property of the learning system and of *competency* as subject to learning and change, and Leonard-Barton's (1992) description of core capability as the knowledge-set that distinguishes and provides a competitive advantage.

Organizational knowledge differs from knowledge resident in physical memory (files, computer, etc.), and in individual human capital (knowledge and skill resident with individuals within the organization). It is the team-knowledge which transcends individual members and exists in the

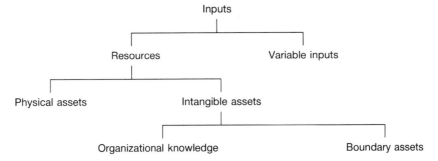

Figure 5.1　*Classification of production inputs*

form of organizational routines (Nelson and Winter, 1982).[12] Generally, organizational knowledge is more *tacit* (Polanyi, 1962) and firm-specific than physical memory and individual human capital.

Barney (1986b), Crémer (1989) and Fiol (1991) characterized this resource as *organizational culture*. For instance, Crémer (1989) defined *corporate culture* as the stock of knowledge which is common to a substantial portion of the employees of the firm, but not to the general population from which they are drawn.

The concept of organizational knowledge also helps us make an admittedly simplistic first-level differentiation within the data–information–knowledge–wisdom continuum proposed by Bartlett. While *data* exist in the available state of nature, *information* is perceived data, *knowledge* is assimilated information, and *wisdom* is knowledge integrated into a world-view.

Boundary resources　These are the relationship-specific intangible assets which link the firm with external constituencies. Some examples would be consumer loyalty, worker human capital, public trust, and so on.

Boundary assets have the interesting characteristic that while the flows which accumulate these assets are provided by the firm and the assets themselves are inputs to the firm production function, the asset-stocks are 'owned by' the external constituencies (since they vest with the external constituency). For instance, worker human capital resides with the worker, public goodwill belongs to the public, consumer trust is embedded in the consumers.

These assets can be likened to bridges spanning organizational boundaries. In Scott's (1981) terminology, while organizational knowledge lies at the core of an organization, boundary resources are the boundary-spanning assets. Thus, we classify production inputs as shown in Figure 5.1.

Capabilities

These are the potential applications of resources. Resources and capabilities are closely related terms – access to a resource leads to a capability, a capability arises from the possession of a resource. While resource is a fixed asset, capability is the potential input from the resource stock to the production function. Our definition matches Grant's definition of capability – 'the capacity for a team of resources to perform some task or activity' (1991: 119). Hence, a multi-use resource is a multi-capability resource.

Further, a capability may draw upon several of a firm's resources. If a firm wishes to develop a particular capability, it may be necessary for it to simultaneously develop the multiple resources which all contribute to the capability. One asset may need another *cospecialized asset* (Teece, 1982) in order that a capability they jointly contribute to develops. The circumstance of assets being cospecialized is a special case of multi-resource capability when the resources are complementary. We can also consider positive scope-effects (the asset *interaction effect* mentioned by Dierickx and Cool, 1989) – there is a positive synergy among the resources, so that the capability generated by their being jointly present is greater than the sum of capability they would have generated separately. On the other hand, we can also contemplate substitute resources (one resource may be able to offer the same capability as another), and negative scope effects (there may be negative synergies among resources).

Competencies

These are higher-order routines which develop and configure organizational resources. Given its resources, an organization has to optimize on available capabilities. However, being a social system, an organization has the ability to change its resource mix, and even 'self-design' this change (Boulding, 1956). Competencies are the guidelines and blueprints used in this process of organizational self-design.

Competencies are higher-order routines – *search routines* in Nelson and Winter's (1982) terminology – since they operate on resources, which include organizational knowledge stored in the form of first-order routines. Further, the definition is recursive, since competencies include not only the search-routines but also the meta-routines which help develop and mold these routines, and the meta-meta-routines, and so on.

The competencies concept is a throwback to the Lippman and Rumelt (1982) discussion of the choice among production functions, and the creation of new production functions, and captures some flavor of the Teece et al. discussion of *dynamic capabilities* and *core competencies* – 'the mechanisms by which firms accumulate and dissipate new skills and capabilities' (1990: 19).

However, our definitions are at variance with Collis' (1991) terminology. He defined *core competence* as 'the vector of irreversible assets along which the firm is uniquely advantaged' (Collis, 1991: 51), and described *organizational capability* as the dynamic routines acquired by the organization. Collis' core competence is organizational resource according to us, and his description of organizational capability is competence in our grammar.

Broadly, competencies operate on resources in two ways – refinement and renewal:[13]

- *Refinement*: This is incremental accumulation of the resource.
- *Renewal*: This is the discovery of new, more efficient production functions. The timing for such discovery is stochastically unpredictable, and it depreciates existing resources.

This dichotomization is rooted in the distinction drawn by Kuhn (1970) between normal science and scientific revolution. Subsequently, this polarity surfaced in the study of intangible assets, specifically R and D research – product versus process innovations, cost reduction versus radical patent race (Dosi, 1982). Tushman and Anderson (1986) distinguished incremental technological advances from technological breakthroughs, which could be knowledge-enhancing or knowledge-destroying. Henderson and Clark (1990) also remarked that incremental innovation feeds on and reinforces the existing problem-solving capabilities of existing organizations, while radical innovation forces them to ask a new set of questions and employ new problem-solving approaches. Dosi and Marengo (1992) generalized this polarity beyond technology to organization by referring to two kinds of competencies, when they described routines for *exploitation* and *exploration*.

Refinement competency, for instance, helps accumulate organizational knowledge incrementally through *learning by doing*. Empirically, Rubin (1973) quoted a dated, but still relevant, study of thirty-two Wisconsin company executives by McLennan (1967), which found that informal on-the-job training was considered the most effective method of skill and knowledge development. However, if an organization focuses only on refinement, its ability to flexibly adapt to changing circumstances becomes limited, since organizational resources become too specific. Strategic resources may become constraints if circumstances change – core capabilities may become *core rigidities* (Leonard-Barton, 1992).

Renewal competency, on the other hand, leads to the spawning of unanticipated products (Prahalad and Hamel, 1990) and the *Schumpeterian revolutions* hypothesized by Barney (1986c). However, this competency may lead to the undermining of existing assets, especially embedded knowledge (Henderson and Clark, 1990). Nonaka (1988) described *organizational self-renewal* as a process of dissolving an existing organizational order and creating a new one. Thus, renewal involves *creative destruction* (Schumpeter, 1950) – moving to a more productive organizational transformation function, but at the cost of depreciating existing resources.

To borrow the terminology of evolutionary ecologists, intraorganizationally (Hannan and Freeman, 1977),[14] a firm experiments with a set of resources. The ecological (competitive) environment signals which capabilities are useful for the organization and which are not. Based on environmental stimuli, the firm selects strategic resources and prunes out ineffectual resources. The firm then retains effective resources over a nontransitory interval of time. In this entire cycle of *experimentation–selection–retention*, selection is forced by the environment, retention ability is akin to *refinement competency*, and experimentation ability is akin to *renewal competency*.

Relevance of the Resource Perspective to General Management

Strategic Resource

Resources yield *sustainable competitive advantage* if they meet the following conditions:

- The resource is *scarce*.
- The resource has *restricted mobility*.
- There is ex-ante *asymmetry* among the firms with respect to the resource.

Scarcity and imperfect mobility Rents arise from ex-post asymmetry among (potentially) competing firms. The cause of this asymmetry is unequal access to or information about a fixed resource. A scarce resource will generate rents if it offers returns greater than its cost in the factor market. A scarce resource must have restricted mobility, since, if the resource were perfectly mobile, its factor market value would reflect its scarcity value, and the firm would get zero rent from appropriating the resource. A resource is rendered immobile due to *asset specificity* (Williamson, 1975). In a revisit to this argument, Rumelt (1984) pointed out that alternate use of the resource may involve high transaction costs. Teece (1982) offered a similar argument in positing that *cospecialized assets* tend to be transaction specific in nature, and hence, may not be contracted for in the market.[15] Conner (1991) stressed that the linkage of an input to the firm's existing asset base was central to rent creation. Rumelt (1984), Teece (1986), and Dierickx and Cool (1989) also mentioned that a factor may be untransferable because the market for an asset may not even exist, since property rights on the asset may not be inalienable.

In order to retain scarcity, a resource must be *inimitable* (Rumelt, 1984) and *nonsubstitutable* (Dierickx and Cool, 1989). In order to restrict imitability and substitutability of its scarce resources, a firm may use *isolating mechanisms* (Rumelt, 1984), also called *mobility barriers* (Caves and Porter, 1977).

Hence, a scarce asset with restricted tradability generates rents – what fraction of these are appropriated by the firm's owner and what fraction accrue to the asset supplier has to be bargained (Collis, this volume; Ghemawat, 1991b). Repeated bargaining may be less efficient than ex-ante long-term contracting between the firm owner and the asset supplier. Thus, we may witness long-term relations between the asset supplier and the firm owner. Essentially, the more a party has sunk in relationship-specific investment, the less its relative bargaining power is and the less its share of the rents. Some first level observations would be:

- The more firm-specific the asset, the more the firm owner can appropriate rents from its use.
- The more the asset is supraindividual, belonging to a team rather than to a specific individual, the more the firm owner can appropriate rents from asset-use.
- The more the incumbency advantage of an asset supplier compared with a potential supplier outside the firm, the more the rent the incumbent asset supplier can extract.
- The more the ambiguity about who specifically supplies the asset, the more the rent the firm-owner can extract.

Ex-ante asymmetry   If access to a particular resource were definitely going to yield positive rents to all comers, the race among firms wishing to appropriate the resource would dissipate the rents. Lippman and Rumelt (1982) showed that *causal ambiguity* – ex-ante uncertainty about firm efficiency – leads to ex-post stable interfirm profitability differences and above normal industry returns. The reason for this is that uncertainty leads to an asymmetry – the firms come to possess heterogeneous reservation prices for the resource. If the competing firms are asymmetrically placed in terms of initial endowments, *first-mover advantage* may yield positive rents (Tirole, 1988). Thus, in order for positive rents to emerge, the firms have to be asymmetrically positioned ex-ante, either in terms of expectations or in terms of resource accessibility.

To summarize, if a resource is freely available it will not generate rents. If there is competitive symmetry in access to a scarce resource, one firm cannot expect ex-ante to necessarily gain any competitive advantage from access to the resource. However, if a firm has advantageous access to (or information about) a scarce resource, rents will accrue to the firm. If the resource is mobile across firms, the resource provider will appropriate all such rents in the factor market. However, if the resource is firm-specific, the rents will be shared between the firm owner and the resource provider. Thus, in order for a resource to yield rents to a firm owner, it must be scarce, it must have restricted mobility, and the firm must have advantageous access to the resource.

Source of Rents

Ghemawat (1991b) referred to Arrow (1968) in highlighting that a factor would command marginal rents equal to its marginal contribution to the firm, unless the factor market were imperfect. Only in such a case can a wedge be drawn between the returns a firm gets from the factor, and the rents the factor can command in the factor market. Thus, in order for a resource to be strategic, its factor market must be imperfect.

For a firm to generate rents from such a resource, it must acquire the resource at a cost lower than the returns it yields. This is possible only if the firm is either lucky or leverages on an ex-ante asymmetry. Barney (1986a) pointed out that for symmetrically-placed firms, positive rents will be generated by firm resources acquired from the environment only if a firm is fortunate, or if it has better information.[16] He defined *strategic factor markets* as imperfectly competitive markets in which some firms have systematically better expectations about the value of a resource, and drew on the *resource-dependency* argument (Pfeffer and Salancik, 1978) to claim that the strategic task for an organization was to acquire resources from the environment through better information. However, possessing better expectations is as much an asymmetry as possessing unequal initial endowments. Hence, only chance can lead resources to yield differential rents if the firms are perfectly symmetric ex-ante.

If the cause of superior returns is luck, there is very little strategic insight possible (except, perhaps, in development of procedures for encouraging experimentation and reducing risk-aversion). On the other hand, if there is an ex-ante asymmetry in a resource which trades imperfectly, firms can contemplate strategic actions. The issue of strategic interactions given asymmetry in information about or access to sunk resources has been extensively studied in the industrial organization literature. As a sampling, witness theoretical works by Fudenberg and Tirole (1984) on strategic interactions, Dixit (1980) on capacity as a strategic variable, Milgrom and Roberts (1982) on using information asymmetry for limit pricing, and Dasgupta and Stiglitz (1980) on R and D.

Dierickx and Cool (1989) identified asset-stocks, which had to be developed within a firm due to market failure, as strategic resources. The underlying assumption is that the problem of market failure is much more acute for stock inputs than variable inputs.[17] Variable inputs may face market failure at one instant, but at another, if the cause of the market failure (small numbers, for instance) disappears, market failure in the factor market also vanishes instantaneously.[18] However, since resources are developed over time, market failure at one instant can deleteriously affect the resource market intertemporally. In the extreme, if the asset property rights are not inalienable, this may prevent a resource market from even existing.

Furthermore, since resources develop only over time, while variable inputs can be traded at any instant, resources tend to involve longer and greater commitment from the firm than do variable inputs. As Dierickx and Cool (1989) discussed, firm-specific assets which have developed over time cannot be instantaneously imitated, and involve an element of intertemporal sunkenness, owing to *time-compression diseconomies* – convex adjustment costs.

Within the general class of resources, intangible assets are even more susceptible to market failure, owing to the intensely firm-specific nature of these assets – not only in application, but also in generation. These resources tend to be more tacit, involving significant time-compression diseconomy,[19] and generated by more socially complex and ambiguous phenomena than physical assets, making them less susceptible to imitation and substitution.

Owing to their graver degree of market failure and greater degree of sunkenness, in general, intangible assets are more strategic than other resources, especially physical assets.[20] This conclusion is at variance with Barney's (1986a) assertion that potential rents would accrue from 'strategic factor markets', and is more in the spirit of Dierickx and Cool (1989), who focused on internally developed asset-stocks as strategic resources. The linkaging of sunkenness with the strategic importance of the input follows a time-honored industrial organization tradition – the more that a firm can commit to an action, by sinking funds irreversibly to accomplish it, the more strategic the action becomes (Caves, 1984). Since entry barriers are also exit barriers, once an intangible asset is acquired, a firm can credibly claim that it cannot reversibly divest itself of this asset.

Within the class of intangible assets, while organizational knowledge is 'owned' by the firm, boundary assets are not. Since boundary assets are built and used by the firm, but stored in the external constituency, they are susceptible to opportunism – the constituency may extract rents by threatening to withhold the asset from the firm. A worker may demand higher wages as his or her human capital grows through job learning; the local public may not part with its entire valuation for a goodwill-generating public service provided by the firm; consumers may not pay their entire reservation valuation for a high-quality product. To overcome the risk of opportunism and repeated ex-post bargaining, the firm owner may enter into a long-term contract with the external constituency detailing rent apportionment and ensuring asset development and availability. Since the firm invests in the asset and the external constituency has control over it, at the first level, it appears that the firm owner is in a weaker bargaining position and most of the rents generated by the asset will accrue to the external constituency. This result is diluted if the asset is intensely firm-specific.

On the other hand, rents generated by organizational knowledge directly accrue to the firm owner. Since it is relatively less susceptible to bargaining losses, less mobile and more tacit (being more in the 'core' of the organization), we would expect organizational knowledge to be even more strategic than boundary assets.

Short Run vs Long Run Strategy: The Role of Competencies

Caves (1984) recognized that competitive strategy focuses on short run optimization. He suggested that the firm operates in the short run and is contractually encumbered with a variety of fixed facilities. Strategic choice then expresses the top coordinator's attempt to maximize the rents to these fixed factors over the planning horizon. The pursuit of competitive advantage can be characterized as a sequence of long-lived and irreversible resource commitments.

Ghemawat (1991b) used this perspective to relate product-market competitive strategy with the resource-based perspective. In his formulation, product market decisions are taken in the short run, given fixed factors, while factor-market decisions are taken with a longer horizon. The mapping may not be exactly one-to-one, since there may be long-run product market variables such as advertising brand name, and there may be short-run factor market variables, for instance, traded inputs. However, at a coarse-grained level, it seems generally correct to look on resource commitments as longer-run decisions, and product market moves as comparatively short run.

However, there is another temporal aspect to strategy. If we were to distinguish among the short run (when most inputs are fixed), the medium run (when committed resources are fixed), and the long run (when there is no fixed factor and there is no strategic resource), product-market decisions tend to be strategic only in the short run; resource-driven decisions are strategic only in the medium term; and the crucial long-term decisions concern competencies.

In the short term, the firm optimizes on available resources. However, in the medium term, these resources are themselves being altered by the competency meta-routines, as the organization shapes its choice-set. While capabilities are resources in the short term, they tend to become constraints in the medium run.

Competencies themselves change, but they tend to evolve very slowly. Organizational ecologists (Hannan and Freeman, 1984) argue that the process of organizational selection favors firms with high performance reliability and accountability, which requires highly reproducible organizational structures ('routines' in evolutionary terminology), and this condition of reproducibility generates inertial processes. Hence, ecological-evolutionary selection process favors organizations with inertial competencies. Hence, while resources are fixed in the short run, competencies are fixed in the medium term. Thus, in the short run, the issue is optimization given fixed resources; in the medium term, the issue is the evolution of these resources, given that the organization has chosen to develop them; and in the long term, the issue is how competencies themselves should evolve so as to yield optimal decision rules on resource-development.

It is in contemplating this temporal aspect of strategy that the role of history becomes crucial. The past constrains the firm along a particular trajectory, but at every point on this trajectory, the firm has the flexibility to shape its future. At any given time, a firm faces a realm of possibility, and a realm of the impossible. Whatever a firm may do, it cannot enter the realm of impossibility. However, within the realm of possibility lie a variety of alternatives. The action taken at each instant opens a new realm of possibility and offers choices for the future. The action of the firm may affect which possible future the flow of events indeed follows. Insofar as the firm is able to influence the flow of events within the realm of possibility, not only is the firm constrained by history, but it also shapes its future.[21] Thus, while we concur with Teece (1984) that 'history matters', we assert that within the constraints of history, a firm makes strategic choices which shape its future. While history is an invariant given in the short term, it is moldable in the long term. It is in choosing among alternatives and charting the trajectory for the future that competencies become crucial, for not only do they help accumulate organizational resources, but they also change the nature of these resources. An organization with a rich repertoire of competencies is a *learning organization* (Senge, 1990) – adaptive in coping with changing circumstances and generative in creating new situations and circumstances. The long-term issue, therefore, is how to develop an optimal repertoire of competencies.[22]

The Strategic Relevance of Resource-based Frameworks

If superior returns are to be had from better information, practitioners must be able to identify and leverage strategic resources, especially intangible assets. Toward this purpose, a framework to help practitioners apply the resource-based perspective must be developed. Stevenson (1976) discovered that it may be non-trivial for the organizational coalition to develop a shared view on what the strategic resources are, and shared understanding may be a major goal for working with a framework. Wernerfelt (1984 and 1989), Amit and Schoemaker (1993), Grant (1991) and Stalk et al. (1992) have offered frameworks to help practitioners apply the resource-based perspective. However, once the framework is widely applied, it will lose its strategic edge, unless ex-ante asymmetries exist (Schoemaker, 1990).

Moreover, as discussed earlier, the quest for generic success factors (management skill, corporate culture, organizational systems, etc.) is bound to fail, since generic factors cannot be the source of competitive advantage. Since strategic assets are idiosyncratic, the *contingency* of a situation will dictate which resources are strategic in the given circumstance (Lawrence and Lorsch, 1967).

Organizational Form and Systems

Rigorous and robust predictions are possible only if they are backed by the microfoundations of tractable models. How intangible assets develop, and what parameters influence this development, is an important question which has received comparatively little attention in the resource-based framework.

Within organization theory, agency theorists, who have looked at the vertical structure of the firm as a sequence of principal–agent relations, have begun explicitly considering molding organizational structure, incentives and control to optimally manage organizational knowledge. For instance, Jensen and Meckling (1990) addressed the need to collocate authority with organizational knowledge.

In the Carnegie tradition, Aoki (1980) described an organization with more horizontal and less vertical linkages than a hierarchical organization as being a configuration which helps the firm utilize its knowledge more effectively. In comparing the *J-form organization* (Japanese organizations with a preponderance of horizontal linkages) with the *H-form organization* (US hierarchical organizations with mainly vertical linkages), he stated that the operating unit of a J-form organization has the ability of *ex-post adaptation* – the ability to learn rapidly from current circumstances and change according to them.

Prahalad and Hamel (1990) remarked that a firm should be organized not as a collection of Strategic Business Units (SBUs), but as a collection of competencies, and such a focus in organizing will help develop and flexibly leverage core competencies. They also remarked that such a focus will prevent 'hollowing out' of corporations, and may provide a rationale for building alliances to share capabilities.

Another intriguing issue is whether organizational forms and systems promoting refinement are very different from those supporting renewal. Burns and Stalker (1961) indicated that such was indeed the case several years ago. While *mechanistic* organizational systems provided stability and efficiency, *organic* systems encouraged innovation. Wilson (1966) suggested that organizational forces which generate innovation proposals conflict with forces which secure their adaption and implementation. It would be useful to enquire whether this mutual exclusivity of competencies still exists, or whether organizations can simultaneously promote both competencies.

However, considerable work still needs to be done to develop a theory of the firm consonant with the resource-based view, such that it may underpin a resource-based view of strategy.

Notes

I am grateful to Professors C.A. Bartlett, R.E. Caves, P. Ghemawat, C.A. Montgomery, and H.H. Stevenson for their comments and suggestions.

1 Conner (1991) classified the economists' perspectives on the role of a firm into five streams – the neoclassical perfect competition theory, which looks at firms as combiners of inputs; the structure–conduct–performance paradigm which looks at firms as output-restraining oligopolies; the Schumpeterian view of firms as contributing to creative destruction; the Chicago view of firms as efficiency-seeking; and the transaction cost view of firms as alternative institutional structures to markets.

2 This argument derives from Simon's (1945) behavioral assumption of bounded rationality. Given limited ability to account for all possible future states of nature (and the increasing cost of writing a more complete, more complex contract which takes more contingencies into account), the contracting parties may choose to leave the contract incomplete.

3 In a similar vein, Ghemawat defined *commitment* as 'the tendency of strategies to persist over time' (1991a: Ch. 2).

4 Reed and DeFillippi (1990) classified the features underlying causal ambiguity as *tacitness* (noncodifiable accumulation of skills resulting from learning by doing), *complexity* (resulting from multiple interdependent skills and assets), and *specificity* (transaction-specific assets).

5 These changes – imitation and substitution, resource mobility, depreciation, technology and market changes – may be evolutionary or revolutionary. However, Barney (1986c) asserted that the rent-streams from strategic assets would continue unless 'a structural revolution in the industry' occurred. He referred back to an older tradition in calling such structural revolutions *Schumpeterian shocks*.

6 I am grateful to Professor Caves for this insight.

7 However, the traditional debate – whether asymmetry leads to market power which leads to deadweight losses, or whether unequal efficiency leads to the efficient firms getting higher returns and becoming bigger – has largely been entirely sidestepped in the more recent empirical industrial organization. The favored approach of the 'new economic industrial organization' has become conducting intensive longitudinal studies of one industry at a time, focusing not only on industry structure, but on conduct also. (See Bresnahan (1989) for a review.)

8 See Peteraf (1993) and Barney (1991) for one side of the view, and Ghemawat (1991a), for the other. Empirically, Schmalensee (1985) discovered that profit differences are attributable mostly to industry effects, and firm effects are insignificant. Hansen and Wernerfelt (1989) found that industry effects and organizational effects were both significant, and roughly independent. Scott and Pascoe (1986), Wernerfelt and Montgomery (1988) and Kessides (1990) discovered significant firm-specific effects, although they all found that industry effect strongly dominated firm effect.

9 As Caves remarked, 'We can't have a differential without something to differ from'.

10 The flows are by-products since they are not the primary revenue-generating products of the firm.

11 Following the Fiol and Lyles (1985) distinction between lower-level and higher-level learning, which is akin to the Argyris and Schön (1978) distinction between single loop and double loop learning, we are referring here to lower-level learning only.

12 Leonard-Barton (1992) further fine-grains knowledge residing in teams into three types – technical systems, managerial systems, and norms and values.

13 The terms *refinement* and *renewal* were first used by Bartlett.

14 This is in the tradition of Burgelman (1991), who borrowed the ecology perspective to study the process of strategy making within an organization.

15 Defining assets as cospecialized is an alternate characterization of asset specificity, since asset specificity arises because an asset gets linked with other firm resources in an idiosyncratic manner.

16 This was essentially a revisit to Demsetz' (1973) comment that superior performance may arise from a combination of uncertainty and luck or atypical insight.

17 Dierickx and Cool's (1989) assertion that traded assets cannot yield rents since their value can be realized in the relevant factor markets rests on the assumption that factor markets are perfect. Hence, while they restricted their framework to only the circumstance when the asset is nontradable, a weaker assumption of an imperfect factor market is sufficient to qualify the asset as strategic.

18 Williamson (1975) identified the environmental factors of uncertainty and small numbers, and the human factors of bounded rationality and opportunism as combining to cause market failure.

19 In the study quoted by Rubin (1973), more than half the managers who were surveyed indicated that it had taken them more than three years to acquire job knowledge from their organizations (McLennan, 1967).

20 Among the various intangible assets which have been hypothesized as underlying sustained competitive advantage are *organizational culture* (Barney, 1986b; Fiol, 1991) and *top-management skill* (Castanias and Helfat, 1991).

21 The argument in this paragraph is derived from Nanda (1989). In subsequent discussions with Malnight and Stevenson, we had coined the phrase *the cone of possibility* to describe and develop this concept.

22 Stevenson attempted to address these higher levels of analysis – how does a firm decide which competencies to develop, and to what purpose – with the concept of the value-matrix: a firm has to not only create value, but also define and distribute it. The process of creating value relates to leveraging resources, but the process of defining values relates to molding competencies.

References

Akerlof, G. (1970) 'The market for lemons: Qualitative uncertainty and the market mechanism', *Quarterly Journal of Economics*, 84: 488–500.

Amit, R. and Schoemaker, P.J. (1993) 'Strategic assets and organizational rent', *Strategic Management Journal*, 14(1): 33–46.

Andrews, K.R. (1971) *The Concept of Corporate Strategy*. Homewood, IL: Dow Jones Irwin.

Aoki, M. (1990) 'Toward an economic model of the Japanese firm', *Journal of Economic Literature*, 28: 1–27.

Argyris, C. (1985) *Strategy, Change, and Defensive Routines*. Boston, MA: Pitman.

Argyris, C. and Schön, D. (1978) *Organizational Learning: A Theory-in-Action Perspective*. Reading, MA: Addison-Wesley.

Arrow, K.J. (1968) 'Optimal capital policy with irreversible investment', in J.N. Wolfe (ed.), *Value, Capital, and Growth*. Edinburgh: Edinburgh University Press.

Bain, J.S. (1956) *Barriers to New Competition*. Cambridge, MA: Harvard University Press.

Baldwin, C.Y. and Clark, K.B. (1991) 'Capabilities and capital investment: New perspectives on capital budgeting', Harvard Business School Working Paper No. 92–004.

Barnard, C.I. (1938) *The Functions of the Executive*. Cambridge, MA: Harvard University Press.

Barney, J.B. (1986a) 'Strategic factor markets: Expectation, luck, and business strategy', *Management Science*, 32(10): 1231–1241.

Barney, J.B. (1986b) 'Organization culture: Can it be a source of sustained competitive advantage?' *Academy of Management Review*, 11: 656–665.

Barney, J.B. (1986c) 'Types of competition and the theory of strategy: Toward an integrative framework', *Academy of Management Review*, 11: 791–800.

Barney, J.B. (1989) 'Asset stocks and sustained competitive advantage: A comment', *Management Science*, 35(12): 1511–1513.

Barney, J.B. (1991) 'Firm resources and sustained competitive advantage', *Journal of Management*, 17(1): 99–120.

Bartlett, C.A. and Ghoshal, S. (1988) 'Organizing for worldwide effectiveness: The transnational solution', *California Management Review*, 1: 54–74.

Bartlett, C.A. and Ghoshal, S. (1989) *Managing Across Borders*. Boston, MA: Harvard Business School Press.

Baumol, W., Panzar, J. and Willig, R. (1982) *Contestable Markets and the Theory of Industry Structure*. New York: Harcourt Brace Jovanovich.

Becker, G. (1975) *Human Capital*. New York: Columbia University Press.

Boulding, K.E. (1956) 'General systems theory: The skeleton of science', *Management Science*, 2: 197–208.

Bower, J.L. (1970) *Managing the Resource Allocation Process*. Boston, MA: Harvard Business School Press.

Bresnahan, T.E. (1989) 'Empirical studies of industries with market power', in R. Schmalensee and R.D. Willig (eds), *Handbook of Industrial Organization*, vol. II. New York: North-Holland. pp. 1011–1057.

Burgelman, R.A. (1983) 'A model of the interaction of strategic behavior, corporate context, and the concept of strategy', *Academy of Management Review*, 8(1): 61–70.

Burgelman, R.A. (1991) 'Interorganizational ecology of strategy making and organizational adaptation: Theory and field research', *Organizational Science*, 2(3): 239–262.

Burns, T. and Stalker, G. (1961) *The Management of Innovation*. London: Tavistock.

Castanias, R. and Helfat, C. (1991) 'Managerial resources and rent', *Journal of Management*, 17(1): 155–171.

Caves, R.E. (1980) 'Industrial organization, corporate strategy and structure', *Journal of Economic Literature*, 18: 64–72.

Caves, R.E. (1984) 'Economic analysis and the quest for competitive advantage', *American Economic Review*, 74(2): 127–132.

Caves, R.E. and Porter, M.E. (1977) 'From entry barriers to mobility barriers', *Quarterly Journal of Economics*, 91: 241–261.

Chandler, A.D., Jr (1962) *Strategy and Structure: Chapters in the History of the American Industrial Enterprise*. Cambridge, MA: MIT Press.

Chatterjee, S. and Wernerfelt, B. (1991) 'The link between resources and type of diversification: Theory and evidence', *Strategic Management Journal*, 13: 33–48.

Coase, R. (1952) 'The nature of the firm', reprinted in G.J. Stigler and K. Boulding (eds), *Readings in Price Theory*. Homewood, IL: Irwin. pp. 331–351.

Collis, D.J. (1991) 'A resource-based analysis of global competition: The case of the bearings industry', *Strategic Management Journal*, 12: 49–68.

Conner, K.R. (1991) 'A historical comparison of resource-based theory and five schools of thought within IO economics: Do we have a new theory of the firm?' *Journal of Management*, 17(1): 121–154.

Crémer, J. (1989) 'Common knowledge and the coordination of economic activities', in M. Aoki, B. Gustafson and O.E. Williamson (eds) *The Firm as a Nexus of Treaties*. London: Sage.

Cyert, R.M. and March, J.G. (1963) *A Behavioral Theory of the Firm*. New York: Prentice Hall.

Daft, R. (1983) *Organization Theory and Design*. New York: West.

Dasgupta, P. and Stiglitz, J. (1980) 'Uncertainty, industrial structure, and the speed of R and D', *Bell Journal of Economics*, 11: 1–28.

Demsetz, H. (1973) 'Industry structure, market rivalry, and public policy', *Journal of Law and Economics*, 16: 1–9.

Demsetz, H. (1974) 'Two systems of belief about monopoly', in H. Goldschmid, H.M. Mann and J.F. Weston (eds), *Industrial Concentration: The New Learning*. Boston, MA: Little, Brown.

Dierickx, I. and Cool, K. (1989) 'Asset stock accumulation and sustainability of competitive advantage', *Management Science*, 35(12): 1504–1511.

Dixit, A. (1980) 'The role of investment in entry deterrence', *Economic Journal*, 90: 721–729.

Dosi, G. (1982) 'Technological paradigm and technological trajectories: A suggested interpretation of the determinants and direction of technical change', *Research Policy*, 11: 147–162.

Dosi, G. and Marengo, L. (1992) 'Toward a theory of organizational competencies', paper presented at Harvard Business School.

Dosi, G., Teece, D.J. and Winter, S.G. (1991) 'Toward a theory of corporate coherence', in G. Dosi, R. Giametti and P.A. Toninelli (eds), *Technology and the Enterprise in a Historical Perspective*. Oxford: Oxford University Press.

Eccles, R. and Crane, D. (1988) *Doing Deals: Investment Banks at Work*. Boston, MA: Harvard Business School Press.

Fayol, H. (1949 [1919]) *General and Industrial Management*. Tr. C. Storrs. London: Pitman.

Fiol, C. (1991) 'Managing culture as a competitive resource: An identity based view of sustainable competitive advantage', *Journal of Management*, 17(1): 191–211.

Fiol, C.M. and Lyles, M.A. (1985) 'Organizational learning', *Academy of Management Review*, 10(4): 803–813.

Freidson, E. (1986) *Professional Powers: A Study of the Institutionalization of Formal Knowledge*. Chicago, IL: University of Chicago Press.

Fudenberg, D. and Tirole, J. (1984) 'The fat cat effect, the puppy dog ploy, and the lean-and-hungry look', *American Economic Review*, 74: 361–366.

Garvin, D.A. (1988) *Managing Quality*. Boston: Harvard Business School Press.

Ghemawat, P. (1991a) *Commitment: The Dynamic of Strategy*. New York: Free Press.

Ghemawat, P. (1991b) 'Resources and strategy: An IO perspective', mimeo.

Grant, R.M. (1991) 'The resource-based theory of competitive advantage: Implications for strategy formulation', *California Management Review*, 3: 114–135.

Grossman, S.J. and Hart, O.D. (1986) 'The costs and benefits of ownership: A theory of vertical and lateral controls', *Journal of Political Economy*, 94: 297–336.

Gulick, L. and Urwick, L. (eds) (1937) *Papers on the Science of Administration*. New York: Institute of Public Administration, Columbia University.

Hannan, M.T. and Freeman, J. (1977) 'The population ecology of organizations', *American Journal of Sociology*, 82: 929–964.

Hannan, M.T. and Freeman, J. (1984) 'Structural inertia and organizational change', *American Sociological Review*, 49: 149–164.

Hansen, G.S. and Wernerfelt, B. (1989) 'Determinants of firm performance: The relative importance of economic and organizational factors', *Strategic Management Journal*, 10: 399–411.

Hayes, R.H. and Garvin, D.A. (1982) 'Managing as if tomorrow mattered', *Harvard Business Review*, 3: 71–79.

Henderson, R. and Clark, K.B. (1990) 'Architectural innovation: The reconfiguration of existing product technologies and the failure of established firms', *Administrative Science Quarterly*, 35: 9–30.

Hofer, C. and Schendel, D. (1978) *Strategy Formulation: Analytical Concepts*. St. Paul, MN: West Publishing.

Itami, H. (1987) *Mobilizing Invisible Assets*. Cambridge, MA: Harvard University Press.

Jaikumar, R. (1989) 'Japanese flexible manufacturing systems: Impact on the United States', *Japan and the World Economy*, 1: 113–143.

Jaikumar, R. (1990) 'An architecture for a process control costing system', in R.S. Kaplan (ed.), *Measures for Manufacturing Excellence*. Boston, MA: Harvard Business School Press.

Jensen, M. and Meckling, W. (1976) 'Theory of the firm: Managerial behavior, agency costs, and ownership structure', *Journal of Financial Economics*, 3: 305–360.

Jensen, M.C. and Meckling, W.H. (1990) 'Knowledge, control and organization structure', mimeo presented at Nobel Symposium No. 77 on *Contracts: Determinants, Properties and Implications*, Stockholm.

Jovanovic, B. (1979) 'Firm-specific capital and turnover', *Journal of Political Economy*, 87: 1246–1260.

Kessides, I.N. (1990) 'Internal vs. external market conditions and firm profitability: An exploratory model', *Economic Journal*, 100(402): 773–792.

Kuhn, T.S. (1970) *The Structure of Scientific Revolutions*. Chicago, IL: University of Chicago Press.

Lawrence, P.R. and Lorsch, J.W. (1967) *Organization and Environment*. Boston, MA: Harvard University Division of Research.

Learned, E.P., Christensen, C.R., Andrews, K.R. and Guth, W. (1969) *Business Policy*. Homewood, IL: Irwin.

Leonard-Barton, D. (1992) 'Core capabilities and core rigidities: A paradox in managing new product development', *Strategic Management Journal*, 13(summer special issue): 111–125.

Lippman, S.A. and Rumelt, R.P. (1982) 'Uncertain imitability: An analysis of interfirm differences in efficiency under competition', *Bell Journal of Economics*, 13: 418–438.

McLennan, K. (1967) *Managerial Skill and Knowledge*. Madison, WI: University of Wisconsin Press.

Milgrom, P. and Roberts, J. (1982) 'Limit pricing and entry under incomplete information', *Econometrica*, 50: 443–460.

Montgomery, C.A. and Hariharan, S. (1989) 'Diversified expansion by large established firms', *Journal of Economic Behavior*, 15(1): 71–89.

Montgomery, C.A. and Wernerfelt, B. (1988) 'Diversification, Ricardian Rents, and Tobin's Q', *Rand Journal of Economics*, 19: 623–632.

Nanda, A. (1989) 'The field of business policy research', Harvard Business School Working Paper.

Nelson, R.R. and Winter, S.G. (1982) *An Evolutionary Theory of Economic Change.* Cambridge, MA: Harvard University Press.

Nohria, N. and Eccles, R.G. (1991) 'Corporate capability', Harvard Business School Working Paper No. 92–038.

Nohria, N. and Garcia-Pont, C. (1991) 'Global strategic linkages and industry structure', *Strategic Management Journal*, 12: 105–124.

Nonaka, I. (1988) 'Creating organizational order out of chaos: Self-renewal in Japanese firms', *California Management Review*, 3: 57–73.

Parsons, D.O. (1986) 'The employment relationship: Job attachment, work effort, and the nature of contracts', in O. Ashenfelter and R. Layard (eds), *Handbook of Labor Economics*, vol. II. New York: Elsevier. pp. 818–830.

Penrose, E.T. (1981) *The Theory of the Growth of the Firm.* New York: M.E. Sharpe.

Peteraf, M.A. (1993) 'The cornerstones of competitive advantage: A resource-based view', *Strategic Management Journal*, 14(3): 179–191.

Pfeffer, J. and Salancik, G.R. (1978) *The External Control of Organizations: A Resource Dependence Perspective.* New York: Harper and Row.

Polanyi, M. (1962) *Personal Knowledge.* New York: Harper Torchbooks.

Porter, M.E. (1980) *Competitive Strategy.* New York: Free Press.

Porter, M.E. (1985) *Competitive Advantage.* New York: Free Press.

Posner, R. (1975) 'The social costs of monopoly and regulation', *Journal of Political Economy*, 83: 807–827.

Prahalad, C.K. and Hamel, G. (1990) 'The core competence of the corporation', *Harvard Business Review*, 3: 79–91.

Pratt, J. and Zeckhauser, R. (1985) *Principals and Agents.* Boston, MA: Harvard Business School Press.

Prescott, E. and Visscher, M. (1980) 'Organization capital', *Journal of Political Economy*, 88: 446–461.

Reed, R. and DeFillippi, R.J. (1990) 'Causal ambiguity, barriers to imitation, and sustainable competitive advantage', *Academy of Management Review*, 15(1): 88–102.

Rubin, P.H. (1973) 'The expansion of firms', *Journal of Political Economy*, 81(4): 936–949.

Rumelt, R.P. (1984) 'Towards a strategic theory of the firm', in R.B. Lamb (ed.), *Competitive Strategic Management.* Englewood Cliffs, NJ: Prentice Hall. pp. 556–570.

Rumelt, R.P. (1987) 'Theory, strategy, and entrepreneurship', in D. Teece (ed.), *The Competitive Challenge.* Cambridge, MA: Ballinger. pp. 137–158.

Schmalensee, R. (1985) 'Do markets differ much?', *American Economic Review*, 75: 341–351.

Schoemaker, P.J. (1990) 'Strategy, complexity, and economic rent', *Management Science*, 36(10): 1178–1192.

Schumpeter, J.A. (1950) *Capitalism, Socialism, and Democracy.* New York: Harper and Row.

Scott, J.T. and Pascoe, G. (1986) 'Beyond firm and industry effects on profitability in imperfect markets', *Review of Economics and Statistics*, 98(2): 284–292.

Scott, W.R. (1981) *Organizations: Rational, Natural and Open Systems.* Englewood Cliffs, NJ: Prentice Hall.

Selznick, P. (1957) *Leadership in Administration.* New York: Harper and Row.

Senge, P. (1990) 'The leader's new work: Building learning organizations', *Sloan Management Review*, 32(1): 7–23.

Simon, H. (1945) *Administrative Behavior.* New York: Free Press. (Expanded 3rd edn, 1976.)

Snow, C.C. and Hrebiniak, L.G. (1980) 'Strategy, distinctive competence, and organizational performance', *Administrative Science Quarterly*, 25: 317–336.

Stalk, G., Jr (1988) 'Time – the next source of competitive advantage', *Harvard Business Review*, 4: 41–51.

Stalk, G., Evans, P. and Shulman, L.E. (1992) 'Competing on capabilities: The new rules of corporate strategy', *Harvard Business Review*, 70(2): 57–69.

Stevenson, H.H. (1976) 'Defining corporate strengths and weaknesses', *Sloan Management Review*, 17(3): 51–68.

Taylor, F.W. (1911) *The Principles of Scientific Management*. New York: Harper.

Teece, D.J. (1982) 'Toward an economic theory of the multiproduct firm', *Journal of Economic Behavior and Organization*, 3: 39–63.

Teece, D.J. (1984) 'Economic analysis and strategic management', *California Management Review*, 26(3): 87–110.

Teece, D.J. (1986) 'Firm boundaries, technological innovation and strategic management', in L.G. Thomas III (ed.), *The Economics of Strategic Planning: Essays in Honor of Joel Dean*. Lexington, MA: Lexington Books.

Teece, D.J., Pisano, G. and Shuen, A. (1990) 'Firm capabilities, resources, and the concept of strategy: Four paradigms of strategic management', CCC Working Paper No. 90–8.

Tirole, J. (1988) *The Theory of Industrial Organization*. Cambridge, MA: MIT Press.

Tushman, M.L. and Anderson, P. (1986) 'Technological discontinuities and organizational environments', *Administrative Science Quarterly*, 31: 439–465.

Wernerfelt, B. (1984) 'A resource-based view of the firm', *Strategic Management Journal*, 5: 171–180.

Wernerfelt, B. (1989) 'From critical resources to corporate strategy', *Journal of General Management*, 14: 4–12.

Wernerfelt, B. and Montgomery, C.A. (1988) 'Tobin's Q and the importance of focus in firm performance', *American Economic Review*, 78: 246–250.

Williamson, O.E. (1975) *Markets and Hierarchies: Analysis and Antitrust Implications*. New York: Free Press.

Wilson, J.Q. (1966) 'Innovation in organization: Notes toward a theory', in J.D. Thompson (ed.), *Approaches to Organizational Design*. Pittsburgh, PA: University of Pittsburgh Press.

6

Core Capabilities and Information Technology:
An Organizational Learning Approach

Rafael Andreu and Claudio Ciborra

One of the fundamental learning processes taking place in organizations is that leading to the development of core competence. Adopting the perspective of the resource-based view of the firm (RBVF), which focuses on the firm's resources and capabilities to understand business strategy and to provide direction to strategy formulation, this chapter emphasizes the learning aspects of capability development and explores how Information Technology (IT) can contribute to it.

As a standardized resource widely available, IT can participate in the fundamental process that transforms resources into capabilities and eventually into core capabilities – through the development and implementation of appropriate IT-based Information Systems (IS). In this way, IT/IS can become – embedded in core capabilities – an active component of the firm's competitive advantages.

The process by which resources end up being components of core capabilities in firms is a learning process that can be described and understood using RBVF concepts. Furthermore, the development of IT strategic applications (also-called 'strategic information systems', or SIS) follows patterns that closely parallel the structure of that learning process. For this reason we propose an organizational learning model based on the RBVF, and use it to describe and better understand how IT can contribute to core capabilities development.

The chapter is organized as follows: The second section summarizes the RBVF framework, including the concepts of capabilities and core capabilities and the organizational processes that lead to them. The third section presents an organizational learning model: an interpretation of capability development that emphasizes situated learning and knowledge accumulation. The fourth section describes and explains a few well-known IT/IS applications that have contributed to core capability formation in different firms using the proposed model, thus showing its appropriateness. The fifth section suggests guidelines about how IT/IS can be used to contribute to the effectiveness of the learning processes involved. Short conclusions follow.

The Resource-based View of the Firm (RBVF) Framework: An Overview

The RBVF conceives a firm as seeking to acquire hard to imitate, valuable resources and capabilities, such that managers must identify, develop and deploy resources and capabilities that provides sustainable competitive advantage and, thus, superior profits for the firm (Amit and Schoemaker, 1993). The firm's quest for differentiation is a process that develops distinctive capabilities, also-called *core capabilities*. Core capabilities are those that beneficially differentiate a company from competitive firms (Leonard-Barton, 1992). A capability has *strategic potential*, and thus becomes core, with potential for competitive advantage, when it is: (1) *valuable* – it exploits opportunities and/or neutralizes threats in a firm's environment (Barney, 1991); (2) *rare* – the number of firms that possess a particular capability is less than the number needed to generate perfect competition in an industry (Hirshleifer, 1980); (3) *imperfectly imitable* – for instance, because of unique conditions in its acquisition process, because the link between the capability and sustainable advantage is causally ambiguous (Lippman and Rumelt, 1982), or because it is socially complex; and (4) *with no strategically equivalent substitutes* – that is, with no alternative ways of achieving the same results.

Core capabilities develop in organizations through a fundamental transformation process by which standard resources, available in open markets (where all firms can acquire them), are used and combined, within the *organizational context* of each firm, with *organizational routines* to produce *capabilities*, which in turn can become core and the source of competitive advantages if the above conditions are met. Since this transformation process takes place within an organizational context and uses specific organizational routines, the resulting (core) capabilities are highly dependent on them. As the process unfolds, the *path-* or *acquisition-dependency degree* increases, making the results more and more idiosyncratic to the firm in which they develop. Hence, the transformation is a path-dependent learning process. We consider now, in more detail, its major phases.

Although iterative and evolving, the process starts with a set of existing *resources*. A *resource* is any available factor owned or controlled by a firm (Amit and Schoemaker, 1993). Alternatively, resources are those tangible and intangible assets which are tied semipermanently to the firm (Werner-felt, 1984). We may add that resources are assets available in the firm without specific organizational effort. IT is understood as a resource in this sense.

Capabilities are developed by combining and using resources (and/or other capabilities) with the aid of *organizational routines*. An *organizational routine* is a particular way of doing that an organization has developed and *learned*, and in the utilization of which that organization is very efficient and effective, to the point of becoming almost automatic, a 'natural' reflection of its 'way of being'. These routines are depositories of organizational knowledge acquired through learning (Dosi et al., 1990; Grant, 1992; Nelson and Winter, 1982); consequently they have a strong tacit dimension which makes them difficult to imitate and change.[1]

Capabilities are seen in the RBVF literature from many different perspectives. Teece et al. (1990) defines capabilities as a set of differentiated skills, complementary assets, and routines that allow success in a particular business. Others define capabilities vis-à-vis resources, such that *capabilities* refer to a firm's capacity to deploy combinations of *resources*, through organizational processes to produce a desired outcome (Amit and Schoemaker, 1993). Unlike resources, capabilities involve a firm's human capital developing, carrying and exchanging information. Consequently, developing capabilities involves organizational learning: learning how to combine and use resources, and also the learning already embedded in the organizational routines employed.[2] The interplay among resources organizational routines, and capabilities is very rich: existing capabilities can be made more sophisticated by combining some of them into new ones with the aid of organizational routines; new organizational routines may also develop by combining old ones with available capabilities. At a given point in time an organization is characterized by specific and interrelated sets or 'stocks' of resources, capabilities, and organizational routines.

Since learning takes place within a firm's organizational context, core capabilities are *path-dependent* – their *specificity degree* is high. This is crucial for making them difficult to imitate and hence resulting in advantages sustainable and durable. *Path-dependency* means that the way a firm owns an asset (a capability) depends on the process through which it acquired it (Collis, 1991; Dierickx and Cool, 1989; Dosi et al., 1990). The concept of *specificity degree* relates to the idea of 'special purpose'. As capabilities develop through a process that uses idiosyncratic routines and takes place in a specific organizational context, the results become less and less 'general purpose', that is, less and less efficient/effective if they are taken away from where they originated (Montgomery and Wernerfelt, 1988).

Figure 6.1 summarizes the process. It is complex and not necessarily planned for; many times it 'just happens'. Planning and making it happen, however, are genuine management activities, as discussed below. In general, the degree of specificity and path dependency increases from bottom to top in Figure 6.1, as more learning and selection are involved.

The Capability Development Process

The transformation process that produces core capabilities from standard resources involves learning. Learning is important because (1) it implies path-dependency and specificity in the resulting core capabilities, and (2) consequently, it is one of the causes of their inimitability, which is crucial for competitive advantage. By analyzing in detail the learning processes

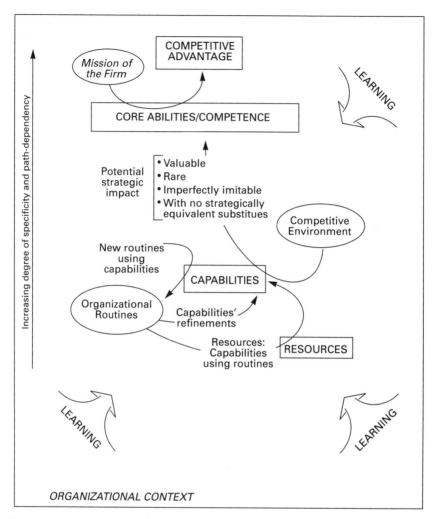

Figure 6.1   *The capability development process: From resources to competitive advantage*

involved we will derive practical suggestions on how to harness IT/IS as a key component of a firm's core capabilities.

The first transformation step develops capabilities from standard resources. Two different types of learning take place at this step. The first aims at *mastering the use of standard resources*, and produces what we call *efficient work practices*. Individuals and groups in the firm learn how to use resources to solve problems in the context of a given organizational situation. The quest for better work practices may even trigger a search for new resources, more appropriate for the practices being developed. Or, the appearance of new resources (say technological innovations) may motivate individuals and groups to 'take advantage of them' by developing new work practices. Thus, there is in fact a *learning loop* between resources and work practices. We call it the *routinization learning loop*. The environment in which learning occurs is an organizational context, which influences the learning process and is in turn influenced by its result; that is, new working practices become part of the context, thus increasing the knowledge base of the organization and enhancing its learning abilities (Giddens, 1984; Muñoz-Seca and Riverola, 1994; Orlikowski, 1992). Such an organizational context has the characteristics of a *formative context* (Ciborra and Lanzara, 1990).[3] Work practices are 'formed' within it, and receive their meaning and scope from it. Work practices resulting from this learning loop are concrete, detailed, specific and operative, close to the concept of *skills*; they are instances of what have been called *modus operandi* (Bourdieu, 1977) – in fact, they tend to lose their value when taken away from the specific situation in which they were developed and are afterwards used. From a different perspective, work practices are the first step in the firm's 'internalization' of resources. Mastering the usage of a spreadsheet by an individual or a team in a specific department, to solve a concrete problem, is an example of this type of learning.

The second type of learning creates capabilities from existing work practices. Several characteristics of this learning are important: (1) it involves combining work practices and organizational routines; (2) the result has a strong *potential* connotation, as capabilities convey what an organization is *capable* of doing if properly triggered – that is, capabilities involve *generalizing* work practices and putting them in a wider context that defines *how* they work, so that they are instances of *opus operatum* (Bourdieu, 1977); (3) the result – capabilities – is easily described in terms of *what* they do and *how* they do it, but *for what* they do it is taken for granted, not necessarily well defined and rarely challenged; and (4) since needs for new routines or work practices can be detected during the process, it also becomes a learning loop which we call the *capability learning loop*. The objectives of the learning involved in both these loops are close to the concept of *static efficiency* (Ashby, 1956; Ghemawat and Ricart, 1993; Klein, 1977).

To summarize, learning at this basic level results in a continuously improving set of capabilities – specialized and idiosyncratic ways of using resources for given purposes (to solve given problems). These purposes are functionally well defined and stable over time, although how they are attained may change even drastically, for example with the emergence of a radically new technology (resource) or a revolutionary new use of an old resource (Penrose, 1959). The driving force for continuous capability improvement is static efficiency, and the change agents are individuals and groups in the organization, who become the repositories of the resulting capabilities. The learning processes often occur spontaneously, although the organizational climate and context, and the incentives, power and motivational systems are ultimately responsible for differences in the quality of the process from one organization to another. Although they are

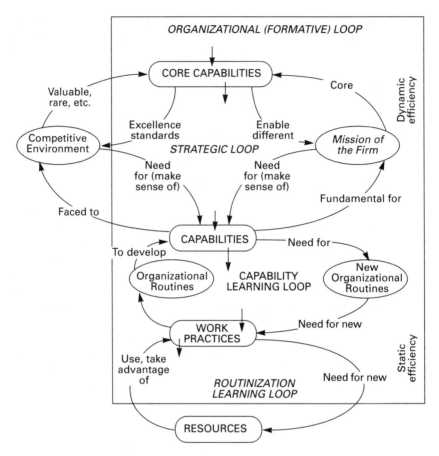

Figure 6.2 *Learning in the capabilities and core capabilities development processes*

efficient, a sense of *why* capabilities exist is lacking, or at least the reasons for their existence are seldom challenged at this level. This sense develops as they evolve into core capabilities through yet another learning loop (see Figure 6.2).

In the next learning process capabilities evolve into core capabilities, those that differentiate a company strategically, fostering beneficial behaviors not observed in competitors (Leonard-Barton, 1992). There are two main reference points against which capabilities can be calibrated to check their potential to become core: *the competitive environment* and *the firm's mission*. When faced with its competitive environment, individuals and groups in a firm learn why some capabilities have strategic potential (they are rare, valuable, etc.) – in other words, they solve the problem of developing distinctive capabilities by using available capabilities in order to take advantage of opportunities in the environment, to avoid threats, etc. A converse influence, from core capabilities to capabilities also exists through the competitive environment, as (1) core capabilities of different firms competing in a given environment (industry) define the 'standards of excellence' in that environment, and so they point out what capabilities each firm should develop in order to compete effectively; and (2) it is when confronting the competitive environment that a sense of *why* capabilities are important is acquired, thus clarifying their role and scope. In addition, capabilities are difficult to imitate in part because of the learning involved in the routinization and capability loops: to develop similar capabilities, competitors must go through those learning loops.

A firm's mission is also relevant for identifying core capabilities. In its context capabilities acquire meaning, as some of them emerge as fundamental for carrying it out. Capabilities fundamental in this sense are candidates to become core. Again, there is a converse influence. Core capabilities can enable new missions which, if accepted as such, trigger new capabilities-to-core capabilities transformations. All these interrelationships give rise to another learning loop linking capabilities and core capabilities; we call it the *strategic learning loop* (Figure 6.2). Some of the dynamics in this loop are close to what has been called 'renewing a firm's capabilities', and described as fundamental for long-term competitive strength (Haspeslagh and Jemison, 1991).

The strategic learning loop also takes place within the firm's organizational (formative) context, and so it is influenced by the context. Furthermore, its outcome – core capabilities – in turn reshapes the context itself. At this level capabilities can be described and understood not only in terms of *what* they do and *how* they do it, but also in terms of *why*, beyond the static efficiency criterion that dominates the other two learning loops. In a context where it is clear which capabilities are core and why, these loops are given added motivation and direction (for example, in the search for new organizational routines or resources); we are in the realm of *dynamic* efficiency. For example, competitive environment changes can render a highly efficient (in the static sense) capability worthless because it becomes irrelevant to the competition under the new conditions. Continuously checking the interrelationships among capabilities, core capabilities, competitive environment, the mission of the firm, and organizational context, and responding to the challenges that arise as the firm and its environment evolve over time, are the essence of the strategic learning loop.

Finally, it must be noted that inertia belongs to the very nature of organizational contexts, as a consequence of the learning involved in their continuous development and updating (Kim, 1993). Consequently, *drastically changing* the context is difficult, although sometimes necessary (for example, to respond to radical environment or mission shifts). However, drastic changes in the mission of the firm are not likely to happen, as its evolution also occurs within the organizational context. Hence, revolutionary changes in the organizational context or the mission of the firm require *radical learning* – becoming aware of what the context is and explicitly stepping out in order to innovate in a radical manner. As core capabilities

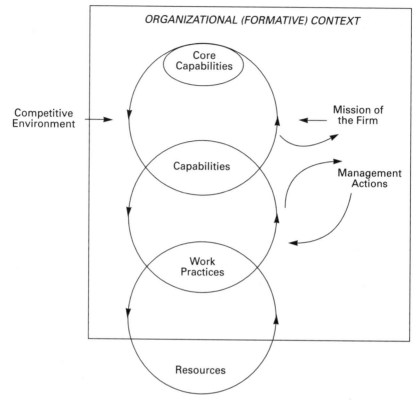

Figure 6.3   *Basic learning processes in the core capabilities formation process*

are components of the organizational context, radical learning means learning how to do radically new things (in the bottom learning loop of Figure 6.2) that are *important in radically new ways* (which implies activity in the top learning loops) (Argyris and Schön, 1978).

Figure 6.3 is a summary of Figure 6.2. We conceptualize the RBVF framework as involving three learning loops, which develop firm's capabilities and core capabilities starting with resources, using organizational routines, and taking into account the firm's competitive environment and its mission. One basic loop routinizes work practices using resources; a second one combines work practices and organizational routines to form capabilities; and the third gives meaning to capabilities in the context of the firm's competitive environment and mission, thus identifying core capabilities. The knowledge of which capabilities are both distinctive and fundamental to competing in a given market is strategic in nature, and becomes part of the organizational (formative) context in which all firm's activities – including learning – occur. Those learning loops tend to unfold spontaneously, and they depend strongly on the individuals' and groups' perceptions of the environment, the mission of the firm, and their own learning abilities. Management actions aim at giving to the learning processes the appropriate direction at a given point in time (Argyris, 1993).

The Case of IT/IS

We now turn to IT/IS. By IT we mean all computer and telecommunications technologies available in open markets, where firms can acquire them. IT is an enabling technology, although it may also play the role of a constraint, in the sense of 'not being enabling enough' (Scott Morton, 1991).

In this section we use the learning model just introduced to explain how IT and its applications – information systems – can help develop core capabilities in firms. The topic relates to Strategic Information Systems (SIS), since these help to shape core capabilities in the companies that develop them. The goal is to show that the full cycle, from resources to a firm's core capabilities, when one of the resources employed is IT, follows the pattern suggested by the model.

One well known SIS is ASAP, launched by AHS Corporation (now Baxter Healthcare). ASAP started as an operational, localized response to a customer need (Short and Venkatraman, 1992). Because of difficulties in serving a hospital effectively, a manager of a local AHS office started to give prepunched cards to the hospital's purchasing department, so that ordering clerks could transfer orders expeditiously through a phone terminal. This local, ad hoc solution gradually led to linking more customer hospitals in the same way, eventually through PCs. AHS management realized the positive impacts on profits of such an electronic link with customers, and allocated resources for its further development (Ciborra, 1992, 1994). The parallel of this process with the basic structure of Figure 6.2 is clear. Initially, IT was a resource used in a new work practice to solve a localized client's problem. It was an unsophisticated response to a specific operative problem. Generalizing the solution and making it available to more clients is a clear example of what in the learning model is the development of capabilities. The *potential* characteristic is present, and organizational routines used in the relationships with clients are not only brought into play, but also refined as the second learning loop of the model would predict. Furthermore, the capability had strategic potential, as it was valuable and difficult to imitate, in particular by some of the AHS's competitors. It was *valuable* because ASAP effectively contributed to the positioning of AHS as the 'prime vendor' (Short and Venkatraman, 1992) for hospitals in an environment where very important competitors (for example Johnson and Johnson) couldn't play the same game, at least in the short run, because they were organized in too many decentralized divisions to respond quickly enough. Thus, ASAP actively contributed to the competitive positioning of the firm by exploiting an environmental opportunity – the so-called 'incumbent's inertia' (Lieberman and Montgomery, 1988) of a major competitor. A valuable organizational and competitive positioning fit was built in the system, which became a major ingredient in the core capabilities' arsenal of AHS. Furthermore, the system evolution led to a shift in 'distinctive business competence' (Short and Venkatraman, 1992) that helped to *sustain* competitive advantage.

A different illustration of IT/IS impact on core capabilities is Mrs. Fields' Cookies (Richman, 1987).[4] Mrs. Fields' business started to commercialize the cookies that Mrs. Fields had prepared at home for years. The first store was under tight personal control of Mrs. Fields herself, who designed not only the cookie recipes, but also a definite approach to sales, promotion, store style, and even personnel recruitment and management. As the number of stores grew, a computerized information system was developed using commodity technology. The system was a bread-and-butter application, that recorded operations data from the stores and reported them to headquarters for centralized control. Although it allowed the company to run the operation with a remarkably low number of staff workers, it evolved into a system with a fundamentally different kind of main impact: it turned into *a way to convey to all stores the 'Mrs. Fields way of doing things'*, independently of the (typically highly mobile and not well trained) personnel, and also a means by which all personnel could communicate – as often as they liked and on a person-to-person basis – with Mrs. Fields herself. The case again illustrates how work practices – initially developed with the aid of commodity IT – were followed by a period of generalization, in which the organizational routines used by Mrs. Fields in the first stores were 'encapsulated' and transmitted to a few other stores, and finally were spread the 'Mrs. Fields way' throughout more than a thousand stores. It also illustrates an interesting and fundamental characteristic of IT/IS. To the extent that the communications infrastructure and systems put in place were a central ingredient of the company's core capabilities (because of their impact in replicating the Mrs. Fields way throughout the organization), they were an important part of the organizational context; furthermore they contributed in effectively transmitting the context to the whole organization. Thus, IT/IS can be instrumental not only in shaping up the firm's core capabilities, but also in effectively incorporating them into the firm's organizational context, thereby making them apparent to all organizational levels and giving meaning to all learning processes which otherwise would operate more 'in a limbo' (Ciborra and Lanzara, 1990).

Another interesting case deals with changing the organizational context. IT/IS, consistently with the structure of the above learning model, can effectively contribute to make the shift actually happen in organizations. Consider what a Spanish Savings Bank did recently. In order to make branch managers responsible for all their activities, as dictated by a decentralization move that top management wanted quickly implemented, they used an existing IS that permitted each branch manager to check, as often as he or she wanted, his or her performance against objectives.

Under the application's new use, any branch manager can now check, in real time, how *any other branch* is doing against its objectives. Strong competition among branches developed, thereby contributing to the emergence of a new 'way of doing things' at the branches, consistent with what management wanted to implement. The existing IS was a basic one developed for control purposes. Once a fundamental shift in the firm's organizational structure was decided upon, it became central for a completely different purpose, similar to that with Mrs. Fields, but different in a fundamental aspect: the organizational context to be communicated was radically new. Thus, IT/IS can also play an active role in the difficult task of making the slowly evolving organizational contexts change faster.

All the examples show that the proposed organizational learning model is useful for describing how IT/IS can contribute to core capabilities development and thereby become part (even a fundamental one) of the resulting core capabilities of a firm. Although more field research is needed to support this claim, the model helps us to understand how IT/IS can contribute effectively to firms' learning and competitiveness. This, together with the management actions needed to govern the learning processes, set a basis for consistently analyzing how IT/IS can be used to actually contribute to the unfolding of the learning processes themselves, a perspective rarely employed in IT/IS analysis but which can significantly enrich it, as discussed in the following section.

The Role of IT/IS in the Learning Processes

The most obvious role of IT/IS in the processes of Figure 6.2 is as a component of capabilities. In fact, many of the organizational routines employed for coordination purposes in the formation of capabilities are nothing more than information handling routines (for example, the organizational routines needed to implement just-in-time (JIT) techniques).

Other IT/IS roles have to do with the learning processes discussed in the preceding section. Below we systematically explore and discuss these roles, and illustrate them with examples.

IT/IS as Ingredients of Capabilities

Conceivably, IT/IS can be part of capabilities in the following ways:

- *In the form of data and information manipulation procedures (IT-based or not)*: Any useful procedure learned by the organization is an example: data gathering in transactions, information preparation for control purposes, database design and access, and so on.
- *As part of well coordinated 'primary value chain activities-information subsystems'* (Porter, 1985) *combinations that are part of a capability*: Any support to primary activities through IS/IT is a good example of what we mean: CAD/CAM systems that help in design activities,

production planning and programming systems, systems to support JIT production, and so on.

- *As part of well coordinated 'support value chain activities-information subsystems' combinations*: Any support through IS/IT of support activities of the value chain would be a good example, for instance, IS support to the firm's control system, all kinds of Decision Support Systems (DSS) used in management activities, and Electronic Information Systems (EIS) (see Rockart and de Long, 1988). A documented example is that of Phillips' 66 (Applegate and Osborn, 1989), where an EIS was used to enable new capabilities in oil trading to develop at lower levels in the organization than had been the case previously.

IT/IS in the Routinization and Capability Learning Loops

IT/IS can contribute to the routinization and capability learning loops in several ways, facilitating the learning that takes place and spreading it to all the individuals and groups involved. For example it can do the following:

Support the firm's capability creation process   Although few IS specifically designed for this purpose seem to exist today, the idea is not an unfeasible dream; data gathered during the continuously ongoing process of capability development can conceivably be stored and made available to future processes of the same sort, with the goal of making future learning more effective.[5] Tools such as knowledge-based procedures and similar artificial intelligence techniques (in particular the so-called *case based reasoning*, or CBR) can be used for this purpose, as can other less sophisticated approaches (such as documenting experiences in a way similar to the lab notebooks typical of experimental scientific research). Another way is through IS that facilitate experimentation with new resources, in particular with new sources of information (for instance, by making information relevant to the capabilities' objectives available) and with IT (for example, by allowing the use of new technologies in pilot projects, etc.); see Tyre and Orlikowski (1993). Still an additional way may come about through the so-called 'electronic brainstorming' processes (Gallupe and Cooper, 1993).

Share work practices and facilitate communication within groups and among groups   An 'individual' capability effectively shared among the individuals of a group is often a new capability in itself. At the same time, a good communication base facilitates the creation of more efficient capabilities in a way directly relevant to the goal of the routinization learning loop as understood in this chapter. Also, a way of effectively sharing work practices and capabilities has to do with the training of individuals and groups in order to make them effective as users. Finally, the sharing of capabilities not only contributes to the creation of new ones, but also to the goal of spreading them in the organization, thus effectively helping to communicate and share the organizational context to the extent that those capabilities are relevant to it (see below).[6] Groupware is a technology directly relevant for all these purposes, in all its forms. Even straightforward applications based on simple electronic mail infrastructures may be very effective in facilitating work practice sharing, and in putting different capabilities, 'owned' by different individuals or groups even geographically dispersed, to work effectively together in ways not feasible before.

Facilitate reflection, experimentation, and training on routines and work practices   Work practices, routines and basic capabilities must not only be shared and spread in order to become effectively available to all individuals and groups in the firm that can benefit from them, but they must also be understood by them – that is, to be effectively learned, it must be understood why they work and what the basic fundamentals behind their reasons for being applied are; the distinction is close to the difference between the so-called operational learning and conceptual learning (Kim, 1993). SIS can contribute to this goal, be it by facilitating experimentation through the use of simulations, or making expert systems available that permit their users to check their solutions or intuitions against those inspired in capabilities already developed, or, more directly in training, through computer assisted instruction (CAI) systems that can even be based on the real systems used in actual capabilities or routines support systems (for instance, transactional procedures used in clerk training in banks, etc.). All kinds of DSS are good examples of the kind of IS support meant in this subsection.

Support and enable capability diffusion   It is a matter of what Boynton (1993) calls 'systems of scope', that is, systems that help in the 'sharing of global knowledge' in the firm, that in this sense take advantage of economies of scope. For example, J.C. Penney, the large department store firm in the United States has put in place a video link infrastructure that permits the store managers (more than 1500 across the United States) to be actively involved in the purchasing decision-making process *without losing the know-how of the experienced central purchasers* who used to make all the decisions centrally and then ship the materials they had purchased to the stores for sale. With the new system in place better decisions can be made by taking explicitly into account the local knowledge that store managers have about their markets, without renouncing the economies of scale inherent in a centrally organized purchasing department and the experience and knowledge of the central purchasing function. Eventually, as store managers learn about purchasing, they can take at least part of the involved responsibility on themselves, thus leading the organizational structure to a new, more decentralized form that is likely to be more effective than the old one. In effect then, not only available and relevant know-how is made accessible to whoever can take advantage of it, but new capabilities develop in the stores that enable the decentralization of decision making. Another example would be using expert systems to make expertise, knowledge, and know-how available in all relevant places in the organization. We believe that seeing all these IT/IS-based actions as contributing to the learning processes of Figure 6.2 gives a completely new perspective on where to look at, understand, and consequently plan, design and implement IS.

IT/IS in the Strategic Loop: Helping Capabilities to Become Core

IT/IS can be instrumental in making capabilities become core (that is, making them rare, valuable, difficult to imitate, and with no strategically equivalent substitutes). Some guidelines to achieve this purpose are as follows (Feeny and Ives, 1989):

Look out for IT/IS applications that help to make capabilities rare   At the beginning of the computerized reservation systems in the airline industry, such systems were rare as only a few of the competitors, who took the lead in deciding to develop them, had them. In the Savings Banks industry in Spain, for quite some time only one offered twenty-four hour debit card service because its telecommunications and IT base were rare, the result of a bold investment decision made well ahead of its competitors.

Concentrate on IT/IS applications that make capabilities valuable   The ASAP-AHS example is a case in point; that application contributed to the competitive positioning of the firm while exploiting an environmental opportunity (the 'incumbent's inertia' of a major competitor). Similar comments can be made of the Federal Express COSMOS system (Smith, 1991). Several procedures have been proposed for precisely the identification of this type of IT/IS applications (Andreu et al., 1992; Gongla et al., 1989).

Identify IT/IS contributions that make capabilities difficult to imitate   Core capabilities can be difficult to imitate for several reasons (in AHS, for instance, organizational impediments on the competitors' side made their responses slow). The IT/IS-based part of core capabilities can also contribute to their inimitability. Reservation systems pioneers in the airline industry couldn't be easily copied simply because at the time those systems were complex – they required advanced software techniques not available to every player in the industry (and even if they had been, they still would have had to be learned, through the two bottom loops in Figure 6.2). More recently, a Savings Bank in Spain developed a system that allows one to use its debit cards and ATM network to make ticket reservations for theater or opera shows, sporting events, concerts, and so on. For this purpose it developed, in a join venture with a computer manufacturer, a special purpose ATM that displays complete theater layouts to choose seats and so on. Owning part of the special purpose ATM design, this bank was able to impose delays in the machine becoming available to competitors, thus making its approach to the entertainment business distribution channel more difficult to imitate than it would had been otherwise.

Concentrate on IT/IS applications with no clear strategically equivalent substitutes To the extent that the functionality of applications cannot be achieved by other means, IT contributes to the lack of substitution. One of the competitors of the bank just mentioned tried to achieve the same functionality and also sell tickets at its branches, using its telecommunications network for seat reservation purposes. However, instead of basing it on ATMs, customers must go to the counter, ask the clerk and wait for a layout of the theater to be printed out before being able to make their choices; they must then tell the clerk, who makes the reservations and the corresponding payment – while other customers wait in line probably to make more mundane banking transactions (and while maybe another customer at a different branch just took the tickets in the meantime). It is unclear that this bank is competing effectively; some say that its approach is jeopardizing its banking business.

IT/IS Supporting and Communicating the Organizational Context

We have already mentioned above, in passing, that IT/IS can play an active role in the diffusion of knowledge and know-how relevant for capabilities throughout the organization. For example:

IT/IS applications that support the organizational context These are applications that actually shape the organizational context. A good example is the systems put in place by Mrs. Fields' Cookies, as discussed above.

Communicating the organizational context to all levels in the organization The organizational context must not only be supported in the sense of making it *exist*, but it also must be effectively communicated and disseminated to the whole organization, so that it works as a true context in the sense of this chapter. We have already mentioned above systems of scope in this regard. The same J.C. Penney example described there is relevant here, to the extent that the newly organized purchasing function forms part of the (new) organizational context of the company. There are many other illustrative examples, for instance, Bank One, a successful banking organization in the United States that has put in place video links between headquarters and the branches for the purpose, among others, of facilitating the rapid and effective dissemination of the bank's competitive approach to all employees in the branches, as well as to customers. In a different setting, American Crown (Vitale, 1988) also used IS to make its salesforce well aware, in an operational way, of what is important in its competitive outlook that should consequently be emphasized in the day-to-day operations of the company.

Systems that help shift organizational contexts From time to time it becomes necessary in companies to change the current context, in order to make a new competitive positioning effective. IT/IS applications can effectively contribute to make the shift happen in the organization. One example is the Spanish Savings Bank mentioned above. Another example is that of Otis Elevator (McFarlan and Stoddard, 1986), a subsidiary of United Technologies Corporation, which implemented a centralized IS for customer service called Otisline – the information access patterns available under the new system set the basis for significant changes in both the assignment of responsibilities and the associated control system.[7]

Conclusions

We have drawn upon a stream of different research programs to address in a new way the by now classic problem of how to make a better use of IT in business organizations. First, the resource-based view of the firm has been invoked to indicate that whatever we do using a commodity resource such as IT to increase a firm's competitiveness, we must aim at transforming a standard resource into a firm's core capability. Second, a due consideration of the literature on organizational learning has helped us to build a structured model of this strategic transformation process. We have identified different learning loops which range from the concreteness of learning-by-doing to the strategic, and at times radical, reflection on the firm's capabilities, mission, and environmental opportunities. Third, the recent sociological theories of structuration (Giddens, 1984) have helped us in showing not only the continuous interplay between transformation, learning, context, but also where these processes take place, and how to exploit their strategic relevance. The studies and cases of Strategic Information Systems have shown how our learning-based model can actually be used to recount the spontaneous emergence of strategic applications of IT/IS and discuss the limits of their sustainability.

We are firmly convinced that further research can lead to a new approach toward design and development of IT/IS applications geared to the dynamics and varied nature of organizational learning processes that take place within and across the firm's boundaries.

Notes

1 Other definitions of the organizational routine concept have been proposed in the literature. Grant (1992), for example, defines them as regular, predictable patterns of activity made up of a sequence of coordinated actions by individuals. Furthermore, they are conceived as dynamic entities that continuously evolve; Collis, for example, describes the managerial capability of improving and upgrading firm efficiency and effectiveness as dynamic routines (1991). (See also Kogut and Zander, 1992; Lado et al., 1992.)

2 As discussed in the following section, learning, as understood in this chapter, is the result of problem solving. In other words, it is through problem solving that people in organizations create mental models useful to solve a family of problems. Furthermore, such models enhance the learning capabilities of the people and organization involved, thus potentiating future learning. (See Muñoz-Seca and Riverola, 1994.)

3 A formative context is defined as the set of preexisting institutional arrangements, cognitive frames and imageries that actors bring and routinely enact in a situation of action

(Ciborra and Lanzara, 1993). That groups are influenced by their organizational entourage is widely recognized – the parts of an organization's memory that are relevant for organizational learning are those that constitute active memory – that is, what an organization pays attention to, how it acts, and what it remembers from its experiences (Kim, 1993).

4 The fact that this company has had trouble after its first very successful years is irrelevant for the argument that follows.

5 The following would prevent 'situational learning': An individual encounters a problem, improvises on the spot, and moves on to the next task, forgetting to codify the learning for later use (Kim, 1993).

6 This helps to avoid 'fragmented learning' (Kim, 1993), which happens when knowledge is only retained by individuals, and not the organization as such, in which case, loss of the individuals means loss of the learning as well – see also note 1.

7 This is a direct consequence of the IS being one of the management systems in the firm, in such a way that it must remain in equilibrium with the rest of them (the control and incentives systems, the organizational structure, etc.) – breaking the equilibrium by drastically changing the IS is a way of provoking changes in the rest; to the extent that this is done with the goal of shifting the organizational context, it is clear that the IS is contributing to that purpose.

References

Amit, R. and Schoemaker, P.J.H. (1993) 'Strategic assets and organizational rent', *Strategic Management Journal*, 14(1): 33–46.

Andreu, R., Ricart, J.E. and Valor, J. (1992) *Information Systems Strategic Planning: A Source of Competitive Advantage*. NCC Blackwell: Oxford.

Applegate, L.M. and Osborn, C. (1989) 'Phillips' 66 Company: Controlling a company through crisis', Harvard Business School Case No. 9–189–006.

Argyris, C. (1993) *Knowledge for Action*. San Francisco, CA: Jossey-Bass.

Argyris, C. and Schön, D. (1978) *Organizational Learning: A Theory of Action Perspective*. Reading, MA: Addison-Wesley.

Ashby, W.R. (1956) *Introduction to Cybernetics*. New York: John Wiley.

Barney, J. (1991) 'Firm resources and sustained competitive advantage', *Journal of Management*, 17(1): 99–120.

Bourdieu, P. (1977) *Outline of a Theory of Practice*. Cambridge: Cambridge University Press.

Boynton, A. C. (1993) 'Achieving dynamic stability through information technology', *California Management Review*, 35(2): 58–77.

Ciborra, C. (1992) 'From thinking to tinkering: The grassroots of strategic information systems', *The Information Society*, 8: 297–309.

Ciborra, C. (1994) 'The grassroots of IT and strategy', in C. Ciborra and T. Jelassi (eds), *Strategic Information Systems: A European Perspective*. New York: John Wiley.

Ciborra, C. and Lanzara, G.F. (1990) 'Designing dynamic artifacts: Computer systems as formative contexts', in P. Galiardi (ed.), *Symbols and Artifacts*. Berlin: De Gruyter.

Collis, D. (1991) 'A resource-based analysis of global competition: The case of the bearings industry', *Strategic Management Journal*, 12: 49–68.

Dierickx, I. and Cool, K. (1989) 'Asset stock accumulation and sustainability of competitive advantage', *Management Science*, 35(12): 1504–1511.

Dosi, G., Teece, D.J. and Winter, S. (1990) 'Toward a theory of corporate coherence: Preliminary remarks', mimeo.

Feeny, D. and Ives, B. (1989) 'In search of sustainability – Reaping long term advantage from investments in information technology', *Journal of Management Information Systems*, 7(1): 27–46.

Gallupe, R.B. and Cooper, W.H. (1993) 'Brainstorming electronically', *Sloan Management Review*, 35: 27–37.

Ghemawat, P. and Ricart, J.E. (1993) 'The organizational tension between static and dynamic efficiency', *Strategic Management Journal*, 14(4): 59–73.

Giddens, A. (1984) *The constitution of society: Outline of the theory of structuration.* Berkeley, CA: University of California Press.

Gongla, P., Sakamoto, G., Black-Hock, A., Goldweic, P., Ramos, L., Sprowls, R.C. and Kim, C.K. (1989) 'SPARK: A knowledge-based system for identifying competitive uses of information technology', *IBM Systems Journal*, 28(4): 628–646.

Grant, R.M. (1992) *Contemporary Strategy Analysis: Concepts, Techniques, Applications.* Cambridge, MA: Basil Blackwell.

Haspeslagh, P.C. and Jemison, D.B. (1991) *Managing Acquisitions: Creating Value Through Corporate Renewal.* Oxford: Polity Press.

Hirshleifer, J. (1980) *Price Theory and Applications.* Englewood Cliffs, NJ: Prentice Hall.

Kim, D.H. (1993) 'The link between individual and organizational learning', *Sloan Management Review*, 35(1): 37–50.

Klein, B.H. (1977) *Dynamic Economics.* Cambridge, MA: Harvard University Press.

Kogut, B. and Zander, U. (1992) 'Knowledge in the firm, combinative capabilities, and the replication of technology', *Organization Science*, 3: 383–397.

Lado, A., Boyd, N.G. and Wright, P. (1992) 'A competency-based model of sustainable competitive advantage: Towards a conceptual integration', *Journal of Management*, 18(1): 77–91.

Leonard-Barton, D. (1992) 'Core capabilities and core rigidities: A paradox in managing new product development', *Strategic Management Journal*, Special Issue, 13: 111–126.

Lieberman, M. and Montgomery, D. (1988) 'First mover advantages', *Strategic Management Journal*, 9: 41–58

Lippman, S. and Rumelt, R. (1982) 'Uncertain imitability: An analysis of interfirm difference in efficiency under competition', *Bell Journal of Economics*, 13: 418–438.

McFarlan, F.W. and Stoddard, D.B. (1986) 'Otisline', Harvard Business School Case No. 9–186–304.

Montgomery, C.A. and Wernerfelt, B. (1988) 'Diversification, Ricardian rents, and Tobin's q', *RAND Journal of Economics*, 19(4): 623–632.

Muñoz-Seca, B. and Riverola, J. (1994) 'The improvement dynamics: Knowledge and knowledge generation', IESE Technical Note No. 0–694–044.

Nelson, R.R. and Winter, S.G. (1982) *An Evolutionary Theory of Economic Change.* Cambridge, MA: Belknap.

Orlikowski, W.I. (1992) 'The duality of technology: Rethinking the concept of technology in organizations', *Organization Science*, 3(2): 398–427.

Penrose, E. (1959) *The Theory of the Growth of the Firm.* London: Basil Blackwell.

Porter, M. (1985) *Competitive Advantage.* New York: Free Press.

Richman, T. (1987) 'Mrs. Fields' secret ingredient', *INC. Magazine.*

Rockart, J. and de Long, D.W. (1988) *Executive Support Systems.* Homewood, IL: Dow-Jones-Irwin.

Scott Morton, M.S. (ed.) (1991) *The Corporation of the 1990s: Information Technology and Organizational Transformation.* Oxford: Oxford University Press.

Short, J.E. and Venkatraman, N. (1992) 'Beyond business process redesign: Redefining Baxter's business network', *Sloan Management Review*, 34(1): 7–21.

Smith, F. (1991) 'The distribution revolution: Time flies at federal express', in J. Blackburn (ed.), *Time-Based Competition*, Burr Ridge: Business One Irwin.

Teece, D., Pisano, G. and Shuen, A. (1990) 'Firm capabilities, resources and the concept of corporate strategy', Consortium on Competitiveness and Cooperation Working Paper No. 90–9, U. of California at Berkeley, Center for Research in Management.

Tyre, M. and Orlikowski, W.I. (1993) 'Exploiting opportunities for technological improvement in organization', *Sloan Management Review*, 35(1): 13–26.

Vitale, M. R. (1988) 'American crown', Harvard Business School Case No. 9–188–052.

Wernerfelt, B. (1984) 'A resource-based view of the firm', *Strategic Management Journal*, 5(2): 171–180.

7

Organizational Capability as a Source of Profit

David Collis

A common theme of many business texts for practitioners is the need to build an effective organization. While the precise type of effectiveness has been variously identified as 'organizational capability' (Stalk et al., 1992; Ulrich and Lake, 1990), 'corporate renewal' (Beer et al., 1990), 'the fifth discipline' (Senge, 1990), and 'continuous improvement' (Pascale, 1990), the implicit assumption of these texts is that possessing some sort of organizational capability can be a source of economic profit.

Even the corporate strategy literature is now moving to embrace this assumption, as demonstrated by its recent identification of intangible firm 'capabilities' (Baldwin and Clark, 1990; Barney, 1986; Teece et al., 1994) as a subset of the 'core competences' (Prahalad and Hamel, 1990, 1994) or 'resources' (Amit and Schoemaker, 1993; Barney, 1992; Peteraf, 1993; Wernerfelt, 1984) that are the source of sustainable competitive advantage (the strategy term for durable intra-industry differences in performance).

Such a proposition is alien to many economists, not in the least because of economics' historical reluctance to treat the firm as anything but a black box. Traditionally, economists have not recognized organization – the process by which the technical production function is translated into physical output – as an independent source of profit, because it does not enter into either the formulation of the firm's maximization problem or the determination of equilibrium market outcomes (see Varian, 1978, for the standard microeconomic treatment).

As economists have shifted their attention inside the firm in recognition of the deficiencies of their previous treatment (see, for example, Tirole, 1988; Milgrom and Roberts, 1992), the managerial literature raises for them the fundamental question of whether or not there is theoretical validity to 'organizational capability' (however defined) as a source of economic profit.

It is this issue of theoretical validity that is addressed in this chapter. The first section draws on the *theory of profit* and recent treatments of sustainable competitive advantage to identify the necessary conditions for the existence of economic profit. The next section defines *organizational capability* in a way that fulfills those conditions. The normative *implications* of this analysis are drawn out in the third section. The fourth section concludes.

A Theory of Profit

Prior to outlining the conditions which must hold for profit to exist, it is necessary to dispense with two definitional preliminaries. The first is to identify the time period and the range of future states of nature over which supranormal returns must extend for them to be considered profits rather than temporary disequilibrium quasi-rents. (Or, in the language of business strategy, for how long and under what circumstances must a competitive advantage endure for it to be termed sustainable?) Clearly, we do not wish to include only those profits that last until infinity and are robust enough to endure in any future state of nature. Conversely, we would not want to include any and all instantaneous quasi-rents. The former is too restrictive as no profits are likely to endure in all feasible future states of nature, for instance, after a nuclear war. The latter is not sufficiently restrictive and renders the distinction between profit and quasi-rent meaningless. Profit instead should be of intermediate robustness and durability.

The definition adopted here, which captures the two important exogenous dimensions that threaten to dissipate profit streams (uncertainty and time), is that profit exists when supranormal returns can be maintained by competent management against rational competitors in all states of nature with probability $> \varepsilon$ of occurring.[1] Increasing ε, which might be on the order of one percent, implies a less 'sustainable' competitive advantage.

Second, it is necessary to distinguish profit from rent since both will generate durable supranormal returns. Economics has long wrestled with the attempt to make this distinction (see, for example, the entry on profit in the *New Palgrave*, Eatwell et al., 1987). The distinction made here lies in the source of the heterogeneity that produces superior economic return. The classical Ricardian theory of rent, derived from the paradigm of the return to land, defined rent as a return to an inframarginal factor in fixed supply (Ricardo, 1951). This requires the factor of production earning rent to be in exogenously fixed supply, and to be of heterogeneous quality so that an inframarginal asset exists. While land clearly meets both these criteria, most factors of production which are essentially homogeneous and in elastic supply do not. Instead, such fungible factors earn profits (quasi-rents) when the return in their current application is higher than the opportunity cost of their use in other applications (Marshall, 1920). This requires product market heterogeneity, because only a differentiated product market position can generate such a return, and a temporary inelasticity in the supply of the factor. Thus, the distinction is between rents which arise from intrinsically heterogeneous factors, and profits which accrue to heterogeneous product market positions built from homogeneous factors of production.[2]

This distinction is important if we are to move beyond the simple assertion that a firm's organizational capability is, like land, a unique, intrinsically superior resource that earns rent. Instead, we must be able to demonstrate that organizational capability is a source of profit.

Conditions for the Existence of Profit

There are five conditions which must hold for a profit to exist. The first (and most studied) condition relates to the product market, and requires that the firm possess a valuable and unique (what I will call singular) product market position (see Porter, 1980, 1985, for a more complete analysis). More recently, scholars have identified four factor market conditions that threaten either the singular product market position itself, or the stream of profits to be earned from that position: imitation and substitution affect the former, appropriation and dissipation the latter (see Barney, 1992; Dierickx and Cool, 1989; Peteraf, 1993). More specifically, the singular product market position must not be subject to imitation by other firms acquiring the equivalent resources from the factor market; the singular product market position must not be able to be substituted by the employment of alternative factors of production; the stream of profits must not be appropriated by the factors of production themselves; and the ex-post profits which accrue to the singular product market position must not have been dissipated in the ex-ante competition to acquire the resources needed to achieve that position.

Importantly, both the product and the factor market conditions must hold for a profit to exist (see, for example, Day and Wensley, 1988). Profits are a flow measure of competitive differences in the performance of product market activities. But flows are by definition transitory, and so any such differences must be attributable to underlying asset stock asymmetries (asymmetries with respect to the factor market) if they are to be durable. Conversely, any asset stock asymmetries among competitors must translate into differences between competitors in the performance of product market activities (a singular product market position), if they are to generate a flow of profits.[3]

Product market   The first condition for the existence of profit is that a firm occupies a singular product market position, so that the return to a factor of production it employs is greater than the return that factor can earn in any other use. Asymmetric product market positions result from exploiting phenomena such as scale economies or experience that give rise to nonconvex production functions, or from offering a preferred combination of product characteristics, whether vertically or horizontally differentiated from competitors. In the corporate strategy literature, these are equivalent to the successful pursuit of the low cost, differentiation and focus strategies, respectively (Porter, 1980, 1985).[4]

Imitation Inimitability is the requirement that an essentially homo-geneous factor of production be temporarily in inelastic supply. Most of the previous research on the factor market conditions for the existence of profit have focused here, and six possible constraints on imitation have been identified – physical, legal, time, economic, reputation, and uncertain imitability. These correspond to 'isolating factors' (Rumelt, 1984) or 'friction forces' (Schoemaker, 1990), and function as 'phenomena that limit the *ex post* equilibrium of rents among individual firms, that make competitive positions stable and defensible' (Rumelt, 1984: 367). Table 7.1 lists these six constraints, along with an illustration of the assets whose supply they can limit, and a comparison with the lists offered by previous authors.[5]

The first two constraints on imitation give rise to rents. Assets of inherently varied quality that are bounded in supply by a *physical* constraint, like natural resources and location,[6] are heterogeneous factors that earn Ricardian rents. Similarly, if *legal* institutions (for example patents and regulations) prohibit imitation, then, barring illicit behavior (which certainly does occur), the supply of factors to that particular product market is effectively constrained and monopoly rents accrue to the singular product market position.

The third cause of nonimitability – *time* compression diseconomies (Dierickx and Cool, 1989) – bridges rent and profit. As Dierickx and Cool illustrate, growing a beautiful lawn is possible, it is just that such imitation takes a long time. Thus, while an asset subject to time compression diseconomies that has to be accumulated internally rather than acquired on a tradable factor market, is not ultimately unique, it can be in fixed supply at a point in time.

The fourth cause of nonimitability, and a cause that does give rise to profit from traded factor inputs, is the *economic* notion of 'commitment opportunities' (Caves, 1984), or 'irreversible investments' (Collis, 1986). It is derived from the theory of entry barriers that attributes entry deterrence to the sunk cost investments that commit an incumbent to a market (Schelling, 1960; the summary of theoretical work in Tirole, 1988, and Schmalensee and Willig, 1989).

While the existence and extent of sunk costs is an empirical matter (Shepherd, 1984; Spence, 1983), the theory of contestability has demon-strated that their existence is critical to the endurance of abnormal returns because it is only sunk costs that deter profit equalizing hit-and-run entry (Baumol et al., 1982).[7] Ironically, it is the commitment to stay in an industry because the assets are worthless (or worth less) elsewhere which prevents others entering and so generates profit for the incumbent.[8]

Although the analysis of sunk costs is typically applied to entry deterrence, it is also relevant to the explanation of the inimitability of a position of competitive advantage. The work of Caves and Porter (1977) extends the notion of entry barriers to mobility barriers between different strategic groups within a single industry. By exploiting different commit-

Table 7.1 *Causes of inimitability*

	Constraint	'Irreversible' assets	Dierickx and Cool 'Asset stock accumulation'	Rumelt 'Isolating mechanisms'	Ghemawat 'Sustainable advantage'	Schoemaker 'Friction forces'
R	Physical	P Natural resources		Unique resources	(A) Inputs	Resource asymmetries
E		P Location				
N	Legal	P Government regulation		Legal restriction on entry	(O) Public policy	
T		P Patents		Patents and trademarks		
P	Time	P/ I	Time compression			
			Diseconomies			
R	Economic	P Fixed assets	Asset mass Economies/ Interconnectedness	Specialized assets	(S) Scale, scope	Asset specificity Production economies Sunk cost
O		P Accumulated customers		Switching and search costs		Transaction costs
F		I Brand name		Reputation and image	(A) Markets	
I		I Accumulated learning		Consumer and producer learning	(S) Experience	Information assymetries
T		I Accumulated R and D		Special information	(A) Know-how	
		I Organizational capability tacit knowledge		Team-embodied skills		Organizational culture
	Reputation	I Reputation		Reputation and image	(O) Defense	Histories and reputation
	Uncertain imitability	—	Causal ambiguity	Causal ambiguity	(O) Response lag	Complexity and instability, bounded rationality, and creativity

P = Physical; I = Intangible; (A) = Access; (O) = Public Policy; (S) = Size.
Sources: Rumelt, 1984; Ghemawat, 1986; Schoemaker, 1990; Dierickx and Cool, 1989

ment opportunities, each strategic group creates barriers against imitation by industry incumbents in other groups. This reasoning, extended to a market leader competing against firms within its own strategic group, can explain the existence of a sustainable competitive advantage. A firm that builds a singular product market position through superior investment relative to all competitors in a valuable irreversible asset (including other incumbents that have a positive level of investment in the asset), has made a commitment to the market which establishes a barrier to imitation by rendering the expected return to duplication of its investment negative.

As in the case of entry deterrence, this constraint on imitation requires the advantaged firm to have made sufficient investment in the relevant irreversible asset, relative to the market size, to effectively deter imitation. It is, therefore, ultimately the limit on the size of any market at a point in time that deters imitation by creating a limit to the demand for the factor of production.

The two conditions that in turn make investment sunk, or irreversible, are specialization and durability (Ghemawat, 1991). Specialization is required because it is only firm or industry specific assets, such as paper machines that cost several hundred million dollars and make limited grades of paper, that represent a sunk cost. By contrast, general purpose assets such as buildings, standard machine tools and computers, can be instantaneously and costlessly redeployed to other markets, which places us back in the world of contestability with the concomitant absence of profit.[9]

If an asset has only partial liquidation value(s) when used elsewhere it can, therefore, be a source of profit as it provides a positive $(1-s)$ degree of specificity or commitment. This is analogous to the durability of the asset – the second requirement for the existence of sunk costs. As Eaton and Lipsey (1980) observed, there must be some durability to an asset to distinguish it from transitory expenditures which are not sunk. While depreciation rates (δ) of assets clearly vary (as does s), provided both are fractional there is some irreversibility to investment in an asset and it can function as a barrier to imitation.

The fifth cause of factor supply inelasticity or inimitability is *reputation*. Examples from the theory of repeated games demonstrate that in the presence of uncertainty, a reputation for aggressive retaliation by a market leader, for example, can limit competitive investment (Milgrom and Roberts, 1982). Therefore this dynamic reputational effect, as opposed to the previous static prepositioning argument, can also explain how firms earn profits.

The last potential cause of inimitability, *uncertain imitability* (or causal ambiguity), has figured prominently in most treatments of profit since Lipmann and Rumelt's original discussion of the concept (Barney, 1985; Lipmann and Rumelt, 1982; Reed and DeFillippi, 1990). The basic premise of causal ambiguity is that the source of the singular product market positions is either impossible to disentangle, or impossible to know how to recreate, and so is impossible to imitate.

However, the notion of causal ambiguity as an explanation of *durable* intra-industry performance is flawed because it implies that no one in the firm itself understands the causes of its success – otherwise, they could trade this information to potential imitators. Given that the firm itself 'knows not what it does right', any adaptation undertaken to accommodate change in the external environment is as likely to destroy, as it is to sustain its advantage. Thus the firm's ignorance contains the seeds of its destruction.[10] Moreover, experimentation by imitators will ultimately replicate or surpass the firm's advantage in a Schumpeterian gale of creative destruction (Schumpeter, 1934), simply because the firm does not know how to adapt its behavior to this particular experiment. Thus uncertain imitability by itself can only be a temporary source of inelastic factor supply – it cannot explain profit.

If, instead, the source of profit is tacit knowledge (which cannot be articulated or written down, Polanyi, 1962), then even if it is known that this tacit knowledge is the source of profit, it can still be inimitable. Tacit knowledge, by definition, can only be acquired through the same process of investment as the original firm undertook (to use the common analogy, everyone must practice in order to ride a bike). It cannot be instantaneously acquired on a traded factor market. Thus if investment in the tacit knowledge itself is specialized and durable, that is, it is irreversible or subject to time compression diseconomies, it can be subject to the same constraint on its supply as other irreversible investments, and so can be a source of profit.

Substitution The second factor market condition for the existence of profit is the absence of substitute assets capable of replicating the singular product market position. Instances of substitution abound. For example, a steel firm supplying beer cans, having built a profitable market position immune to imitation by other steel companies, would nevertheless have seen that position substituted by aluminum can manufacturers, whose investment was undeterred by the existing assets of the steel firms.

The threat of substitution is omnipresent, and suggests that firms should invest in multiple assets if they are to preserve their future profit stream. It also identifies the exploitation of alternative assets as a strategic prescription for disadvantaged firms which, by definition, cannot simply imitate profitable market positions. How to generate creative insights, such as the introduction of branding to an industry (Perdue chicken) or the reconfiguration of an industry's value chain (Federal Express, Iowa Beef Packers) through conceiving new alternatives, superior framing, etc., remains far more problematic (Collis, 1988; Schoemaker, 1990) than it is sometimes made to appear (Prahalad and Hamel, 1994).

Appropriation For a firm to benefit from a sustainable competitive advantage, suppliers of the factors of production must not be able to appropriate the profit stream that accrues to its singular product market position. Unfortunately, the distribution of any profit stream is the result of a bargaining process with suppliers of all the factors of production, which has no general or simple outcome. Profit accrues to the collection of all factors of production as an ongoing system, and cannot readily be attributed either to a particular factor of production or to the firm itself. It is, therefore, bargaining that plays a central role in the distribution of profit.

The outcome of this process depends on the relative power of the involved parties (Raiffa, 1982) and is affected by a number of variables, including the inherent tradability of the factor (the more tradable a factor, the closer the value it extracts will be to the opportunity cost in its next best use); the potential for collective action to form exclusionary coalitions with other factors (since the bargaining process is essentially a search within the core of the cooperative game, Moulin, 1988); the credible strategic commitments that a factor can make; and other structural characteristics (noted by Porter, 1980). Additionally, bargaining positions are affected by any prior assignment of property rights. Indeed, the bargaining process is really about the assignment of the property rights to the firm's stream of profits, not about payments to factors, and so raises the issue of power relations inside the organization (Aoki, 1988; Marx, 1906).

Previous authors have argued that appropriation is determined by the inherent tradability of the asset that generates the singular product market position. Thus nontradability, stickiness, or immobility feature prominently in their definition of such assets (or resources) (Dierickx and Cool, 1989; Ghemawat, 1991; Gilbert, 1989; Peteraf, 1993). However, tradability is unlikely to fully govern appropriation for two reason – collective bargaining and transaction costs – even when the abnormal returns are rents to a heterogeneous factor of production.

First, as Robinson and Eatwell observe, even the classical explanation of rent:

> requires complete equality of bargaining power between the parties, and free competition within each group. If the landowners agreed among themselves to keep rents up, they could force the workers down to a level of income at which they would work just as hard for a smaller return. If the workers had sufficient reserves to last out, they could reduce rents. (1973: 87)

Second, the factor market transaction by itself does not actually realize the above normal returns. These only arise when the related activities of production, marketing, distribution, and so on, are physically performed on a day-to-day basis. These may well involve complementary or cospecialized assets which have independent claims to the profit stream (Teece, 1987). Even if it does not, and all the other activities are performed by perfectly competitive factors, such as unskilled labor, the physical process of hiring incurs transaction costs which creates an asymmetry between existing employees and an otherwise homogeneous pool of labor. Thus, even tradable factors of production, which are sources of rent (not profit), are unlikely to fully appropriate in a single factor market transaction the superior product market returns they generate.[11]

Conversely, those assets which generate singular product market positions but which cannot be traded on factor markets – such as firm-specific learning (which is valueless outside the firm), or collective tacit knowledge (which cannot be traded because it is a supra-individual phenomenon) – do not always generate profits that are appropriable by the firm. Those assets are accumulated internally, not purchased on factor markets, but still vest in individuals. Thus, each individual possesses some bargaining power by virtue of the threat to withdraw from the organization and reduce the profit stream. The distribution of profits in this case will again result from bargaining between the firm, whose reservation price is the profit it will lose if an employee quits, and the employee whose reservation price is the value (presumably low) that his knowledge has elsewhere. The need for continual bargaining with labor to retain its involvement (and hence the intangible assets) maintains the overall threat of appropriation, even though the asset itself cannot be traded.

Nontradability of an irreversible asset does not therefore guarantee full appropriation of the profit stream by the firm. Rather, the factors of production bargain over the appropriation of a complex set of current and future profits. The outcome of this is both indeterminate and fundamental to maintaining the stream of profits because of the need for the continuing involvement of all factors of production in the organization.

Dissipation   The fourth and last factor market condition for the existence of profit is that the ex-ante competition to invest in the factor of production, which then becomes in inelastic supply, does not dissipate the ex-post profits that accrue to the singular product market position. Profit dissipation will occur as the result of rational behavior in the backwardly iterative game of preemption – played either in physical factor markets (Fudenberg and Tirole, 1985), or in strategic factor markets, such as market share and those that are not acquired, but accumulated internally (Barney, 1985, 1989; Dierickx and Cool, 1989).[12]

The extreme version of this line of reasoning (Powell, 1992; Reed and DeFillippi, 1990) holds that anything that is common knowledge cannot be a source of profits, because investment will occur at the instant the profit from any known potential future singular product market position turns positive. In this view, profits only exist because firms either possess proprietary information about sources of profit – or else luck, animal spirits, or random deviations from past behavior (whether intentional or accidental) led one firm to make the appropriate investment before others, and at least on some occasions, after the instant when future profits would be completely dissipated (Barney, 1985).

In such a world, profit would be a return to the entrepreneurial function in the presence of uncertainty (Knight, 1921), and insights, like bolts of lightning, would strike lucky firms every so often – allowing them to create a singular, profit generating product market position. Predicting which entrepreneur would win would be impossible, and no strategic prescriptions would exist beyond locking oneself in a darkened room and waiting for the bolt to strike (except perhaps for continuous experimentation, see Waterman, 1987). This is a nihilistic view, in which purposeful and calculative behavior is irrelevant and all firms can be treated as random actors. Schoemaker, who has gone furthest along this path, argues that even superior analytical techniques can only be of temporary value, because once superior modes of analysis become common knowledge, they lose their strategic value (Schoemaker, 1990). In place of competitive strategic analysis, Schoemaker therefore proposes only general heuristics to guide decision making in the uncertain world.

However, it is unnecessary to go this far to seek an explanation for the existence of profit, because asset stock asymmetries among firms limit profit dissipation, even in the presence of common knowledge.

The premise of this argument is that firms are always strategically asymmetrical because, at every point in time, their accumulated stocks of irreversible assets are different. Thus, the first mover advantage in the factor market, represented by a superior current asset stock level, allows an advantaged firm to appropriate future product market profits. Ghemawat, for example, demonstrates that even without efficiency differences conditional on size, an asymmetric asset stock position cumulates (Ghemawat, 1990). Mills also shows how in the presence of any sunk costs, profits are not dissipated by the preemptive investment timing game (Mills, 1988).

Any underlying asset stock asymmetry is also bolstered by the presence of dynamic nonconvexities in asset accumulation. Others have identified this as a constraint on imitation (Dierickx and Cool, 1989; Ghemawat, 1991), but it does not by itself deter imitation. It allows the firm with the superior asset stock to invest to achieve a singular product market position without dissipating the resulting profits. Dynamic nonconvexities arise through organizational inertia, time compression diseconomies (as documented, for example, in software development), or if there are scale economies in the rate of asset accumulation (either with respect to the asset being accumulated, or with respect to stocks of interconnected or cospecialized assets; Dierickx and Cool, 1989). In such instances, a firm's current superior stock of a factor ensures that it can preempt investment by others and still earn profits. Competition in the factor market does not, therefore, always dissipate profits in the product market, even in the presence of common knowledge about the source of those profits.

It is also for this reason that history matters. The history of a firm acquiring physical assets and accumulating organizational learning determines the idiosyncratic bundle of irreversible tangible and intangible assets it inherits today (Wernerfelt, 1984).[13] Because of their irreversibility, these assets function as state variables in a firm's dynamic optimization problem (Collis, 1993). Their current level, therefore, determines the future path of investment. As a consequence, they constitute a valuable object for strategic analysis. Each firm can, and should, rationally analyze the pattern of investment necessary to exploit its differentiated endowment of specialized, durable assets. Thus, irreversible assets do indeed make a firm's evolution 'path dependent' (Arthur et al., 1987; Dosi et al., 1990).[14]

This analysis suggests a world of infinite regress. A firm will capture profits from product market position A because it had a superior stock of durable specialized asset Y at an earlier date. It had that because in the past, it invested to capture profits from a product market position B because it had a superior stock of durable, specialized asset Z . . . until, because at the beginning of time the firm had an advantage in durable specialized asset X, it is now what it is, and its future (which will include a series of profit generating product market positions) is what it is ordained to be. The difference in starting positions determines a firm's optimal course for ever, and allows it to successfully exploit a series of profit generating market positions.

This is an overly deterministic view of the world given uncertainty and bounded rationality. Accidents of fate dictate that the particular path a firm follows is never completely prescribed the moment it comes into being. While it is true that a first mover's superior stock of valuable irreversible assets allows it to pursue a reasonably wide range of options that will sustain its advantage across a broad range of future states of nature, when either the dispersion of uncertainty (the range of future states of nature) or bounded rationality (the range of possible options) becomes large relative to the size of the asset stock advantage, rational analysis cannot be guaranteed to generate a single evolutionary path.

Summary

The theory of profit described above accounts for the existence of profit when a firm possesses a singular product market position that is immune to the factor market threats of imitation, substitution, appropriation and dissipation. This is achieved when a firm has a superior investment relative to competitors and the current economic capacity of the market in a valuable, specialized, durable and preferably nontradable asset.

Organizational Capability

The list of irreversible assets, identified as being potential sources of profits, was divided into physical and intangible (or invisible, Itami, 1987) assets in Table 7.1.

Organizational capability is one of these intangible assets. It is defined here to be the firm's dynamic routines that enable it to generate continuous improvement in the efficiency or effectiveness of its performance of product market activities (see also Teece et al., 1994). It is the firm's collective tacit knowledge of how to initiate or respond to change, that is built into the organization's processes, procedures and systems, and that is embedded in modes of behavior, informal networks and personal relationships (for a more detailed account of internal corporate decision making see Cyert and March, 1963; Simon, 1957).

Importantly, such an organizational capability, like any tacit skill, is not instantaneously acquired on a tradable factor market (Dierickx and Cool, 1989). Rather, it is acquired over years of investment (in computer and telephone systems, HRM policies, etc.), as well as through the accumulation of knowledge gleaned in the performance of day-to-day activities by all the members of the firm.

Such an idiosyncratic capability of an organization involves the ability to optimally manage the transformation of inputs into outputs over time. For this reason, it is the 'managerial' factor of production that is needed to alter the mix of other factor inputs, either on its own initiative or in response to exogenous change. In fact, organizational capability becomes Marshall's fourth factor of production (Marshall, 1920); the 'entrepreneurial' factor in the Schumpeterian dynamic competitive economy (Schumpeter, 1934: 143); the mobilizing of resources to exploit an opportunity (Stevenson, 1985); or as Lipmann and Rumelt model it, the production of new production functions (Lipmann and Rumelt, 1982; see also Nelson and Winter, 1982).

To demonstrate that organizational capability defined this way can be a source of profit, rather than merely an asset that is a unique capability that earns a rent, we must show it can meet the five conditions for the existence of profit.

The product market condition is that organizational capability be valuable, that is, be able to create a *singular product market position*. To achieve this, organizational capability cannot simply be represented by any unique 'culture' (of informality, collegiality or whatever). Nor are organizational capabilities that produce static optimality (for example the appropriate plant layout or the optimal marketing mix) the source of profit, since they can be replicated in a finite period of time (although the existence of the corresponding x-inefficiency over long periods of time has often been observed, Leibenstein, 1966). Rather the capability must be dynamic, allowing the organization to continuously improve the performance of its product market activities, continually advancing the production frontier (Nelson and Winter, 1982).

Consider, for example, the organizational capability which yielded a firm a unique product feature today, such as a new special effect button on a VCR. Such static product market phenomena can be relatively costlessly copied, as the rapid reverse engineering skills of many firms demonstrate. Instead, the valuable capability is the accumulated know-how, embedded in the firm's routines, which allows the company to introduce the next product feature more quickly or cheaply than any competitor (as, for example, Sharp has done in liquid crystal displays (LCDs; Collis, 1993). It is, therefore, such dynamic routines which are the true source of value

(Dosi et al., 1990), not the static routines, because they enable the firm to possess a singular product market position at every point in time.

The *inimitability* of organizational capability is not achieved because organizational capability is causally ambiguous (although previous treatments would seem to disagree). Although organizational capability involves supra-individual 'tacit' knowledge, and is difficult for outsiders to observe because of the complexity and detail of the systems, processes, procedures, and so on, from which it is constructed (Barney's (1992) socially complex phenomenon), it *must* ultimately be 'known' if it is to be sustained in a dynamic environment.

As stated earlier, observability does not make organizational capability imitable. Managers cannot move from one firm to another and replicate what they did in their previous organization. No one individual can know all there is to know about the organization, not only because of bounded rationality, but also because organizational capital is ultimately both tacit and supra-individual (in Teece's (1982: 44) words 'organizational memory is not reducible to individual memory'. Contracts outlining terms and conditions of employment, for example, which a manager might be able to replicate, only specify the job content in general terms. An individual's exact mode of behavior, which lies within a 'zone of indifference' (Leibenstein, 1966), and how he or she interacts with others, is critical to the effective functioning of the organization. Thus, contracts alone cannot capture all the essential features of an individual's behavior. The intangible organizational capability of a whole unit cannot be partially parceled up, sold, or reproduced elsewhere ('the transfer of productive expertise requires the transfer of organizational as well as individual knowledge'; Teece, 1982: 45). Another organization can replicate it only by going through a process of investment identical to the one undertaken by the original organization.

It is this requirement for imitators to go through a comparable investment process in order to acquire the desired tacit knowledge that ultimately leads to inimitability. First, because accumulating tacit knowledge is often subject to time compression diseconomies because attempts to speed up the arrival of a capability built out of network relationships will be met by decreasing returns. Compressing a set of personal experiences, for example, increases stress and will be detrimental to the sequential learning process that is an integral part of organizational capability. Second, because when investment in organizational capability is irreversible, it can function as a credible deterrent to imitation.

To be irreversible, organizational capability must be a durable and specialized asset. It is durable simply because the network of relationships on which it is based decays slowly. It is specialized because it involves investment in firm-specific human capital by every individual in the organization, each of whom has developed a unique expertise by virtue of membership in the organization. They have over time learned not only the requisite functional skills – the optimal way to perform the task – but also the inappropriate methods (which will be avoided in all future reconfigurations) and, most important, the ability to interact effectively with, and correctly interpret the behavior of the rest of the organization in pursuit of a particular strategy (Ghemawat and Cost, 1993). Because these skills are specific to the firm and its strategy, they are valued less if deployed another way.

However, the requirement that organizational capability be specialized[15] also helps refine its definition. Organizational capability must be rooted in and developed for the industry in which it is applied. It cannot merely be a fungible general management skill. Such a generic capability can be instantaneously and costlessly redeployed to other industries under the threat of imitation and so, as outlined earlier, cannot function as a deterrent to imitation. Indeed, most general management capabilities are essentially static optimization skills, such as accounting and tight control of working capital, and therefore are not the all important dynamic adjustment skills tailored to a particular industry. Firms with an organizational capability must have built it from industry specific knowledge, mastering the detail of, and installing the dynamic routines unique to continuous improvement in that industry alone.[16]

Indeed, to be truly irreversible, organizational capability must also be specialized to a particular strategy. If organizational capability allows a firm to improve performance in multiple directions, the threat of competitive imitation of its current singular product market position could be met by developing an alternative product market position. Only if the organizational capability is committed to building a specific product market position, such as the low cost position, is it irreversible and so an effective deterrent to imitation.

Importantly, this suggests that to meet the condition of inimitability, the valuable dynamic routines captured in organizational capability must be capable of only locally advancing the production frontier (Nelson and Winter, 1982). Organizational capability must not allow firms to switch costlessly from one location on the frontier to another, or to globally advance the production frontier. If it did so, its very flexibility would lead to its demise as a source of profit.

The threat of *dissipation* is overcome not only because of asset stock asymmetries, but also because an organizational capability is often enhanced as it cumulates experience at improving the firm's static routines.[17] As a consequence, any initial competitive asymmetry in its level is reinforced by increasing returns to the process of change from asset mass economies and interconnectedness. These nonconvexities provide strong reasons why a firm that has a superior organizational capability can rationally expect to make the necessary investments to sustain that capability while avoiding the threat of profit dissipation.

Appropriation by another factor of production is, however, a real threat to the realization of profit from organizational capability. As was described earlier, intangible assets, such as organization capability, are vulnerable to appropriation by the individuals in whom the collective skills reside.[18] Two factors, however, do limit the threat of appropriation of profits that are the result of organizational capability. The first is the number of individuals involved, and the second is the degree of tacitness to the organizational capability.

The limit to appropriation as the number of individuals involved in organizational capability increases is relatively straightforward. If the capability is specific to a single individual, it is easy for him or her to appropriate profits. The large sums paid to CEOs such as Michael Eisner at Disney, or David Geffen of Geffen Records and then MCA, can be attributed to their success at appropriating part of the profits that accrue to their abilities to build and sustain unique capabilities in the organizations they run. The fact that these individuals do not appropriate all of the profits they generate confirms that tradability of a profit generating asset does not guarantee full appropriation of its profits.

It is also possible for a small team to appropriate profits from its organizational capability. A group of senior executives or a research team can either covertly or explicitly threaten to trade their skills on the factor market if they do not fully appropriate the returns their collective capability generates. However, as the number of individuals involved increases, the likelihood that bargaining among them will result in their fully appropriating the profit stream decreases. This occurs because the size of the 'core' will decrease as subgroups exist that can still generate most of the profit (Moulin, 1988).

Similarly, the more tacit the collective capability, the less likely it is that labor will appropriate the profit. First, the ability of employees to trade their capability on factor markets is restricted by the market failure surrounding all information, but tacit knowledge in particular. Second, the tacitness of the collective knowledge restricts cooperative bargaining. Knowing individual reservation prices is impossible because individual contributions cannot be disentangled. Moreover, because the capability vests in the collective organization, trading or threatening to trade the skill on the factor market must involve the willing consent of the whole organization.

The irony is, of course, that the more tacit the organizational capability and the greater the number of individuals involved (which makes both appropriation and imitation less likely and profits more secure), the closer such capability comes to being causally ambiguous. Its causal ambiguity, in turn, constitutes the seeds of its own destruction. However, it should be clear that within broad bounds the profits to an observable but inimitable organizational capability will not be fully appropriated by the members of the organization in which the unique skill rests.

The final factor market threat to the extraction of profit from organization capability is the case of *substitution*, where new strategies invalidate old routines. The best example of this is perhaps Ford and General Motors (see also Henderson and Clark, 1990). In the early 1920s, Ford built an invulnerable market position around the production of a low cost automobile – the Model T. This was achieved not only by enormous preemptive physical investments – the almost completely vertically integrated River Rouge plant – but also by building an organization capable of continual cost reduction. Estimates of the experience curve between 1909 and 1923 show a 15 percent reduction in price for each doubling of accumulated output, while direct labor hours followed an 80 percent experience curve between 1913 and 1921 (Abernathy and Wayne, 1974). The capability to first build such a unique organization, and then to relentlessly improve its cost performance, was certainly a source of profit. It was, however, completely invalidated by General Motors' introduction under Alfred Sloan of product differentiation. The physical assets, and equally, if not more important, the organizational capability at Ford, was at a stroke substituted by the need to compete over product development. The difficulty Ford had in adapting its organization to the new era was illustrated by the nearly twelve month shutdown at River Rouge to retool in 1927, and by the permanent loss of market leadership (from a market share peak over 50 percent in the early 1920s to less than 30 percent by the 1930s). Having built an inimitable organization capable of continual cost reduction, Ford's profit-generating asset was substituted by General Motors' strategy which required a completely different sort of organizational capability.

This sort of substitution is almost inevitable, and its threat is omnipresent. Indeed, because organizational capability can only generate profit to the extent that it is committed to a single strategy, substitution is almost unavoidable. The only way to overcome it would be to build an organization capable not only of continuous improvement in a single direction, but also adaptable enough to be able to proactively change the direction of improvement as well. While this sort of organizational readaptation is observed (Bartlett and Ghoshal, 1989; Collis, 1991), it is relatively rare, far more demanding, and ultimately, as argued earlier, far more likely to invite imitation of the original capability.

The application of the theory of profit laid out earlier demonstrates, therefore, that a superior specialized organizational capability that generates continuous improvement in the performance of the activities needed to support a particular product market position (in the dynamic routines that continually advance the local production frontier) can be a source of profit.

Implications

The first implication of recognizing organizational capability as a source of profit is that we should have empirical observations of its occurrence. Practical examples of organizational capability include the ability to continually reduce development cycles for new products (Hayes et al., 1988) or the more recent broader approach of 'competing in time' (Stalk and Hout, 1990); the superior skill in transferring learning from one part of the organization to another (Clark, 1989); superior research and development capability (Henderson and Cockburn, 1994); better coordination of multinational activities (Bartlett and Ghoshal, 1989); and more effective management of change (Kanter, 1983). Each of these capabilities enables firms with the same or inferior inputs of capital and labor to simply outperform their competitors (see the examples in the steel, automobile and other industries quoted in Baldwin and Clark, 1990). Perhaps the best examples have been demonstrated in the tobacco and ready-to-eat cereals industries (Thomas, 1989a, 1989b), where there have been found to be pronounced stable asymmetries in the competence of firms to launch new brands. These asymmetries have lasted for forty to eighty years and, at least in the case of tobacco, can be shown to be independent of size. Such capabilities have been the source of durable intra-industry differences in performance – notably for Kelloggs and Philip Morris – and so confirm the existence of durable differential corporate capabilities (in this case of initiating and improving brand positioning).

Analytically, the theory provides a rationale for treating internal organization not merely as the function of an administrative hierarchy, but as a source of profit in its own right. In this it recalls the initial work of Andrews on corporate strategy (Andrews, 1971). He outlined the internal and external factors that give rise to a profit-earning 'distinctive competence'. While much research has since been conducted on the external product market conditions, it is only recently – under the guise of the 'resource-based' view of the firm – that the *internal* factor market conditions have been examined. The latter approach highlights the importance of organization and justifies both the search for normative prescriptions for building a superior organizational capability, and academic research into the extent, limits and sources of such a capability.

More immediately, the theory challenges the notion that organization structure is contingent on the choice of strategy (Chandler, 1960). Rather, organization structure and managerial processes may themselves constitute a viable strategy. If organizational capability can be an independent source of profit, one strategy is to build a unique organization capable of continuous improvement in a particular direction. Indeed in many businesses, such as high-technology disk drives, the organizational capability almost becomes the strategy (Wheelwright, 1994). Succeeding in an environment where the product generations change every few years cannot be achieved without the organizational capability to continually innovate and bring products to market rapidly. In such industries, this capability, rather than positioning the product correctly or controlling a channel of distribution, may well become the source of profit (Collis, 1994).

At this stage, the normative prescriptions suggested by the theory must be derived from the recognition that organizational capability is a complex social phenomenon, that the skills must be industry specific rather than generic, and that continual investment in the capability is required.

However, we do not really know yet how to develop a valuable organizational capability. A complex web of organizational phenomena, from the formal organization structure and management information systems to incentive schemes and personnel evaluation practices, affect behavior inside the organization. These phenomena occur in ways that defy our current analytic abilities (although organizational economics is certainly advancing our knowledge of the phenomena; Barney and Ouchi, 1988; Milgrom and Roberts, 1992). Thus we cannot detail the steps necessary or the organizational arrangements required to create an effective organizational capability.

At a more macro level, however, it is possible to speculate on how to build organizational capability, without being specific as to which organizational design parameters to alter in order to achieve it. Organizational capability involves continuous improvement. To be able to institutionalize this requires an organization capable of three tasks which map closely into Nelson and Winter's description of evolution – search, evaluate/choose, routinize procedures (Nelson and Winter, 1982) and the TQM approach of plan/do/act/check (Juran, 1988; see also Garvin, 1993). The first is the ability to innovate; change is essential for improvement; mechanistic repetition of behavior cannot produce improvement beyond the immediate learning effect. Adam Smith's pin factory would rapidly have reached the limits of performance without some change to the division of labor (Smith, 1970/1776). Indeed, dividing up the task into smaller elements is itself an organizational innovation. The Boston Consulting Group's experience curve, for example (Henderson, 1972), always recognized the need for explicit managerial intervention to change the production process – it was never conceived of as an automatic effect, independent of proactive managerial initiative. Thus the first task is to build the insight and creativity that generates new ideas, and an organizational ethos and incentive scheme that encourages and rewards innovation.

The second critical factor in building organizational capability is the ability to learn. If changes are made but the organization fails to understand whether the change was beneficial or detrimental, or fails to adopt the superior approach, change, even good change, will be wasted. Thus individuals and groups must have sufficient awareness of their environment, goals and performance to be able to learn the consequences of their actions and so adopt or reject whatever innovations they make (Senge, 1990). The third factor is the ability to transfer learning and information within the organization. While individual learning alone might be of temporary value, most dynamic routines are group-centered. As such, whatever is learned, wherever it is learned, must be transferred to other appropriate personnel and institutionalized if the organization as a whole is to continually improve its performance (Walsh and Ungson, 1991).

Organizational processes, systems and procedures should therefore be set to accommodate these three tasks – innovation, learning, and information transfer – while at the same time ensuring that the static administrative routines needed to carry out the current activities of the organization are adequately performed. What levels to set for each of the many organizational parameters that affect such behaviors remains the unresolved issue, although it is their impact on the allocation of decision rights, reward systems, and the distribution of information within the firm that will ultimately determine their effect (Jensen, 1983).

As a last and even more speculative suggestion, it might be that only continual tension or conflict (Pascale, 1990) within the organization can build the required dynamic routines. Continually stretching individuals (Itami, 1987) by underinvesting in their numbers and the precise specification of their tasks, while overinvesting in their firm-specific human capital might maintain the appropriate pressure to perform, while providing the training that enables them to respond effectively (Prahalad and Hamel, 1994).

Conclusions

This chapter laid out a theory of profit and demonstrated that organizational capability, defined as the dynamic routines that produce continual improvement in the efficiency or effectiveness of the performance of product market activities, could be an independent source of profit. Thus its primary contribution is to the recent work on the resource-based view of the firm in general (Barney, 1992; Peteraf, 1993), and to the research on organizational capability or dynamic capabilities, in particular (Teece et al., 1994). By adding to long-established notions of distinctive competence, industrial organization's treatment of commitment and the importance of factor market asymmetries as explicators of durable intra-industry differences in performance, this analysis identifies the characteristics of organizational assets which can generate profits.

More generally, the chapter represents an integration of industrial economics' treatment of commitment (Ghemawat, 1991) with the emerging strategy literature on the resource-based view of the firm. The two approaches are consistent with one another, because ultimately they require similar conditions for the existence of profit.

In developing the argument that organizational capability, appropriately defined, can be a source of profit, a number of important precepts were also discussed:

- Defining economic profit as existing when supranormal returns could be maintained in all states of nature with some specified probability of occurring.
- Distinguishing profit from rent by defining rent as the inframarginal return to an intrinsically heterogeneous factor of production, and profit as a return to heterogeneous product market position built from investment in fungible factors of production.

- Establishing the five conditions for the existence of profit – that a singular product market position is invulnerable to the factor market threats of imitation, dissipation, appropriation and substitution.
- Disproving causal ambiguity as a durable source of profit in the presence of any exogenous change.
- Observing that irreversible assets are the fundamental determinants of strategic position and that, as a consequence, each firm's evolution is path dependent (history matters), and normative strategic analysis is valuable.
- Suggesting that bargaining over the appropriation of profits is integral to the distribution of any profit stream, regardless of the source of those profits.

This chapter also serves a normative purpose by articulating the set of conditions that determine whether a particular organizational capability can create a sustainable competitive advantage. If some firms are able to build an organization that can locally advance the production frontier more rapidly than competitors, they will indeed earn profits for a period of time. By suggesting that such a capability must be industry specific, and committed to the pursuit of one strategy, this chapter contributes to normative prescriptions for building organizational capability. The next critical step should be to analyze the specific organizational structures and policies that enable firms to build the organizational capabilities that both economic principles and the strategic perspective now recognize as a source of profit.

Notes

This chapter benefits enormously from many discussions with Pankaj Ghemawat, Cynthia Montgomery and David Yoffie. Support from the Division of Research at the Harvard Graduate School of Business Administration is also acknowledged.

1 Barney's equilibrium notion of sustainability, explicitly excludes the Schumpeterian shocks that overturn competitive advantage (Barney, 1991).

2 Efficiency rents can therefore, in principal, be distinguished from monopoly profits (Peteraf, 1993).

3 This analysis indicates that debate over the relative importance of resources and activities as determinants of competitive position is unnecessary (Porter, 1991). There is an essential duality between 'activity' flows and 'resource' stocks – one is the income statement, the other the balance sheet (Dierickx and Cool, 1989). The flows involved in the performance of activities directly change asset stock levels as they consume and/or generate resources. Advertising expenditures, for instance, build brand loyalty. Conversely, it is the current stock of resources that determines the necessary level of activity by a firm in each period. The appropriate amount of advertising expenditure, for any firm, is determined by its stock of brand loyalty. Thus, a firm's profit can be attributed either to its lower current advertising expenditures or to its superior brand loyalty.

4 Restrictions on the relationship between the shapes of the cost and demand functions are required for profitable product market positions to exist. Not all industries will support durable intra-industry differences in firm performance, and some industries will support multiple profitable positions for firms pursuing different strategies.

5 An important distinction that previous authors have confounded has to be made between

the constraints themselves and the related assets. While the two are clearly related, they are conceptually distinct.

6 Location in attribute space is conceptually similar because only one firm can hire Michael Jackson for advertising purposes and benefit from that, supposedly superior, positioning.

7 Scale economies per se, for example, are not sufficient to deter entry and sustain profits, as Stigler observed years ago in his critique of Bain's original conception of entry barriers (Bain, 1956; Stigler, 1968). Similarly, Dierickx and Cool's (1989) notion of asset mass economies and interconnectedness do not deter imitation unless the incumbent's investment is sunk.

8 Note that there must be exit barriers in an industry if it is to support persistent interfirm differences in performance. As Eaton and Lipsey (1980) observed, all entry barriers are exit barriers.

9 The important investments in airline computerized reservations systems, for instance (which the recent sale prices of several hundred million dollars show have generated large profits), are not the computers, but the idiosyncratic software programs developed over thirty years and the external linkages to the travel agent network (Copeland and McKenney, 1988). Conversely, industries lacking idiosyncratic fixed assets, such as dressmaking or wooden table manufacturing, will be fragmented and characterized by normal economic rates of return and a high turnover of companies (Collis and Ghemawat, 1994).

10 Consider, for example, investment fund management. At any point in time one fund has the best twelve-month investment record. Its advantage is certainly 'uncertainly imitable' because its reason for success is unknown even to the fund manager, and sure enough in the next twelve months it loses its superior performance record.

11 In addition, given any uncertainty, capitalizing an unpredictable stream of future returns in a single factor market transaction is unlikely to result in the exact appropriation of those returns.

12 Seemingly irrational behavior also leads to profit dissipation. Often this happens when firms underestimate the investment costs necessary to attain a desirable product market position. The most cited example is Philip Morris, which invested several billion dollars (including operating losses) to move Miller Brewing from seventh to second in the US beer industry. Although now profitable, Miller never overtook the leader Anheuser-Busch and is unlikely ever to recoup its investment.

13 It is these resources which underlie the notion of 'distinctive competence' (Andrews, 1971) and its recently rediscovered form, 'core competence' (Prahalad and Hamel, 1994).

14 This is an essentially Chandlerian view of the importance of first-mover investments in industries characterized by substantial commitment opportunities (Chandler, 1990). Historically, because firms could not develop durable advantages if there were no specialized durable and valuable assets to invest in, the only examples of sustainable superior performance until the mid-nineteenth century were those based on natural resources or government-regulated monopolies, for example, Hudson's Bay Company, East India Company. Chandler documented the changes that led to the development of fixed assets that were product specific and sensitive to scale economies, rather than general purpose and scale insensitive. Also, mass distribution allowed for the creation of consumer brand franchises (Chandler, 1977). As a consequence, the establishment of the firms that remain today the pillars of corporate America became feasible. By making initial investments in the irreversible assets of their industries, first movers like General Electric, Exxon and du Pont established durable profit-generating positions that competent managements have sustained for about a century through continued investment in the valuable irreversible assets (Chandler, 1990).

15 Even with respect to time compression diseconomies, rather than irreversibility, as the source of inimitability, basic organizational requirements for cross-functional consistency support the specialization tendency by suggesting that strategic choices and their requisite organizational capabilities are mutually exclusive. As Caves states, 'a firm's managerial cadre may hope to beat its median-ability competition along one dimension, but not along every dimension' (1984: 9).

16 This analysis accords with Montgomery and Wernerfelt's (1988) findings on the value

and direction of successful diversification strategies. Narrow industry skills earned higher rents in diversification than general management skills.

17 To the extent that organizational capability is both self-replicating and responsible for mutations, it can be interpreted as the gene in a firm's evolution.

18 Merely observing workers earning rents does not, however, imply that they possess an organizational capability. A valuable organizational capability probably does not reside in airline mechanics or newspaper printers. Their high wages more likely result from having appropriated the profits accruing to the near monopoly positions airlines and newspapers created by preemptive investment in particular locations (major hub cities, and one-newspaper cities, respectively).

References

Abernathy, W.J. and Wayne, K. (1974) 'Limits of the learning curve', *Harvard Business Review*, 52(5): 109–119.

Amit, R. and Schoemaker, P.J. (1993) 'Strategic assets and organizational rent', *Strategic Management Journal*, 14: 33–46.

Andrews, K. (1971) *The Concept of Corporate Strategy*. Homewood, IL: Richard D. Irwin.

Aoki, M. (1984) *The Cooperative Game Theory of the Firm*. Oxford: Oxford University Press.

Aoki, M. (1988) *Information, Incentives and Bargaining in the Japanese Economy*. Cambridge: Cambridge University Press.

Arthur, W.B., Ermolieve, Y.M. and Kaniovsky, Y.M. (1987) 'Path dependent process and the emergence of macro structure', *European Journal of Operations Research*, 30: 294–303.

Bain, J. (1956) *Barriers to New Competition*. Cambridge, MA: Harvard University Press.

Baldwin, C.Y. and Clark, K.B. (1990) 'Capabilities, time horizons and investment: New perspectives on capital budgeting', Harvard Business School mimeo.

Barney, J.B. (1985) 'Strategic factor markets: Expectations, luck and business strategy', *Management Science*, 21(10): 1231–1241.

Barney, J.B. (1986) 'Organizational culture: Can it be a source of sustained competitive advantage?', *Academy of Management Review*, 11(2): 656–665.

Barney, J.B. (1989) 'Asset stocks and sustained competitive advantage: A comment', *Management Science*, 35(12): 1511–1513.

Barney, J.B. (1991) 'Firm resources and sustained competitive advantage', *Journal of Management*, 17(1): 99–120.

Barney, J.B. (1992) 'Integrating organisational behaviour and strategy formulation research: A resource based analysis', in (eds), *Advances in Strategic Management*, vol. 8. London: JAI Press Inc.

Barney, J.B. and Ouchi, W.G. (eds) (1988) *Organizational Economics*. San Francisco, CA: Jossey Bass.

Bartlett, C. and Ghoshal, S. (1989) *Managing Across Borders*. Boston: Harvard Business School Press.

Baumol, W.J., Panzer, J. and Willig, R. (1982) *Contestable Markets and the Theory of Industry Structure*. New York: Harcourt Brace Jovanovich.

Beer, M., Eisenstat, R. and Spector, B. (1990) *The Critical Path to Corporate Reversal*. Boston, MA: Harvard Business Press.

Caves, R.E. (1984) 'Economic analysis and the quest for competitive advantage', *American Economic Review*, 74(2): 127–132.

Caves, R.E. and Porter, M.E. (1977) 'From entry barriers to mobility barriers: Conjectural decisions and contrived deterrence to new competition', *Quarterly Journal of Economics*, 91(2): 241–261.

Chandler, A. (1960) *Strategy and Structure*. Cambridge, MA: MIT Press.

Chandler, A. (1977) *The Visible Hand*. Cambridge, MA: Harvard University Press.

Chandler, A.(1990) *Scale and Scope*. Cambridge, MA: Harvard University Press.

Clark, K.B. (1989) 'Product development in the world auto industry', *Brookings Papers on Economic Activity*, 3: 729–771.

Collis, D.J. (1986) 'The value added structure and competition within industries'. PhD dissertation, Harvard University.

Collis, D.J. (1988) 'Entrepreneurship, strategy, and creativity', Harvard Business School Working Paper No. 89–021.

Collis, D.J. (1991) 'A resource based analysis of global competition: The case of the bearings industry', *Strategic Management Journal*, 12: 49–68.

Collis, D.J. (1993) 'Sharp corporation: Technology strategy', Harvard Business School Case No. 793–064.

Collis, D.J. (1994) 'The resource based view of the firm and the importance of factor markets', Harvard Business School Working Paper No. 95–070.

Collis, D.J. and Ghemawat, P. (1994) 'Industry analysis: Understanding industry structure and dynamics', in L. Fahey and R.M. Randell (eds), *The Portable MBA in Strategy*. New York: John Wiley. pp. 171–194.

Copeland, D. and McKenney, J. (1988) 'Airline reservation systems: Lessons from history', *MIS Quarterly*, 12: 353–370.

Cyert, R. and March, J. (1963) *A Behavioral Theory of the Firm*. Englewood Cliffs, NJ: Prentice Hall.

Day, G.S. and Wensley, R. (1988) 'Assessing advantage: A framework for diagnosing competitive superiority', *Journal of Marketing*, 52: 1–20.

Dierickx, I. and Cool, K. (1989) 'Asset stock accumulation and sustainability of competitive advantage', *Management Science*, 35(12): 1504–1511.

Dosi, G., Teece, D. and Winter, S. (1990) 'Toward a theory of corporate coherence', mimeo.

Eaton, B. and Lipsey, R. (1980) 'Exit barriers are entry barriers', *Bell Journal of Economics*, 11: 721–729.

Eatwell, J., Milgate, M. and Newman, P. (eds) (1987) *The New Palgrave*. New York: Macmillan.

Fudenberg, D. and Tirole, J. (1985) 'Preemption and rent integration in the adoption of new technology', *The Review of Economic Studies*, 52: 383–401.

Garvin, D. (1993) 'Building a learning organization', *Harvard Business Review*, 7(4): 78–91.

Ghemawat, P. (1986) 'Sustainable advantage', *Harvard Business Review*, 64(5): 53–58.

Ghemawat, P. (1990) 'The snowball effect', *International Journal of Industrial Organization*, 8(3): 335–351.

Ghemawat, P. (1991) *Commitment*. New York: Free Press.

Ghemawat, P. and Cost (1993) 'The organizational tension between static and dynamic efficiency', *Strategic Management Journal*, 14: 59–73.

Gilbert, R.J. (1989) 'Mobility barriers and the value of incumbency', in R. Schmalensee and R. Willig (eds), *Handbook of Industrial Organization*. Amsterdam: North-Holland, 8(1): 476–535.

Hayes, R., Wheelwright, S. and Clark, K. (1988) *Dynamic Manufacturing*. New York: Free Press.

Henderson, B. (1972) *Perspectives on Experience*. Boston, MA: Boston Consulting Group.

Henderson, R.M. and Clark, K.B. (1990) 'Architectural innovation: The reconfiguration of existing product technologies and the failure of established firms', *Administrative Science Quarterly*, 135: 9–30.

Henderson, R.M. and Cockburn, I. (1994) 'Measuring core competence? Evidence from the pharmaceutical industry', Massachusetts Institute Of Technology mimeo.

Itami, H. (1987) *Mobilizing Invisible Assets*. Cambridge, MA: Harvard University Press.

Jensen, M.E. (1983) 'Organization theory and methodology', *The Accounting Review*, 58: 319–339.

Juran, J.M. (1988) *Juran on Quality Planning*. New York: Free Press.

Kanter, R.M. (1983) *The Change Masters: Innovation and Entrepreneurship in the American Corporation*. New York: Simon and Schuster.

Knight, F.M. (1921) *Risk, Uncertainty, and Profit*. New York: Harper and Row.

Leibenstein, H. (1966) 'Allocative efficiency as X efficiency', *American Economic Review*, 56: 392–415.

Lipmann, S.A. and Rumelt, R.P. (1982) 'Uncertain imitability: An analysis of interfirm differences in efficiency under competition', *Bell Journal of Economics*, 13: 418–438.

Marshall, A. (1920) *Principles of Economics*, 8th edn. London: Macmillan.

Marx, K. (1906) *Capital: A Critique of Political Economy*. Chicago, IL: C.H. Kerr.

Milgrom, P. and Roberts, J. (1982) 'Predation, reputation, and entry deterrence', *Journal of Economic Theory*, 27: 280–312.

Milgrom, P. and Roberts, J. (1992) *Economics, Organization and Management*. Englewood Cliffs, NJ: Prentice Hall.

Mills, D.E. (1988) 'Preemptive Investment Timing', *Rand Journal of Economics*, 19(1): 114–122.

Montgomery, C.A. and Wernerfelt, B. (1988) 'Tobin's Q and the importance of focus in firm performance', *American Economic Review*, 78(1): 246–250.

Moulin, H. (1988) *Axioms of Cooperative Decision Making*. Cambridge: Cambridge University Press.

Nelson, R.R. and Winter, S.G. (1982) *An Evolutionary Theory of Economic Change*. Cambridge, MA: Harvard University Press.

Pascale, R.T. (1990) *Managing on the Edge*. New York: Simon and Schuster.

Peteraf, M.A. (1993) 'The cornerstones of competitive advantage: A resource-based view', *Strategic Management Journal*, 14(3): 179–191.

Polanyi, M. (1962) *Personal Knowledge*. New York: Harper Torchbooks.

Porter, M.E. (1980) *Competitive Strategy*. New York: Free Press.

Porter, M.E. (1985) *Competitive Advantage*. New York: Free Press.

Porter, M.E. (1991) 'Towards a dynamic theory of strategy', *Strategic Management Journal*, 12: 95–117.

Powell, T.C. (1992) 'Strategic planning as competitive advantage', *Strategic Management Journal*, 13: 551–558.

Prahalad, C.K. and Hamel, G. (1990) 'The core competence of the corporation', *Harvard Business Review*, 68(3): 79–91.

Prahalad, C.K. and Hamel, G. (1994) *Competing for the Future*. Boston, MA: Harvard Business School Press.

Raiffa, H. (1982) *The Art and Science of Negotiation*. Cambridge, MA: Belknap.

Reed, R. and DeFillippi, R.J. (1990) 'Causal ambiguity, barriers to imitation and sustainable competitive advantage', *Academy of Management Review*, 15(1): 88–102.

Ricardo, D. (1951) *Principles of Political Economy and Taxation*. Cambridge: Cambridge University Press.

Robinson, J. and Eatwell, J. (1973) *An Introduction to Modern Economics*. Maidenhead: McGraw-Hill.

Rumelt, R.P. (1984) 'Towards a strategic theory of the firm', in R.B. Lamb (ed.), *Competitive Strategic Management*. Englewood Cliffs, NJ: Prentice Hall. pp. 556–570.

Schelling, T.S. (1960) *The Strategy of Conflict*. Cambridge, MA: Harvard University Press.

Schmalensee, R. and Willig, R. (1989) 'Interindustry studies of structure and performance', in R. Schmalensee and R. Willig (eds), *Handbook of Industrial Organization*. Amsterdam: North-Holland, 11(2): 951–1009.

Schoemaker, P.J. (1990) 'Strategy, complexity, and economic rent', *Management Science*, 36(10): 1178–1192.

Schumpeter, J.A. (1934) *The Theory of Economic Development*, Cambridge, MA: Harvard University Press.

Senge, P.M. (1990) *The Fifth Discipline*. New York: Doubleday.

Shepherd, W.S. (1984) 'Contestability versus competition', *American Economic Review*, 74: 572–587.

Simon, H. (1957) *Administrative Behaviour*. London: Macmillan.

Smith, A. (1970 [1776]) *The Wealth of Nations*. London: Penguin Books.

Spence, A.M. (1983) 'Contestable markets and the theory of industry structure: A review article', *Journal of Economic Literature*, 84(21): 981–990.

Stalk, G. and Hout, T. (1990) *Competing against Time*. New York: Free Press.

Stalk, G., Evans, P. and Shulman, L.E. (1992) 'Competing on capabilities: The new rules of corporate strategy', *Harvard Business Review*, 70: 57–69.

Stevenson, H.H. (1985) 'Entrepreneurship', in J.J. Kao and H.H.Stevenson (eds), *Entrepreneurship: Colloquium at Harvard Business School*. Boston, MA: Harvard Business School Press. pp. 253–269.

Stigler, G.J. (1968) *The Organization of Industry*. Homewood, IL: Richard D. Irwin.

Teece, D.J. (1982) 'Towards an economic theory of the multiproduct firm', *Journal of Economic Behavior and Organization*, 3: 39–63.

Teece, D.J. (1987) 'Profiting from technological innovation', in D.J. Teece (ed.), *The Competitive Challenge*. Cambridge, MA: Ballinger.

Teece, D.J., Pisano, G. and Shuen, A. (1994) 'Firm capabilities, resources, and the concept of strategy', Consortium on Competitiveness and Cooperation Working Paper.

Thomas, L.G. (1989a) 'Which brands succeed', Columbia University mimeo.

Thomas, L.G. (1989b) 'Asymmetries in entry competence', Columbia School of Business Working Paper No. FB–89–14.

Tirole, J. (1988) *The Theory of Industrial Organization*. Cambridge, MA: MIT Press.

Ulrich, D. and Lake, D. (1990) *Organizational Capability*. New York: Wiley.

Varian, H.R. (1978) *Microeconomic Analysis*. New York: W.W. Norton.

Walsh, J.P. and Ungson, G.R. (1991) 'Organizational memory', *Academy of Management Review*, 16(1): 57–91.

Waterman, R.H. (1987) *The Renewal Factor*. New York: Bantam Books.

Wernerfelt, B. (1984) 'A resource-based view of the firm', *Strategic Management Journal*, 5(2): 171–180.

Wheelwright, S.C. (1994) 'Product development: The essence of business strategy planning in high-tech environments', Harvard Business School, Working Paper.

Williamson, O.E. (1985) *The Economic Institutions of Capitalism*. New York: Free Press.

Part 3

STRATEGIC CHANGE AND ORGANIZATIONAL LEARNING

The previous parts have shown that learning processes can lead to knowledge and capabilities that provide competitive advantage for organizations. This part focuses on the practical issues of organizational change and the implementation of new strategies. To begin, Beer, Eisenstat and Biggadike (Chapter 8) introduce a new method for implementing strategic change, called 'strategic human resources management' (SHRM), and describe an intensive action research project in which SHRM was used to create strategic change in a large corporation. They suggest that *patterns* of organization and management cannot be changed without discussion of previously 'undiscussable' issues related to how people and departments work together. Managerial behavior and organizational strategy are thus discovered to be inextricably linked together.

Chapter 9 takes a broad look at organizational processes, by revisiting Karl Weick's three components of 'organizing' – enactment, selection and retention. Orton introduces the notion of 'continuing structures' to counter what he terms a common misconception among readers of Weick that organization members can enact whatever reality they want to enact. This chapter also calls attention to the role of institutional memory in shaping the enacted environment in an organization. This detailed analysis of Weick's groundbreaking *theory of organizing* provides a new vocabulary for discussing organizational and strategic change.

Chapter 10 focuses on the problem of creating strategic organizational change, in particular through the use of management consultants. Phills identifies four 'general analytic activities' (GAAs) in which consultants engage – comparison, explanation, prediction and prescription – and each are discussed as components of organizational learning. Drawing from the work of Argyris, as well as from recent developments in cognitive social psychology, Phills also describes barriers to learning, and then discussses implications for practice, for both consultants and managers. The chapter concludes with a brief consideration of important unanswered questions for creating strategic change in organizations.

8

Developing an Organization Capable of Strategy Implementation and Reformulation:
A Preliminary Test

Michael Beer, Russell A. Eisenstat and E. Ralph Biggadike

Despite consensus in the business policy literature that strategy can only be implemented if the organization is aligned with strategy, very little knowledge exists about how to bring about such alignment. Employing a framework from business policy that examines the 'fit' of organization and management practices with strategy, and knowledge about organization change from the fields of organizational behavior and development, a process was developed – Strategic Human Resource Management (SHRM) – through which general managers can implement strategic alignment. This chapter reports preliminary findings from an action research project in one company aimed at evaluating SHRM as a process, and learning from its application about the problem of strategy implementation. Preliminary findings indicate that the SHRM process is very powerful. That is because it combines analysis with an examination of personal and organizational patterns of management. Findings about organizational factors and processes that are important in developing strategic alignment through SHRM are discussed.

There is little dispute among business policy scholars that the general manager's job involves the formulation and implementation of strategy. Research and theory have made it possible for scholars in the field of competitive strategy to stipulate analytic frameworks that help general managers formulate effective strategies (Fahey and Christensen, 1986; Porter, 1980). The business policy field has made substantially less progress in formulating a body of knowledge that is helpful to managers in implementing strategy, the other half of the general manager's job.

It has been long argued that strategy implementation relies on the general manager's capacity to align organizational elements such as structure, control systems, incentive systems, management process, corporate culture and leadership style with strategy (Andrews, 1980; Hamermesh, 1982; Uyterhoeven et al., 1977). Business policy scholars, however, have been unable to stipulate exactly how this alignment occurs.

The literature is replete with references to leadership, communication and education, but provides no clear theory to explain why one approach to implementation may be better than another.

Given increasingly rapid changes in markets and technology, organizations will have to develop the capacity to learn (Hayes et al., 1988). Continuous adaptation will be important, and strategic and organizational change will become increasingly interdependent. Given these developments, understanding how strategic alignment is to be implemented becomes even more important.

This chapter describes preliminary findings from an action research project in a single company aimed at closing this gap in our knowledge about how to implement strategic alignment. The project has two objectives. The first is to create a new social technology for developing an organization capable of implementing and reformulating business strategy – Strategic Human Resource Management (SHRM) – and to evaluate the efficacy of that technology. An essential aspect of the SHRM process involves the use of organizational members as co-investigators in systematically and regularly collecting a range of organizational data. Thus the second objective is to use these data to develop a complete understanding of the factors that facilitate and hinder organizational alignment.

Research and Theory on Strategic Alignment

Two streams of research and theory inform the problem of strategic alignment. Below we review briefly the contributions and limitations of organizational theory and business policy on the one hand, and organizational behavior and development on the other. We show how SHRM integrates these two streams of research, building on their strengths and complementing their weaknesses.

Organizational Theory and Business Policy

A large body of organizational research and theory has established the now well accepted concept of 'fit'. According to this work the effectiveness of the organization – its capacity to interact successfully with its environment – is dependent on the alignment of multiple organizational elements with environment and strategy. Chandler's (1962) seminal work established the relationship between strategy and structure. Since then, other researchers have demonstrated a relationship between environmental uncertainty and organizational form (Burns and Stalker, 1961; Lawrence and Lorsch, 1967), environmental uncertainty and modes of conflict resolution (Lawrence and Lorsch, 1967), the relationship between the organization's task and member predisposition and motivation (Lorsch and Morse, 1974), and the relationship between strategic archetypes, and organizational structure and management style (Miles and Snow, 1978).

The business policy literature has used the idea of alignment as its organizing conceptual scheme (Andrews, 1980; Uyterhoeven et al., 1977).

This literature, as noted in the introduction, argues that it is the general manager's task to assure alignment. It poses this task as an analytic one – develop strategy, diagnose organization and then change it. Often this prescription includes examples of archetypal fit patterns general managers might consider as guides for their own actions. Implementation is a matter of managerial judgments about timing, involvement and communication argue academics like Hamermesh (1982) and Herbiniak (1990), but the particular shape of the process is unspecified. Recommendations of management consultants such as Steel (1991), Wright (1989) and Harker (1991), who write about implementation, also provide analytic frameworks for assessing alignment, but leave the process completely unspecified.

Underlying the recommendations of the business policy literature are some implicit assumptions about the nature of employees and organizations. These are:

- Employees are motivated to change their behavior by rational arguments emanating from the top.
- Employees so motivated possess the repertoire of attitudes, behavior and skills needed to enact the new organizational arrangements.
- When deficiencies in attitudes, skills and behavior exist they can be corrected through follow-up communication and education.

These assumptions have led to an oversimplified approach to implementation, one that emphasizes changes in structure and systems as the principle agents of change, but ignores many of the elements of organization, particularly the so-called 'softer' or behavioral ones. Typical recommendations found in the literature suggest that strategy be defined, appropriate structure and incentive systems developed, and that reorganization follows. People, management process and culture are either ignored or at best presumed somehow to follow. Substantial management experience, as well as recent research, suggests that this laissez-faire approach may preclude alignment of human attitudes, behavior and skill, and thus impede the effectiveness of strategic implementation (Beer et al., 1990).

Consider the experience of the company under study, which led one of the authors to search for a better way to implement the corporation's globalization strategy (Biggadike, 1990). Having identified rapidly growing markets overseas as a major growth opportunity for existing products and developing technology, the company introduced a transnational organization (Bartlett, 1988). Worldwide teams were introduced, with domestic division managers as presidents and relevant country product managers as members. The structure was appropriate, but experience soon showed that worldwide teams were a long way from achieving effective levels of functioning. Staff, skills, style and shared values simply were not aligned (Waterman et al., 1980).

This experience has been repeated many times in other companies. These difficulties in creating alignment are likely to be particularly true as the competitive environment causes organizations to move from control to commitment as the basis for coordinated activity (Beer et al., 1990; Walton, 1987).

In summary, examination of the organizational theory and business policy literature reveals a consensus, one supported by extensive empirical evidence, that all elements of an organization must 'fit', but it also reveals a gap in our knowledge. That gap is in precisely how a general manager is to go about achieving alignment in attitudes, behavior and skills – the culture of the organization. Fortunately another stream of research, theory and practice provides some insights into this problem.

Organizational Behavior and Development

A substantial body of research and theory in these fields has established that cultural norms govern attitudes and behavior in organizations. For example, group norms can influence individual perceptions (Sherif, 1936), as well as levels of productivity (Homans, 1961; Rothlisberger and Dickson, 1939), and organizational culture powerfully influences behavior and attitudes (Deal and Kennedy, 1982; Denison, 1984; Ouchi, 1981; Schein, 1985). All this suggests that fundamental change in organizations is not possible without change in norms. Organizational behavior is difficult to change through rational appeals, incentives and communication aimed at persuading individuals, unless these are part of a broader shift in culture. What this research suggests is that the context for individual behavior, the social system and its norms, must be changed to effect change in attitudes and behavior.

How can norms be changed? To use coercive or top down methods would undermine the very objective of the change – an alteration in employee beliefs and values to which they must be internally committed (Argyris, 1972; Vroom and Yetton, 1973). Yet recent research on organizational renewal supports the notion that conceiving of organization change as a series of human resource programs aimed at educating and motivating individuals also is flawed (Beer et al., 1990).

A process that involves employees in examining the organization's assumptions, belief system and behavior clearly is called for. Unfortunately, research indicates that many of the most significant of these are undiscussible, and their undiscussibility is undiscussible (Argyris, 1990). Organizations form norms that prevent discussing those aspects of the organization that are essential for a cultural transformation to take place.

Organization development (OD), a field concerned with intervention theory and method, has long maintained that organizations cannot be changed without altering cultural norms (Beer, 1980; Bennis, 1969; Bennis et al., 1961; Burke, 1982). A variety of intervention methods have emerged that involve the collection and discussion of previously undiscussible data in meetings specially designed to promote trust and open dialogue (Beer, 1975, 1980). The underlying theory is that internal commitment can only be obtained when the change agent (management) and change target (subordinates) trust each other, valid information is surfaced (not purposefully biased or manipulated), and organizational members are involved in making an informed choice about required changes in their own behavior (Argyris, 1970).

Considerable evidence exists that shows these methods promote internal commitment and learning of new attitudes and behaviors – particularly in small groups, and when the leader values open dialogue. Yet there is also evidence that these methods have failed to transform the culture of large organizations (Beer and Walton, 1987, 1990). In large organizations, OD methods are often resisted for two reasons:

- They are experienced as overly normative – naively prescribing openness, participation, employee involvement, and team management in all situations, regardless of the organization's task or strategy.
- They focus on interpersonal behavior and internal problems of the organization without sufficient connection to strategy, customer and task as the driving forces for change.

It is not surprising that in organizations where results are all important and norms militate against discussing the undiscussible, these characteristics of OD interventions produce resistance, and preclude wide scale application. Even when top management has stated that cultural transformation toward participation and teamwork is its goal, lower level managers resist if they do not see the connection to their business goals (Beer et al., 1990).

Even when organization development has been introduced successfully at a plant or division, culture change has often not spread to other parts of the larger corporation. This generally has been caused by top management's inattention to strategies for spreading and institutionalizing change (Beer et al., 1990; Walton, 1987).

SHRM: An Integration of the Two Research and Theory Traditions

It seems rather clear that each of the theory and research traditions described above offers an important part of the puzzle for achieving strategic alignment. Business policy and organizational theory provide the analytic framework that ties organization to strategy. Organizational behavior and organization development provide a theory of organizational change based on internal commitment and intervention methods that have been shown to produce such change.

What is necessary is a strategy implementation process that both analytically defines the organizational arrangements demanded by the competitive environment, and develops internal commitment to these arrangements. The Strategic Human Resource Management process, developed and researched by the authors, is an effort to do this.

SHRM uses the contributions of both research traditions discussed above, and aims to overcome their inherent weaknesses. It also builds on recent research findings on how corporations transform their fundamental patterns of management to increase competitiveness (Beer et al., 1990). The following hypotheses about strategic organizational alignment or change guided the design of SHRM.

1   Mobilizing energy for change is the key to successful strategic alignment. It is best obtained by focusing organizational members on strategy and task, not on the personal and human resource changes that must inevitably follow (Beer, 1980; Schaffer, 1988).

2   Energy can be mobilized when the top team of the business unit actively engages in a process of defining strategy, and then collects and jointly diagnoses data about barriers to enacting the strategy.

3   Organization-wide commitment to change and learning can only occur when a process connects lower level organizational members and the top team in an iterative process of collecting data, diagnosing, changing and re-diagnosing. This process gives voice, and empowers lower levels to help develop the organization's capability to enact strategy.

4   If strategic alignment is to occur, the business unit's top team (general managers and direct reports) must be willing to discuss its own behavior – including the behavior of the general manager – and must be capable of learning from the discussion. That is because strategic alignment inevitably requires new patterns of coordination throughout the organization, and that is governed by attitudes and behavior at the top.

5   Alignment of all organizational elements (structural and behavioral) must start with a systemic vision of the organizational arrangements required to enact the strategy. Since organizational effectiveness is contingent on managing relevant interdependencies, such a vision must articulate the horizontal (across functions) and vertical (management, employees and union) coordination/cooperation requirements imposed by the strategy. It must explicitly describe the interactions needed to achieve requisite coordination, as well as the workforce commitment and competencies needed to function in the new arrangements.

6   Sustained organizational change occurs when a new organizational context is created – one that 'forces' change in organizational members, but which they perceive to be owned by them, and connected to strategic purpose. Since formal structure and systems changes emanating from the top produce resistance, an initial context must be created through a collaborative redefinition of the ad hoc roles, responsibilities and relationships of the individuals. As people struggle to learn how to work in new arrangements they helped to create, they discover the real barriers to change – those inherent in their deepest beliefs about how things ought to be done. It is only at this point in the change process that management begins to understand the managerial and professional competence required to align the organization. Their planning for recruitment, selection and succession therefore becomes more relevant for the future state to which the organization is moving. Formal

structure and systems changes may be used later in the process to 'lock in' patterns of management to which people already are committed.

There have been other less ambitious efforts to integrate the perspectives of business policy/organizational theory and organizational behavior/ development. Lawrence and Lorsch (1969) developed a diagnostic approach to organization development that required managers to analyze their environment/task before arriving at decisions about organization. They also recommended a data collection, diagnosis and design process for doing so, but their intervention methods were primarily analytic, and did not deal extensively with how to change analysis into personal and organizational change and learning. Moreover, no empirical data exists on implementation of their intervention method. Argyris (1989) designed an educational experience that instructed management teams in competitive analysis and strategy formulation, and in skills for discussing the undiscussible barriers to strategy implementation. While apparently successful in producing discussions of personal and organizational barriers to implementation, the effort stopped short of producing a plan for organization development or an effort to institutionalize the process in the company.

The action research project described below attempts to incorporate missing elements in these early efforts to develop a strategically aligned organization. It also involves the collection of empirical data on the effectiveness of SHRM at the business unit and corporate level.

SHRM at Alpha Corporation

Alpha, with two billion dollars in revenues, has two sectors, each with several autonomous divisions. Many of the divisions were acquired in the 1970s. During the late 1970s and 1980s, the company rationalized its business through an extensive strategic planning process. Under the leadership of its current CEO, who initially came to the company as an external consultant on strategy, the company uses a process-oriented approach to strategy formulation called Strategic Profiling.

A strategic profile of a business is developed by a general manager and his or her staff with the help of a profiler (internal or external consultant) whose role is to ensure that the group answers a series of questions about its competitors, markets, products and customers. Acting as a facilitator and resource, not an expert, the profiler moves the group to consensus on strategy. In many ways, this process shares with organization behavior/ development assumptions about how commitment is developed, and about the role of consultants as helpers rather than experts (Schein, 1969).

Satisfied with the quality of its strategies, the company became increasingly concerned about the capability of its business units to implement them. The predictable difficulties met with in the introduction of a global organization, described above, convinced the CEO and one of the authors that the company needed to turn to the field of organization development and human resources for help. The authors became involved in designing the SHRM process, and implementing it in several divisions of the company, and at the corporate level with top management. The successful experience of the company with strategic profiling, and the CEO's understanding of the importance of process in developing commitment, made Alpha a promising site for assessing SHRM's viability.

The SHRM process builds on the strategic profiling process. It is only after a business unit's top management team has conducted its competitive analysis and defined its strategy that it can begin to examine the organization's capacity to implement it. The stated purpose of SHRM is to 'develop a vital organization capable of implementing and reformulating business strategy'. This is done by engaging the general manager and his or her team in an examination of the organization's strengths and weaknesses, but always in the context of the business strategy defined through the strategic profiling process.

SHRM involves the following steps.

Orientation and Planning

A one day meeting led by two consultant/profilers introduces the top team to SHRM. At this meeting the following occur:

- The purpose and description of the process is presented by the profilers.
- A case study of a business unit whose organization was not aligned with strategy is used to provide a preview of the SHRM process.
- The top team restates its strategy in terms of organizational tasks to be performed, and specifies the particular forms of organizational coordination, commitment and competence required.

Data Collection

The profiler trains members of the employee task force to conduct interviews in all functions, as well as with representatives of other parts of the company with which the business unit is interdependent. The employee task force asks interviewees to describe the specific management practices and organizational arrangements that help or hinder the business unit from achieving each of the strategic tasks identified earlier. What surfaces are issues about the functioning of the top team, such as its role in prioritizing, resource allocation and promoting needed coordination, as is the strategy. The profiler also conducts interviews with the top team to obtain members' views of misalignment in the organization, and of problems in the group's functioning – including the general manager's role and style.

Three-day SHRM Profiling Meeting

Analysis of the organization and behavior of the top team, development of a strategically aligned organizational vision, and the development of a change plan are accomplished in a three-day SHRM profiling meeting. This meeting is especially designed to promote an open dialogue, and personal and organizational learning.

The first day of the meeting is for data feedback. The day begins with a presentation of guidelines for communication that will facilitate the clarification and exploration of potentially controversial information. The profilers ask the top management team to agree that they will not blame or otherwise punish the task force for presenting negative findings. Throughout the meeting, the profilers work to ensure that participants obey these norms, and avoid defensive behavior (Beer, 1980).

The top management team listens to comments from the employee task force. The task force organizes findings around major themes, developed with the assistance of the profilers the previous day. After the task force finishes and departs, the profilers present to the top team a summary of the common themes that arose in the interviews with individuals in the top management team.

If the interviews suggest that the role or style of an individual team member, whether the general manager or functional head, is impeding the group, these issues are discussed as well. Unlike a more traditional organizational development intervention, however, these more behavioral and stylistic issues are addressed only if the members of the group or the profilers perceive them to be impeding the effectiveness of the operating unit to enact its strategy.

The second day of the meeting is reserved for analysis. The analytic model in Figure 8.1 is used in the following manner. The top team lists the key patterns of behavior and skill – at the top and in the organization as a whole – uncovered the previous day as strengths and barriers (Box 1).

An assessment is made – in qualitative and if possible quantitative terms – of the historic effects of these organizational behaviors on financial performance and human outcomes. Then there is an evaluation of how these persistent behaviors affect the organization's capacity to perform its strategic tasks and produce requisite coordination, commitment and competence.

Next the management team is asked to make an explicit and informed choice as to whether the performance and/or strategic consequences of the identified organizational issues are of sufficient scope to warrant continuing the meeting. Consistent with the theory of internal commitment outlined above, business imperatives are regarded as the most viable source of motivation for confronting difficult organizational and human problems, and sustaining change. None of the profile meetings conducted at Alpha were concluded at this point, however (Boxes 2 and 3).

Then a diagnosis of the organization as a system is conducted, to identify causal factors for the behaviors identified as barriers. Corporate policies and practices are examined, as is the division's approach to organizing and managing its people in five major policy areas (Beer et al., 1984) (Boxes 4 and 5).

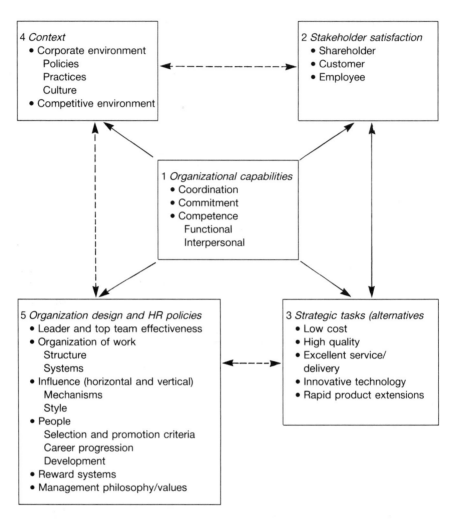

Figure 8.1 *Diagnostic model of organizational effectiveness*

The third day is devoted to the development of the vision and a change plan. The vision is articulated using the same analytic systems framework used to perform the diagnosis. Typically, this results in a consensus on how the top team will change its pattern of management; how critical interdependencies will be managed through ad hoc teams (that is, business, product development or quality teams); what skills are needed in key roles, and which existing employees should be placed there; and what structural, measurement, information, and reward systems might ultimately be put in place to support the behaviors specified. When this is complete, a philosophy of management – stated in value terms – emerges naturally and is articulated.

Finally, a plan is developed for involving the employee task force and the organization as a whole in modifying, refining and implementing the vision.

Review with Higher Management

Following the SHRM profile, the general manager and his or her team meet with higher management, to review what they learned about themselves and their organization, as well as their vision and change plan for strategic alignment. There is also a review of corporate barriers to division effectiveness identified in the profiling meeting. The profilers attend to facilitate this exchange of sensitive information. It is envisioned that higher management will review objectives for organization development that come out of SHRM as part of their routine business reviews.

Ongoing Monitoring and Follow-ups

As the organizational changes developed during the three-day meeting are implemented, the top management team monitors their effectiveness. The employee task force facilitates this process, and is typically empowered to provide the top team with ongoing informal comments on the organization's response to the changes. As difficulties arise, the profilers are available for guidance and consultation. Thereafter, on a periodic basis – typically every other year – more systematic data is collected and analyzed through a SHRM follow-up that is essentially a recapitulation of the process described above.

Research Strategy

Assessment of SHRM is a difficult and complex endeavor that is still underway. We are using several sources of data. First, there is a simple practical test of acceptance and utilization. Is the company continuing to use SHRM over time? While continued use does not provide conclusive evidence of effectiveness or applicability to other companies, it at least suggests that it is possible to employ SHRM under a given set of conditions.

A more convincing test for SHRM is its capacity to cause the organization to realign and change in some fundamental way. This question cannot be answered definitively, because in action research it is virtually impossible to do a controlled experiment with a large sample of divisions and corporations randomly assigned to experimental and control groups. The very nature of the SHRM process itself, however, which involves the systematic and periodic collection of a range of organizational data, allows us to bring far more evidence to bear on the question of the efficacy of the process than is typically the case in field research. An analysis of this evidence allows us to use each organization as its own control in assessing the extent to which the SHRM process has allowed a particular business unit to make progress on previously intractable organizational problems.

In addition, comparisons across several divisions can identify conditions and strategies that are more or less conducive to managing strategic realignment.

Thus the best source of data about the efficacy of SHRM, and the validity of the theory underlying it, comes from the clinical data generated by the process itself. These data allow one to assess the effects of the process on an organization and its managers as perceived by several different actors – including the researchers/consultants, the top managers in the business unit, managers at middle and lower levels who serve on the employee task force that collects data and is involved in monitoring change, and managers outside the business unit. By documenting SHRM profiling meetings, and identifying key turning points across many meetings, there is much to learn about improving the design of SHRM, and about the skills a profiler must possess. By documenting the struggle of managers to align behaviorally and attitudinally in the months and years that follow the SHRM profile, those elements in the social systems that pose the most difficult barriers can be identified, and change strategies for dealing with these barriers can be discovered.

Preliminary Findings

In all SHRM profiles conducted at Alpha Corporation, the diagnosis of data surfaced revealed that it was possible to enhance strategy implementation by realigning the organization and its management practices. All divisions and top management began to plan organizational change. Below we discuss our findings about the dynamics of strategic alignment, and the efficacy of SHRM as a planned process for negotiating these dynamics.

Issues in Aligning Organization with Strategy

The response of several employee task forces and management to SHRM, as well as many of the findings of previous researchers in organizational behavior/development cited earlier, provided support for the hypotheses about strategic alignment that guided the design of SHRM discussed above.

First, hidden and undiscussible data often blocks strategic alignment of the organization. All the profiles, including the corporate profile, raised anxiety levels as the employee task force uncovered data they believed was important for strategic alignment. All employee task forces were very anxious about the feedback process, and had to be reassured. The anxiety of top management teams about receiving comments, even when they had selected the task force and understood the data, though revelatory about their own management practices, was relevant to strategy implementation.

Second, issues raised by SHRM confirmed that organizational alignment is much more than an analytic process that fits structure and systems to strategy. Most of the profiles surfaced issues about the style of the general manager, the effectiveness of the top group, interfunctional coordination, and raised questions about deeply held beliefs and patterns of management. For example, in division Beta, using responses from the employee task force and from profilers' interviews with them, the top team identified numerous problems in their functioning and in interfunctional coordination. They estimated that these produced shortfalls in strategic capabilities, business performance and human outcomes. This was of particular concern because of a growing threat from a foreign competitor. The primary causes of the behavioral and skill problems were diagnosed as work system and influence problems – ineffective management meetings and management process at the top, a functional organization that lacked cross-functional teams, ineffective project team/management skills, low influence on the part of quality assurance and marketing, a powerful R and D function, and nonexistent cross-functional transfers for developing employees capable of team work. Unreasonable demands and close control from sector level management also were identified as causally important.

Third, SHRM profiles in all four divisions and the corporation resulted in a similar diagnostic pattern, suggesting a hierarchy of organization and management issues to be emphasized in diagnosing and taking action. Work systems, the means for processing information and coordinating decisions, were always the first order issues identified as causal to a shortfall in performance or strategic capability. Diagnosis in all divisions profiled showed that ineffectiveness at the top produced organizational behavior that was counterproductive to strategic alignment when cross-functional teamwork was necessary. The capacity of the bottom and top of the organization to develop mutual influence, and one function's capacity to influence another, were also central causal factors in the diagnosis.

Measurement and compensation, though mentioned in all profiles, were second order issues. They were not identified as the root causes of problems in the initial profile, and generally not even in the follow-up. This suggests that they may not be the major cause of misalignment typically assumed, nor the powerful force for change assumed by many academics and practitioners. This is probably particularly true in situations where an open discussion about causes for behavior can alter top management's behavior, and these changes in turn can produce change in the organization without modification of formal systems.

Fourth, a similar generic set of yardsticks seem to be helpful in assessing the effectiveness of an organization – such as the behavior of the leader and top team, the prioritization and resource allocation process, interfunctional coordination and team work, and the effect of interfunctional mobility and coordination on general management depth. These appear to be useful in diagnosing a wide variety of businesses, at least within Alpha Corporation.

Fifth, strategic alignment is an iterative learning process, powered by shared experiences of failure and success. All three divisions we followed over time made plans to make changes that we later learned they did not truly understand. It was not until they experienced difficulties, and were forced to confront their causes, that they began to fully understand the words they had spoken and put to paper in their original plans for change. The shared nature of this experience seemed to result in the development of a collective understanding so necessary for all parts of the organization to change in a coordinated and simultaneous manner.

Additional findings come from observing differences in the effectiveness of SHRM in three divisions, operating in two different sectors, across time. Since the standardization of the SHRM process, differences in response to SHRM itself, as well as differences in organizational and personal change, suggest two key conditions that govern success in alignment.

- The skills of the leader in promoting trust, an open dialogue, and empowerment while providing unmistakable signals about the kind of business and organization he or she values, certainly makes change much smoother and easier.
- New leaders can use SHRM more easily than existing leaders, particularly if they can quickly develop trust. The only new general manager who led SHRM used it to begin a process of change that he recognized was necessary. Jack Gabarro (1987) has shown that in the first three months, managers assess their business and their key managers before taking action. SHRM provided the vehicle to do this for new general managers.

Effectiveness of SHRM

If acceptance and utilization are criteria for evaluating SHRM, it must be judged a success. An increasing level of commitment to SHRM by corporate and business unit executives is developing. The principal evidence for this is the diffusion of SHRM from two initial models to two other business units, top management's own involvement in profiling the corporate organization, follow-up initiatives in the three divisions who undertook SHRM in 1988–1989, plans to conduct more profiles, and the commitment of substantial time and money resources to further the process, including the development of internal profilers. In particular, the corporation's vice presidents for human resources and strategic management have conducted profiles on their own, and are enthusiastic about the value of SHRM in developing the capacity of business units to implement strategy.

Utilization in itself is a necessary but not a sufficient measure of effectiveness as discussed above. The extent to which SHRM promotes successful strategy implementation is a better measure. Below we discuss our findings at the business unit and corporate level.

Business unit level In four business units, management perceived that SHRM contributed to developing the organizational capability needed to compete. Consider the following observation from a general manager of one of the business units that went through the SHRM process:

SHRM allowed us to discuss that which could not be discussed before. It allowed us to discuss the undiscussible. It got things on the table that would have taken me, in a serial sense, years.

Getting feedback from the employees as a mechanism is indispensable. Putting it in a strategic context is important. We were there to discuss behaviors that are consequential. The focus on strategy puts it in context. It wasn't personal. We keep coming back to the strategy. We have discovered things that are going to help us succeed or [that were] preventing us from succeeding as an organization. They are strategic issues – delivering the goods and services to our customers better than our competitors. Once you decided it was strategic, you had to fix it or suffer the consequences, and no one was willing to suffer the consequences of gradual loss of competitive position.

The following observations by a general manager from another division capture the difficulty and benefits of the SHRM process. Recalling his organization's first round of SHRM some two years earlier, he described the profilers as 'going for the jugular', asking people to really get their feelings on the table. 'It was a pretty scary day . . . when we left we didn't feel very good about ourselves'. Yet this manager also suggested that:

We are pleased with the process. We interact differently now. Our level of achievement is higher. We have more responsibility worldwide. We are now able to focus on the task at hand. . . . We have been successful in warding off [a foreign competitor]. We are pleased with results, although it has been a long process. It is a cultural process, which takes time. Since SHRM, we have implemented many changes based on the team concept, and have delegated more to mid-level managers. We see ourselves as getting better.

The case of division Beta, discussed above, also provides support for the effectiveness of the SHRM process. The division created a number of cross-functional teams to manage quality, product improvements and a response to its competitors. An SHRM profiling meeting about three years later revealed significant improvements in cross-functional team work. They were managing quality more effectively, and the organization had successfully responded to the threat by its foreign competitor.

Corporate level   There is a growing conviction among corporate executives that SHRM is a powerful process, capable of unearthing aspects of organizing and managing people that are at the core of the company's capacity to implement its strategies. The firsthand experience with SHRM of the CEO and key executives at corporate headquarters substantially strengthened this conviction. Executives who participated in the corporate profiling perceive that it has:

1   caused the CEO to delegate strategic decisions to the sector level, where the consensus diagnosis suggested it should rest;
2   altered the management process at the top;
3   modified the manner in which a key staff executive is managing his responsibilities for cross-divisional selling; and
4   begun to form a consensus on the managerial competencies the company needs/values, and stimulated examination of the process and policies that will govern their development.

Consider the following comments by three corporate executives with very different roles in the corporate SHRM profile. First, the CEO of the company:

> The concept of SHRM is very important to us because it allows us, as an organization, to examine the way we function, and decide what we have to change in order to become more effective.

Second, the corporate staff executive with cross-divisional selling responsibility, whose approach to enacting his responsibilities came under scrutiny as a result of the SHRM profile:

> The SHRM process was very good. It really got out a lot of things that had to be addressed. Substantive changes have been made, for example, in the role of the Strategy Review Committee (SRC). I don't know how I would have managed going to twenty strategy reviews through this period. Delegating that to the sector presidents, with the SRC reviewing the summary reports by the sector presidents, was a very important tangible difference. I think I have gained a lot of insights by slowing down, and getting more people involved, and helping think through what we need to do.

Third, a strategic planner and profiler, who served as a member of the employee task force that collected data for referral to top management:

> One of the key implementation problems we have had, which I became sensitive to going through the SHRM process, is that we do all this strategy development work, and we do a lot of financial planning, but so often the unknown factor is the people and the system and all of the HR aspects that are needed to implement strategy. This process has convinced me that, just as we need to reduce our planning to specifics in marketing, manufacturing, and technology, so we also need to reduce it to specifics in what we're going to do with regard to people development and staffing and all the HR kinds of issues, or our plans are not going to get implemented.
>
> Until going through this process [SHRM], I would not have been convinced that so much of the stuff we write on paper and so many of our plans are just nonsense without taking stock of where we are in terms of our people capabilities.

Despite the power of the SHRM profiling meeting, and the immediate energy for change it releases, there is some evidence that follow-up and sustained activity will be a struggle. Consider the comments of the staff executive with cross-divisional selling responsibility:

> In retrospect, I think we were and are on the brink of some things that are very, very important. I'm disappointed that we haven't seen more come out. Why isn't there more happening? I really think we're onto the capability of trying to make change. I just don't see enough movement.

Problems with follow-up to the corporate SHRM process were also evident among divisional personnel. Most individuals interviewed noted that substantial improvements were occurring in the overall effectiveness of the corporation in implementing its business strategies. Many, however, did not make the link between these changes and the SHRM process. This came about partly due to the long delay in top management's comments about decisions and actions they took as a result of SHRM.

This problem also occurred at the divisional level, where changes were noted in divisional management by lower levels in the organization, but not necessarily attributed to SHRM. It appears to be difficult to communicate the connection between decisions taken through the SHRM process and improvements in effectiveness. It is essential that this problem be solved if they are to sustain energy among employers for continuous organizational learning through SHRM.

Assessing Causality

Might the positive changes we described at both the corporate and the divisional levels have occurred without the SHRM process? As we pointed out earlier, in action research it is difficult to answer this question definitively. The case of one division whose general manager attributed some of the changes in his division to the early retirement of an autocratic and controlling sector president illustrates the problem of attributing causality. A closer analysis of our findings, however, suggests that a causal relationship between SHRM and the changes we have described probably exists:

- There was consensus among all respondents that changes in business outcomes occurred following the SHRM process.
- The consultant/profilers were able to trace a series of events that directly linked the changes in business performance to the SHRM process. For example, committees that universally were seen as central in addressing particular business problems, explicitly were created during the SHRM meetings.
- In many cases, changes involved problems recognized by individuals prior to the SHRM process. These individuals, however, were unable to mobilize the necessary forces to surface issues and create change until the SHRM process began. The fact that a new division manager, who had correctly analyzed misalignments in his division, found SHRM very helpful in compressing the time it might otherwise have taken to align the division's organization with strategy, suggests that SHRM enables and empowers even those at the top to implement strategic alignment.
- The more closely involved individuals were with the described changes, the more likely they were to make the link between the changes and the SHRM process.

Conclusions

We opened this chapter with the premise that the fields of business policy and organizational theory have failed to produce knowledge about exactly how a general manager can implement strategic alignment. Much of past research and theory provides insights into various alignment patterns that managers ought to consider. It assumes that a proper analysis of strategy and current organizational arrangements, together with knowledge about organizational alignment patterns that are effective, is sufficient as long as communication and education follow.

Our research suggests that this prescription for implementing alignment is inadequate. Our application of SHRM at the business unit and corporate level indicates that in every instance patterns of organization and management could not be changed without discussing what previously had been undiscussible – how people at the top managed and worked as a group, how various departments and functions worked together, who had the power, and who needed more if decisions were to be strategically aligned. In other words, SHRM is not only a linear analytic process, though appropriate analysis and knowledge of effective patterns of alignment are clearly important. It is a process that iterates between progress and regression as individuals and groups struggle to learn new attitudes, skills and behaviors.

SHRM appears, at this stage in the action research project, to be a powerful tool for motivating, guiding and furthering the individual and organizational learning needed for strategic alignment to take place. Its value lies in that it puts process ahead of content. We do not argue that knowledge of typical alignment patterns is not helpful. What is more important, however, is that the top management team, informed by data from lower levels, goes through a process that puts them in touch with the reality of their own behavior and that of the organization. When examined in the context of a jointly defined strategy and requisite coordination, commitment and competence, awareness is followed by internal commitment, which in turn is followed by the struggle to change. Setting up the conditions for change to which people are committed – open dialogue across levels about valid data in an atmosphere of trust – is the key.

By requiring all general managers in the company to go through a process of self-examination and learning like SHRM, top management can hold managers accountable for developing an organization capable of strategy implementation and reformulation, without imposing their organizational solution – something that surely would be resisted. If they develop a supportive climate, top management can engage in an open dialogue about personal and organizational alignment with general managers, thus ensuring a continued struggle to internalize new patterns of management.

We believe that the major barriers to the utilization of a process like SHRM lie in the problems of institutionalizing. We are still investigating these problems at Alpha Corporation. It is only with institutionalization that general managers can receive the help they need in learning, and top management can have access to the information it needs to fulfill its role as a steward of the corporation's most important asset – the organization and people that will implement strategy.

References

Andrews, K.R. (1980) *The Concept of Corporate Strategy*, revised edn. New York: Dow Jones-Irwin.

Argyris, C. (1970) *Intervention Theory and Method: A Behavioral Science View*. Reading, MA: Addison-Wesley.

Argyris, C. (1972) *The Applicability of Organizational Sociology*. London: Cambridge University Press

Argyris, C. (1989) 'Strategy implementation: An experience in learning', *Organizational Dynamics*, 18(2): 5–15.

Argyris, C. (1990) *Overcoming Organizational Defenses*. Reading, MA: Allyn and Bacon.

Bartlett, C. (1988) *Managing Across Borders: The Transnational Solution*. Boston, MA: Harvard Business School Press.

Beer, M. (1975) 'The technology of organization development', in M.D. Dunnett (ed.), *Handbook of Organizational and Industrial Psychology*. Chicago, IL: Rand McNally.

Beer, M. (1980) *Organization Change and Development: A Systems View*. Santa Monica, CA: Goodyear.

Beer, M. and Walton, E. (1987) 'Organization change and development', in M. Rosenzweig and L. Porter (eds), *Annual Review of Psychology*. Palo Alto, CA: Annual Reviews, 38: 339–368.

Beer, M. and Walton, E. (1990) 'Developing the competitive organization: Interventions and strategies', *American Psychologist*, 45(2): 154–161.

Beer, M., Eisenstat, R. and Spector, B. (1990) *The Critical Path to Corporate Renewal*. Boston, MA: Harvard Business School Press.

Beer, M., Spector, B., Lawrence, P., Mills, D.Q. and Walton, R. (1984) *Managing Human Assets*. New York: Free Press.

Bennis, W.G. (1969) *Organization Development: Its Nature, Origins and Prospects*. Reading, MA: Addison-Wesley.

Bennis, W.G., Benne, K.D. and Chin, R. (1961) *The Planning of Change*. New York: Holt, Rinehart and Winston.

Biggadike, R. (1990) 'Research on managing the multinational company: A practitioner's experiences', in C.A. Bartlett, Y. Doz and G. Hedlund (eds), *Managing the Global Firm*. London: Routledge. pp. 303–325.

Burke, W.W. (1982) *Organization Development*. Boston, MA: Little, Brown.

Burns, Tom and Stalker, G.M. (1961) *The Management of Innovation*. London: Tavistock.

Chandler, A.D. (1962) *Strategy and Structure*. Cambridge, MA: MIT Press.

Deal, T.A. and Kennedy, A.A. (1982) *Corporate Culture*. Reading, MA: Addison-Wesley.

Denison, D. (1984) 'Bringing corporate culture to the bottom line', *Organizational Dynamics*, 13(2): 4–22

Fahey, L. and Christensen, H.K. (1986) 'Evaluating the research on strategy content', *Journal of Management*, 12(2): 167–184

Gabarro, J.H. (1987) *The Dynamics of Taking Charge*. Boston, MA: Harvard Business School Press.

Hamermesh, R. (1982) 'Note on implementing strategy', Boston, MA: Harvard Business School. Case no. 383-015.

Harker, W.C. (1991) 'Alignment for success in the 1990s', *Business Quarterly*, 55: 107–112.

Hayes, R.H., Wheelwright, S.C. and Clark, K.B. (1988) *Dynamic Manufacturing: Creating the Learning Organization*. New York: Free Press.

Herbiniak, L.G. (1990) 'Implementing strategy', *Wisdom from Wharton*, The Wharton School, University of Pennsylvania.

Homans, G.C. (1961) *Social Behavior: Its Elementary Forms*. New York: Harcourt, Brace and World.

Lawrence, P.R. and Lorsch, J.W. (1967) *Organization and Environment*. Boston, MA: Harvard Business School Press.

Lawrence, P.R. and Lorsch, J.W. (1969) *Developing Organizations: Diagnosis and Action.* Reading, MA: Addison-Wesley.

Lorsch, J.W. and Morse, J.J. (1974) *Organizations and Their Members: A Contingency Approach.* New York: Harper and Row.

Miles, R.E. and Snow, C. (1978) *Organization, Strategy, Structure and Process.* New York: McGraw-Hill.

Ouchi, W.G. (1981) *Theory Z.* Reading, MA: Addison-Wesley.

Porter, M. (1980) *Competitive Strategy: Techniques for Analyzing Industries and Competitors.* New York: Free Press.

Porter, M. (1985) *Competitive Advantage: Creating and Sustaining Superior Performance.* New York: Free Press.

Rothlisberger, F.J. and Dickson, W.J. (1939) *Management and the Worker.* Boston, MA: Harvard University Press.

Schaffer, R. (1988) *The Breakthrough Strategy: Using Short-term Success to Build the High Performance Organization.* Cambridge, MA: Ballinger.

Schein, E.H. (1969) *Process Consultation: Its Role in Organization Development.* Reading, MA: Addison-Wesley.

Schein, E.H. (1985) *Organization Culture and Leadership.* San Francisco, CA: Jossey-Bass.

Sherif, M. (1936) *The Psychology of Social Norms.* New York: Harper.

Steel, Roy (1991) 'From paper to practice: Implementing the corporate strategic plan', *Business Quarterly*, 55: 119–124.

Uyterhoeven, H.E.R., Ackerman, R.W. and Rosenblum, J.W. (1977) *Strategy and Organization*, revised edn. Homewood, IL: Richard D. Irwin.

Vroom, V. and Yetton, P.W. (1973) *Leadership and Decision Making.* Pittsburgh, PA: University of Pittsburgh Press.

Walton, R. (1987) *Innovating to Compete.* San Francisco, CA: Jossey-Bass.

Waterman, R., Peters, T. and Phillips, J.R. (1980) 'Organization is not structure', *Business Horizons*, 23(3): 14–29.

Wright, N.B. (1989) 'The driving force: An action-oriented solution to strategy implementation', *Business Quarterly*, 54: 51–54.

9

Reorganizational Learning: Some Conceptual Tools from Weick's Model of Organizing

J. Douglas Orton

Managers are finding it helpful to focus attention on organizational processes. Numerous small process changes can interact to increase quality, reduce costs, increase speed and generate profits. In strategy terms, organizations with process competence – an understanding of the complex processes which occur within organizations – have a competitive advantage over organizations with underdeveloped process competence. Consequently, organization theorists and strategy researchers are starting to look more closely at processes such as organizational change, decision making, sensemaking, strategy formulation, strategy implementation, organizational learning and reorganizing. The process this chapter focuses on is the organizational learning which takes place before an organization can announce a decision to reorganize. This process is referred to here as 'reorganizational learning'.

In a detailed study of a single reorganization (Orton, 1994), it was helpful to conduct a review of the meta-process which Weick (1979) labeled 'organizing'. Weick's model of organizing can be described in its simplest formulation as three stages – enactment, selection and retention – connected by feedback loops. In this review, Weick's model of organizing was defined more broadly to include other ideas presented in Weick's 1979 book, other statements by Weick related to the theory of organizing (Weick, 1969, 1976, 1977, 1980, 1984, 1988, 1989a, 1989b, 1993a and 1993b; Daft and Weick, 1984; Orton and Weick, 1990; Webb and Weick, 1979; Weick and Browning, 1986; Weick and Gilfillan, 1971; Weick et al., 1973), and adaptations of Weick's ideas by others (for example, Abolafia and Kilduff, 1988; Porac et al., 1989; Smircich and Stubbart, 1985).

As a result of these analyses, each of the three components of Weick's theory of organizing was reframed as two components. 'Enactment' became 'enacted environments' and 'bracketed enactments'. 'Selection' became 'cause maps' and 'workable realities'. 'Retention' became 'reorganizing packages' and 'residual structures'. Within each of these six stages, there are several conceptual tools which are grounded in Weick's work. The text of this chapter is an attempt to introduce concisely and catalog the conceptual tools which proved to be helpful in a study of reorganizational learning.

Enacted Environments

'Enacted environments' are the limitless influx, repertoire, or frontier of actions, statements, influences and ideas which can shape an eventual reorganization.

Continuing Structures

Weick's (1979) theory of organizing emphasizes, through a feedback loop from retention to enactment, that past structures constrain current actions. Thus, one of the things which organization members might pay attention to if they scan the environment to figure out an appropriate organization design, is the fact that a large part of that environment is a continuing structure which has been shaped by their own previous actions. Kimberly (1984) observed that organization design is better conceptualized as organization *re*design, because there is always some previous structure – minimal or elaborate – which constrains future possibilities. This is the first half of Giddens' (1984) structuration dialectic: yesterday's structures constrain today's actions and today's actions shape tomorrow's structures. Porac et al. (1989) demonstrated, in a study of the Scottish fine wool industry, the processes by which industry members have gradually enacted a continuing structure – in the form of industry norms and practices – which constrain the industry members' actions today. One frequent misreading of the theory of organizing – facilitated by the model's original emphasis on enactment and de-emphasis on the feedback loop from retention to enactment – is that the organization members can enact whatever reality they want to enact. The notion of continuing structures helps correct that misinterpretation of organizing by emphasizing that structures and momentum are inherited.

Fluid Ecological Change

Weick's (1979) theory of organizing occasionally cited ecological change or environmental influences as a fourth component of the theory of organizing; the environment could produce or trigger certain actions. Furthermore, Weick's (1979) theory of organizing proposes that the environment is always evolving, continually changing and emergent. In an extended gloss of a section from Steinbeck, Weick argued that a living fish possesses a more dynamic reality than a dead fish, and living environments and organizations possess a more dynamic reality than can be communicated through quantitative variables. Weick (1993a) also argued that enactments occur in continually changing flows or streams, that organizations generate numerous actions, and that the stream of consciousness in organizations takes the form of streams of people, solutions and problems (see also

Cohen et al., 1972). To describe an enacted environment as fluid is to state that there is a continually changing stream of inputs.

Loose Coupling between Organizations and Environments

Another phenomenon observed in organizing processes is that environments can be loosely coupled to organizations (Glassman, 1973; Weick, 1976). Loose coupling between an environment and an organization does not mean that the two entities are decoupled, but means that the two entities are coupled on some dimensions and decoupled on other dimensions (Orton and Weick, 1990). Manning's (1982) research provides a detailed example of loose coupling between environments and organizations. Manning (1982) studied semiotic loose coupling between a police communication system and an environment of people making emergency phone calls. He reported that dramatic phone calls are 'conventionalized' and frozen into rigidly defined crime codes by police operators, and he defined the telephone operators' task as one of processing, decoding, classifying, encoding and transforming the calls into the code, language, or perspective of the organization. Therefore, by changing the information as it crosses the boundaries into the organization, police communication systems (1) maintain the integrity, consistency and autonomy of their organizations, and (2) loosen the couplings between the organization and its environment. As Glassman (1973) and Weick (1976) theorized, and Manning (1982) illustrated, the link between enacted environments and organizations is not immediate and direct.

Complex Environments

The theory of organizing emphasized that environments are fragmented, particularistic and detailed, and that organization members and organizational researchers can only understand a small part of the barrage of information which environments produce. The more complex the environment, the more fragmented the stimuli the organization receives. Complexity is not seen here as an environmental variable which is correlated with a structural variable such as decentralization or specialization. To say that an environment becomes more complex is to use a shorthand to represent a variety of more specific changes which are translated through environment members to organization members.

Institutional Memory

An important part of Weick's (1979) theory of organizing is often overlooked. In the theory of organizing, there is a feedback loop from retention to enactment, meaning that the retained learning from previous enactments has an influence on current enactments. Another way to make the same point is to define institutional memory as part of the enacted environment. Institutional memory, acquired wisdom and past experience all connote organizational learning from past actions. To define institutional memory as part of the enacted environment is to reframe the environment from a narrow definition as something outside the organization to a broader definition of something which can be inside the organization.

Enactment

An environment is not a distinct, discrete, or exogenous entity acting on organizations, but can be influenced, controlled and created by the voluntaristic strategic choices of organization members and managers. Weick's (1979) descriptions of 'enactment' have been interpreted in three different ways, each of which will be analyzed here. The first interpretation of enactment is that it is similar to perception – there is some environment out there which organization members register, interpret, or perceive. The second interpretation of enactment is that it is similar to action – organization members perform actions which trigger subsequent sense-making. The third, and most accurate, interpretation is lodged in between the first and second interpretation – the actions of organization members create an environment to which they must then respond.

Bracketed Enactments

'Bracketed enactments' are actions, statements, influences, and ideas – selected from enacted environments by organization members for further attention – which lead to eventual reorganizations.

Equivocality

Weick (1979) used an example from Heider (1958) to demonstrate how meaning can be equivocal. If a Russian spy escapes from an English prison, how can observers determine whether the spy is an escaped Russian agent, a freed British double agent, or a freed Russian agent who has been 'turned' into a British agent? Daft and Macintosh (1981) described equivocality as a condition in which the underlying meaning of a signal is not clear to a receiver because the signal has two or more possible meanings. To state that bracketed enactments are equivocal is to suggest that any given bracketed enactment can be interpreted in different ways by organization members.

Bracketing

Bracketed enactments are created when organization members select an action, statement, perception, or influence for further attention (Weick, 1979). Organization members have no direct experience with overarching 'environments' – they have direct experience only with the pieces of the environment that they have selected for further attention.

Raw Materials of Cause Maps

Organization members make sense of variations by incorporating numerous causal attributions into a cause map (Weick, 1979). Researchers find that people generate causal attributions between events and causes which accumulate into patterns of cognitive associations, cognitive maps, or cause maps. Ford (1985) studied the creation of causal attributions and their effects on decision making. He argued that questions such as 'Why are profits down?' and 'Why are costs increasing?' initiate sensemaking. As people find answers to these questions, they construct causal attributions. Bracketed enactments are essential inputs to the creation of causal assertions. A significant, unexplained bracketed enactment is like a vacuum which must be filled by either fact or speculation.

The Map is not the Territory

To bracket part of an enacted environment is to not bracket a much larger part of the environment. The problem of inaccurate mapping is emphasized in Weick's discussions of the aphorism, 'the map is not the territory'. Because the map is not the territory, and different people make different maps of what they believe to be the same territory, organization members spend a fair amount of time believing that other organization members are using inaccurate maps.

Enactments

In the organizing model, 'enactment' is most frequently described as action. The theory of organizing proposes that organization members create variations through behaviors and experiments; organization members can enact variations which define and create constraints on subsequent action. Weick (1979) quoted a Lou Pondy statement that if enactment were intended to refer to nonactions it would be enthinkment. Daft and Weick (1984) listed some of these 'enactment behaviors': experimentation, testing, coercion, invention of environments, learning by doing. The emphasis in enactment is clearly on action, but the door is open for other types of enactments. Weick's descriptions of the organizing model include four general types of enactments: action (interacts, double interacts and strings of action), statements (speech, documents, proposals, ideas and initiatives), influences (environmental, interpersonal, technological and bureaucratic) and ideas (about situations, about desires and about norms). Another source of diversity in bracketed enactments is along the continuum of unintentional to intentional enactments. In an extended analysis of a single enactment process, Abolafia and Kilduff (1988) studied the intentional enactment of a speculative bubble in the silver futures market. Their study helped clarify the wide range of meaning in the term 'enactment' – from evolutionary biology's nonintentional 'variation' to the 'purposive action' of coalitions of investors who create a speculative bubble.

Variation

Systems seem to benefit from numerous and varied bracketed enactments. One of the most articulate advocates of variation has been March (1981), who offered a series of provocative footnotes to traditional models of organizational change. He argued that because there are limits on coordination, attention and control, it is improbable that rationality can be implemented in organizations. Given the combination of enacted environments and bounded rationality, March concluded that '[o]rganizations need to maintain a balance . . . between explicitly sensible processes of change (problem-solving, learning, planning) and certain elements of foolishness that are difficult to justify locally but are important to the broader system' (1981: 570). Foolishness, variation and other producers of bracketed enactments provide information which can be used by organizations in the creation of reorganizations.

Behavioral Commitment and Avoided Tests

The complementary concepts of avoided tests and behavioral commitment help explain why bracketed enactments are important in reorganizing processes. First, bracketed enactments are given impetus through processes of behavioral commitment. Salancik (1977) identified three variables which, if present, increase commitment to decisions: volitionality, visibility and irreversibility. Behavioral commitment received only a brief discussion in Weick's (1979) book, but has since become a more explicit component of the theory of organizing (Weick, 1993a). Behavioral commitment suggests that some bracketed enactments should be more influential than other bracketed enactments, depending on the degree of behavioral commitment which is generated through the conditions identified by Salancik. Because bracketed enactments trigger processes of behavioral commitment, and commitment can lead to learning, it follows that people can avoid learning by not creating bracketed enactments. This avoidance of action is described by Weick as an avoided test. An avoided test occurs when people assume that there are dangers, costs, or limitations on their ability to act (Weick, 1979). One way to slow down reorganizing processes is to actively avoid actions which can trigger behavioral commitment and organizational learning.

Small Wins

One of the common assumptions people make about causality (Einhorn and Hogarth, 1986) is that small causes should lead to small effects and large causes should lead to large effects. This assumption is built around two variables – the size, effort and cost of the cause ('small' or 'large'), and the size, importance and impact ('small' or 'large') of the effect. 'Small wins' are cases in which small causes lead to disproportionately large effects. The mechanics of these 'small wins' include the notion of deviation-amplifying loops, also referred to as vicious circles and virtuous circles (Weick, 1979). The continuing development of the idea of small wins (Weick, 1984) is built on the premise of small enactments which can develop into larger benefits through organizational processes.

Cause Maps

'Cause maps' are local-level sets of explanatory causal attributions which make sense of bracketed enactments.

Retrospective Rationality

Organization members use retrospective rationality to make sense of bracketed enactments. Weick (1979) explained that organization members retrospectively or retroactively interpret experiments, explain events, generate accounts, ascribe intention and discover goals. In an extended elaboration of the notion of retrospective rationality, Perrow described the concept as 'disturbing', 'unnerving' and 'unsettling' because it defies people's sense of order, rationality and intelligent behavior (1979: 135–136). Retrospective rationality can come in a variety of degrees of accuracy. In a mild form of retrospective rationality, the actor rediscovers his or her reasons for action. In a harsher form of retrospective rationality, the actor manufactures justifications for action. Bracketed enactments serve as triggers for retrospective rationality.

Micro-macro

There is a subtle shift in which individuals participate in groups for personal interests but then become committed to the creation and attainment of group goals; organizing moves from individual/psychological to organizational/sociological levels. Weick (1993a) emphasized the micro-macro qualities of the theory of organizing in a recent chapter entitled, 'Sensemaking in organizations: Small structures with large consequences'. In the chapter, he organizes diverse research to demonstrate how (1) individual actions create commitment to social relationships, (2) social relationships generate more commitment, (3) justifications are based on social relationships, (4) reifications of justifications create self-fulfilling prophecies, and (5) efforts to validate justification diffuse to others. The net effect of these linked processes is that micro-level actions can have macro-level consequences.

Discrediting

Weick (1979) wrote that cause maps can be built up from past experience and that these historical cause maps are imposed on equivocal situations.

Weick (1979) also noted that cause maps should be discredited and questioned occasionally. When old cause maps are retained and reapplied to new situations, there is little change, but when old cause maps are questioned and discredited, there should be greater change.

Interpretive Schemes

Cause maps are not manufactured from scratch. Each organization member brings an accumulated interpretive scheme to bracketed enactments. Interpretive schemes (Bartunek, 1984) are used here as an overarching term to capture related ideas of assembly rules, assumptions, beliefs, cognitive consensuality, cognitive logic, cognitive maps, the 'conventional point of view', cultures, dominant reality, frames of reference, ideologies, logics, mental models, myths, norms, prototypes, schemata, scripts, shared meanings, shared paradigms and worldviews. Different groups of people operate under different interpretive schemes. Weick's (1979) discussion of the Naskapi Indians provides a useful illustration of interpretive schemes. The Naskapi heated and cracked the shoulderblades of a caribou to decide which direction they should go hunting. The modern corporate equivalent of caribou bones might be market research. The Naskapi interpretive schemes would filter out market research, and modern corporate interpretive schemes would filter out shoulderblade-cracking. As used here, an interpretive scheme held by an individual or an organization provides a background from which a more specific cause map is created.

Complicated Managers

Weick wrote that the prescription, 'Complicate yourself!' (1979: 273) 'lies at the heart of the organizing formulation as the overall prescription for adaptation' (1979: 261). Complicated organization members contribute requisite variety to reorganizing processes. A system has requisite variety for interpreting a specific system if it can adequately register or sense another system through the accurate internal modeling – through multiple, independent, weakly constrained elements – of the diversity of the other system. Bartunek et al. (1983) traced the development of the proposition that complicated understanding is valuable. In their review, they found that complicated managers outperform less complicated managers because they are capable of registering more organizational complexity and crafting better interpretations of that complexity.

Minority Influence

As people try to make sense of bracketed enactments, some people may construct cause maps which differ from a dominant cause map which may be held by others. Nemeth (1986) demonstrated that the presence of an alternative point of view increased the cognitive effort of other decision makers. A similar argument has been made by Janis (1972), who argued that alternative points of view are a potential antidote against groupthink.

Loosely Coupled Systems

In a review of research on loosely coupled systems, Orton and Weick (1990) argued that a system is loosely coupled if its elements are simultaneously distinctive (decoupled) and responsive (coupled). Orton and Weick argued that loose coupling can produce three direct effects – modularity, requisite variety and discretion – all of which are helpful tools in the creation and maintenance of diverse cause maps. 'Modularity' emphasizes the ability of components in loosely coupled systems to operate without constant interference from other components in the system. 'Requisite variety' emphasizes the ability of the system to accurately register the complexity of environments. 'Discretion' emphasizes the ability of components in the system to act and think autonomously.

Workable Realities

'Workable realities' are temporary perceived correspondences of multiple agendas and interpretations. Workable realities are products of organizational sensemaking which transform individual-level cause maps into organizational-level foundations for collective action in the form of reorganizing packages; a workable reality is not an agreement or a consensus, but is a temporary perceived correspondence of multiple agendas and interpretations which allows a reorganizing package to be created.

Equivocality Reduction

Organization members make sense of the variations they are confronted with through the application of rationality, intentionality and causality. People perceive, interpret, organize, and make sense out of events, opportunities, past experiences and ill-structured problems. Daft and Weick described ways that organizations engage in the activity of sense-making or interpretation, which is also referred to as scanning, monitoring, understanding, learning and equivocality-reduction. They emphasized the importance of interpretation to organizations: 'Information about the external world must be obtained, filtered, and processed into a central nervous system of sorts, in which choices are made. The organization must find ways to know the environment' (1984: 285).

Compromise

Workable realities are built through compromise. Weick (1979) observed that organizing occurs in a social context. The cause maps which are created to explain proposed actions must be palatable to constituencies which are expected to approve those actions. Enactment and organizing processes cannot escape the constraints imposed by other people, who are also in the process of enacting and organizing.

Specific Tasks

Workable realities and organizational learning are not created in the abstract. Instead, they are created around specific tasks (Weick and Orton, 1986). Organizations which are able to break down a complex stream of events, decisions and actions into discrete learning episodes are more likely to learn than organizations which stay at abstract levels.

Time-lagged Sensemaking

The creation of workable realities is complicated by time-lagged sensemaking. Weick argued that organizations enact environments, rather than merely perceive environments, and consequently their 'enacted environment is a sensible rendering of previous events' (1979: 166) which the organizations have shaped. Because the interpretations which are built from these previous events are based on 'anachronistic, dated, belated' stimuli (1979: 166), there is a 'definite time lag and a definite tinge of retrospect to the definitions of the situation' (1979: 166). Feldman (1989) found a manifestation of time-lagged sensemaking in her study of reports by government analysts: policy makers would ask for reports to inform their decisions on a specific problem, but the decisions were often made before the reports were completed.

Stability and Flexibility

Weick (1979) proposed three responses to organizations' need for both stability and flexibility: simultaneity, alternation and compromise. In simultaneity, an organization simultaneously trusts and doubts its retained method of operation. In alternation, an organization alternates between trusting and doubting its retained methods. In compromise, an organization mixes trust and doubt into acceptable compromises.

Environmental Jolts

Workable realities are shaped by environmental jolts. Meyer (1982) described the responses of three hospitals to the environmental jolt of an anesthesiologists' strike. While contingency theories of organizational structure suggested that environmental jolts should lead to similar structural changes, Meyer instead found that the three hospitals developed different responses. One explanation for these differences is that each of the hospitals' different workable realities were reshaped in different ways by the environmental jolt.

Reorganizing Packages

'Reorganizing packages' are sets of reorganizing initiatives – proposals to change formal relationships between individuals, groups, or organizations – which are presented together as deliberate organizational redesigns.

Complex Constructions

Weick (1993b) has recently developed the image of the bricoleur as a person able to piece together a variety of materials. The improvization of the bricoleur is described by Weick as a better explanation of change in organizations than the more architect-like activities implied by the phrase 'organization design'. An organization which creates a reorganizing package acts like a bricoleur and cobbles together a complex construction from a variety of change archetypes. A study of 953 reorganizing initiatives in the Ford White House (Orton, 1994) identified twenty-one change archetypes which could be combined to create a reorganizing package: establish, extend, or terminate; reorganize; grow or shrink; consolidate or fragment; create a liaison or break off a liaison; assert organization; absorb or spin off; upgrade a unit or downgrade a unit; transform; study; impose a system; reestablish; rearrange; and formalize. Reorganizing packages are not single actions, such as 'downsize', but are more complex combinations of several archetypes.

Presentation Pressures

Many of the themes in Weick's approach to organizing emphasize the importance of how actions are interpreted by others. The approach is not just psychological, it is social psychological. There are not just actions, but there are double interacts. Self-fulfilling prophecies in social contexts depend on one person's actions being interpreted by another. Behavioral commitment is premised on the assumption that observers will require a person to justify his or her actions. As Dutton and Dukerich (1991) explained, organization members' actions are affected by their understanding of organizational image and identity.

Multiple Purposes

The creation of a formal reorganizing package can have a variety of organizational outcomes which extend beyond the technical rationales which are usually used to justify a reorganizing package. Weick (1979) cited Cohen and March's four alternative purposes for plans in organizations: symbols, games, excuses for interaction and advertisements. First, plans are symbols which can substitute for substantive action. Second, plans are 'games' or tournaments which filter out ideas which have little support. Third, plans are 'excuses for interaction' which provide a platform for ongoing discussions of current issues. Fourth, plans are 'advertisements' which can be used to attract resources and support.

Forceful Presentation

Reorganizing packages are presented with certainty. There are two forces which work together to create the certainty present in the announcement of reorganizing packages: hierarchy and retrospection. Reorganizing packages come at the end of periods of analysis and are usually announced by people at high hierarchical levels. Retrospection and hierarchy thus interact to filter the uncertainty out of the reorganizing package. Retrospection exaggerates the intentional and rational nature of design because over time people forget about the false starts, discarded options, inadequate information and probabilistic judgments which are used to create the reorganizing package. Hierarchy has a similar effect through a different mechanism. As the reorganizing package is passed up the hierarchy from people who have a lot of time to devote to the creation of the reorganizing package to people who have little time to devote to the creation of the reorganizing package, the messiness of the package is filtered out by communication constraints.

Residual Structures

'Residual structures' are the lingering accumulated effects of a stream of previous reorganizing packages.

Brief Moment of Order

There is a brief moment in a reorganization when the reorganizing package is presented and starts to become a residual structure. Reorganizations are sensible to organization members for only a fleeting moment. At that one moment, the map becomes the territory – through accurate information-processing or through self-fulfilling prophecy (Weick, 1979) – and the organization pauses in its swing from the complexities of strategy formulation to the complexities of strategy implementation.

Reshaping

The theory of organizing's summary question is 'How do I know what I think until I see what I say?' (Weick, 1979: 133). Thus the announcement of a reorganizing package is not the final word on the manner in which the reorganization will be implemented. Reorganizations are reshaped as they are communicated, interpreted and evaluated.

Nested Reorganizations

How long can a reorganizing package stay 'fresh' before it is bumped off the organizational agenda by a subsequent reorganizing package? The implementation of a reorganizing package does not occur instantaneously, but organizations seem to produce a steady flow of reorganizing packages. This creates a condition in which reorganizing processes overlap: yesterday's reorganizing package is not implemented before today's reorganizing package is announced, and today's reorganizing package will be announced even though tomorrow's reorganizing package is in preparation.

Presumption of Logic

Weick et al. (1973) found that jazz musicians expended more effort on a composition if they were told that the music was composed by a serious composer. When musicians act under this presumption of logic, they exert more effort, and the composition sounds better than it would if the musician doubted the logic behind the music and exerted less effort. The preservation of this presumption of logic is important to the process of reorganizing. After the announcement of a reorganizing package, there are efforts to reinforce the hard work, the intelligent conclusions, and the unquestionable rationality of the reorganizing process.

Memory

Weick wrote, 'If an organization is to learn anything, then the distribution of memory, the accuracy of that memory, and the conditions under which that memory is treated as a constraint become crucial characteristics of organizing' (1979: 206). Walsh and Ungson (1991) built on the theory of organizing to explain in great detail how memory is created and retained in organizations: ecological changes or problems serve as equivocal decision stimuli; the stimuli are filtered and encoded and the equivocality is reduced; and information is stored in individuals' cause maps or other cognitive structures, standard operating procedures, and information technologies.

Reorganizational Histories

Reorganizing packages are portrayed here as the condensation of a series of bracketed enactments, but reorganizing packages can also be seen as a series of bracketed enactments which shape a larger pattern which might be called a reorganizational history. For example, from 1908 to 1983, General Motors conducted fifteen major downsizings. One conclusion which can be drawn from a study of this history of downsizing is that General Motors accumulated learning from each of the fifteen downsizings which constrained their approach to the sixteenth downsizing. Organizations do not approach reorganizations with a blank slate of options. Instead, from each previous reorganizing package, they accumulate an overarching reorganizing history which will shape subsequent reorganizations.

Puzzles

Weick (1979) began his book on the theory of organizing with frequent references to the metaphor of puzzles. Because reorganizing packages are shaped from complex environments, loosely coupled enactments and diverse cause maps, they may contain internal contradictions. Because reorganizing packages accumulate and are absorbed into structures, it is likely that structures contain numerous inconsistencies, which can be framed by organizational participants as puzzles. Reorganizing packages can thus trigger consequences, unintended consequences and complicated unintended consequences, or puzzles, within organization structures.

Unintended Consequences

A theme running through the theory of organizing is that although individuals may attempt to act rationally, that does not guarantee that they will be able to predict the eventual outcomes of complex, poorly-understood relationships (Weick, 1979). A reorganization can reorganize components of the organizational structure that were not intended to be reorganized.

Faded Complexity

Residual structures are faded memories. Weick (1979) wrote that there are good memory surfaces in organizations, and bad memory surfaces. Memory surfaces will be influenced by the continuing streams of influences which shape enactments, sensemaking and reorganizing packages. In addition, people attempt to manage memories to serve their own self-interests.

Persistence

Residual structures can persist through generations of organization members (Weick and Gilfillan, 1971). One of the reasons for persistence is that cause maps get built up which justify the existence of residual structural entities and residual structural relationships. A structural entity cannot be turned off like a light switch because it remains connected to other structural entities which have grown accustomed to the existence of the entity. A better metaphor than light switches is that of a family heirloom in which rose petals are placed, after each event which merits roses, and left to slowly disintegrate throughout the decades. Residual structures are never deleted from organizations – they simply remain in increasingly muted forms.

Conclusions: Organizing and Reorganizing

What does this catalogue of conceptual tools from a study of reorganizational learning contribute to organization theory?

First, it is a helpful elaboration of Weick's (1979) theory of organizing. Most researchers who have built on Weick's work have sliced off a portion of the larger set – for instance, double interacts, enacted environments, loosely coupled systems and small wins. A few researchers have tried to use all three components of the organizing model – enactment, selection and retention (Abolafia and Kilduff, 1990; Porac et al., 1989; Smircich and Stubbart, 1985). What I have tried to accomplish in this chapter is to create a highly detailed model which integrates the diverse components of Weickian theory. I think that this restatement of a variety of Weickian concepts can provide a good foundation for the subsequent analysis of additional research on reorganizational learning.

Second, this chapter can serve as a foundation for the analysis of research by micro-sociologists, especially the writing of Giddens and Bourdieu. Weick is more explicitly focused on organizations than Giddens and Bourdieu. Giddens positions himself as a grand social theorist trying to explain the emergence of societies. Consequently, his work does not directly address the dynamics of organizations, which are smaller and more likely to be consciously managed by leaders. Bourdieu is a sociologist-anthropologist trying to explain how economic practices are produced and maintained by societies. Consequently, he has much to say about organizational processes, but his philosophical and cultural roots make it difficult for business school researchers to interpret his work. Many of the organizational researchers who have started to study Giddens and Bourdieu are building upon a base gradually constructed by Weick since 1969. This chapter, then, can serve as a foundation for interpretation of Giddens, Bourdieu, and other sociologists who focus – directly and indirectly – on organizing processes.

Finally, this detailed map of reorganizing processes serves as a proxy for the higher-level root process of 'organizing'. As attention continues to shift from the logic of causality to the logic of processes, researchers are finding 'organizing' to be a more practical focus for attention than 'organizations'. Researchers working on topics such as strategy formulation, organization decision making, reengineering, organizational change and organizational learning are all tapping into the root process of organizing from different vantage points. By offering a model derived from a focus on reorganizing, I hope to contribute to – and solicit the assistance of – organizational researchers studying organizing processes from a variety of perspectives. The study of organizing processes – such as learning, reorganizing and reorganizational learning – deserves a school of researchers as dedicated to their paradigm as population ecologists, institutional theorists and organizational economists are to theirs.

References

Abolafia, M.Y. and Kilduff, M. (1988) 'Enacting market crisis: The social construction of a speculative bubble', *Administrative Science Quarterly*, 33: 177–193.

Bartunek, Jean M. (1984) 'Changing interpretive schemes and organizational restructuring: The example of a religious order', *Administrative Science Quarterly*, 29: 355–372.

Bartunek, Jean M., Gordon, Judith R. and Weathersby, Rita Preszler (1983) 'Developing "complicated" understanding in administrators', *Academy of Management Review*, 8: 273–284.

Cohen, Michael D., March, James G. and Olsen, Johan P. (1972) 'A garbage can model of organizational choice', *Administrative Science Quarterly*, 17: 1–25.

Daft, Richard L. and Macintosh, Norman B. (1981) 'A tentative exploration into the amount and equivocality of information processing in organizational work units', *Administrative Science Quarterly*, 26: 207–224.

Daft, Richard L. and Weick, Karl E. (1984) 'Toward a model of organizations as interpretation systems', *Academy of Management Review*, 9: 284–295.

Dutton, Jane E. and Dukerich, Janet M. (1991) 'Keeping an eye on the mirror: Image and identity in organizational adaptation', *Academy of Management Journal*, 34: 517–554.

Einhorn, H.J. and Hogarth, R.M. (1986) 'Judging probable cause', *Psychological Bulletin*, 99: 3–19.

Feldman, Martha S. (1989) *Order without Design: Information Production and Policy Making*. Stanford, CA: Stanford University Press.

Ford, Jeffrey D. (1985) 'The effects of causal attributions on decision makers' responses to performance downturns', *Academy of Management Review*, 10: 770–786.

Giddens, A. (1984) *The Constitution of Society: Outline of the Theory of Structuration*. Berkeley, CA: University of California.

Glassman, Robert B. (1973) 'Persistence and loose coupling in living systems', *Behavioral Science*, 18: 83–98.

Heider, F. (1958) *The Psychology of Interpersonal Relations*. New York: Wiley.

Janis, I.L. (1972) *Victims of Groupthink: A Psychological Study of Foreign Policy Decisions and Fiascoes*. Boston, MA: Houghton Mifflin.

Kimberly, John R. (1984) 'Anatomy of organizational design', *Journal of Management*, 10: 109–126.

Manning, Peter K. (1982) 'Producing drama: Symbolic communication and the police', *Symbolic Interaction*, 5: 223–241.

March, James G. (1981) 'Footnotes to organizational change', *Administrative Science Quarterly*, 26: 563–577.

Meyer, A.D. (1982) 'Adapting to environmental jolts', *Administrative Science Quarterly*, 27: 515–537.

Nemeth, C.J. (1986) 'Differential contributions of majority and minority influence', *Psychological Review*, 93: 23–32.

Orton, J. Douglas (1994) 'Reorganizing: An analysis of the 1976 reorganization of the U.S. intelligence community'. Unpublished PhD dissertation, University of Michigan.

Orton, J. Douglas and Weick, Karl E. (1990) 'Loosely coupled systems: A reconceptualization', *Academy of Management Review*, 15: 203–223.

Perrow, Charles (1979) *Complex Organizations: A Critical Essay*, 2nd edn. Glenview, IL: Scott, Foresman.

Porac, Joseph F., Thomas, Howard and Baden-Fuller, Charles (1989) 'Competitive groups as cognitive communities: The case of Scottish knitwear manufacturers', *Journal of Management Studies*, 26: 397–416.

Salancik, Gerald R. (1977) 'Commitment and the control of organizational behavior and belief', in B.M. Staw and G.R. Salancik (eds), *New Directions in Organizational Behavior*. Chicago, IL: St. Clair. pp. 1–54.

Smircich, Linda and Stubbart, Charles (1985) 'Strategic management in an enacted world', *Academy of Management Review*, 10: 724–736.

Walsh, James P. and Ungson, Gerardo Rivera (1991) 'Organizational memory', *Academy of Management Review*, 16(1): 57–91.

Webb, Eugene and Weick, Karl E. (1979) 'Unobtrusive measures in organizational theory: A reminder', *Administrative Science Quarterly*, 24: 650–659.

Weick, Karl E. (1969) *The Social Psychology of Organizing*. Reading, MA: Addison-Wesley.

Weick, Karl E. (1976) 'Educational organizations as loosely coupled systems', *Administrative Science Quarterly*, 21: 1–19.

Weick, Karl E. (1977) 'Enactment processes in organizations', in Barry Staw and Gerald Salancik (eds), *New Directions in Organizational Behavior*. Malabar, FL: Robert Krieger. pp. 267–300.

Weick, Karl E. (1979) *The Social Psychology of Organizing*, 2nd edn. Reading, MA: Addison-Wesley.

Weick, Karl E. (1980) 'Psychology as gloss', in R. Kachau and C.N. Cofer (eds), *Psychology's Second Century*. New York: Praeger. pp. 110–132.

Weick, Karl E. (1984) 'Small wins: Redefining the scale of social problems', *American Psychologist*, 39: 40–49.

Weick, Karl E. (1988) 'Enacted sensemaking in crisis situations', *Journal of Management Studies*, 25: 305–317.

Weick, Karl E. (1989a) 'Organized improvisation: 20 years of organizing', *Communication Studies*, 40: 241–248.

Weick, Karl E. (1989b) 'Theory construction as disciplined imagination', *Academy of Management Review*, 14: 532–550.

Weick, Karl E. (1993a) 'Sensemaking in organizations: Small structures with large consequences', in J.K. Murnighan (ed.), *Social Psychology in Organizations: Advances in Theory and Research*. Englewood Cliffs, NJ: Prentice Hall. pp. 10–37.

Weick, Karl E. (1993b) 'Organizational redesign as improvisation', in G.P. Huber and W.H. Glick (eds), *Organizational Change and Redesign: Ideas and Insights for Improving Performance*. New York: Oxford University Press. pp. 346–379.

Weick, Karl E. and Browning, L. D. (1986) 'Argument and narration in organizational communication', in J.G. Hunt and J.D. Blair (eds), *1986 Yearly Review of Management, Journal of Management*, 12: 243–259.

Weick, Karl E. and Gilfillan, D.P. (1971) 'Fate of arbitrary traditions in a laboratory microculture', *Journal of Personality and Social Psychology*, 17: 179–191.

Weick, Karl E. and Orton, J. Douglas (1986) 'Academic journals in the classroom', *Organizational Behavior Teaching Review*, 11: 27–42.

Weick, Karl E., Gilfillan, D.P. and Keith, T. (1973) 'The effect of composer credibility on orchestra performance', *Sociometry*, 36: 435–462.

10

The Epistemology of Strategic Consulting:
Generic Analytical Activities and Organizational Learning

James A. Phills Jr

In the last twenty years a great deal of concern and research has been directed toward the problem of strategic change in organizations (Boeker, 1989; Fombrun, 1992; Gersick, 1994; Hinings and Greenwood, 1988; Johnson, 1987; Lorsch, 1986; Miller and Chen, 1994; Pennings, 1985; Pettigrew, 1985, 1988; Pettigrew and Whipp, 1991; Quinn, 1978; Starkey and McKinlay, 1988; Tichy, 1983). The impetus for much of this work appears to be the difficulty and the importance of getting organizations to adapt their strategic postures to changes in their competitive environment. For example, research on strategic change often begins with observations of firms who have failed to adapt their strategies in response to market signals or changes in the nature of competition in their industry. Some authors cite the failures of the American automobile industry in the 1980s (Lawrence and Dyer, 1983; Mitroff and Mohrman, 1987; Tichy, 1983) and, more recently, the difficulties of giants such as IBM and Sears (Loomis and Mendes, 1993; Solomon and Underwood, 1993).

Reflecting on this difficulty, some writers have described the problem in terms of the inertial tendencies of organizational strategies, structures, configurations and mindsets (Bonoma, 1981; Burgelman, 1991; Fredrickson and Iaquinto, 1989; Haveman, 1992; Miller and Chen, 1994). While there is compelling evidence that at the organizational level inertia is partly due to economic forces (Ghemawat, 1991; Oster, 1982), most management scholars and practitioners appear to view it as a human and organizational problem. In addition, although some scholars argue that inertia is adaptive because of its link to stability and reproducibility (Hannan and Freeman, 1984), far more attention appears to be directed toward the challenge of creating strategic change rather than maintaining strategic stability.

As troubling as these accounts may be, frequently embedded in discussions of inertia is a more disturbing phenomenon. Even when faced with explicit, empirically grounded challenges to their strategic direction, organizations frequently *still fail* to adapt – at least to the degree that outsiders think they should. To the extent that this secondary form of inertia is both prevalent and problematic, it suggests important limitations to technical prescriptions for strategic flexibility that focus on more vigilant environmental monitoring, better competitive analysis, or more robust models of strategy.

Consulting and Competitive Beliefs

In attempting to understand the roots of the primary and secondary forms of inertia, one culprit suggested by research on strategic change is the competitive beliefs (including assumptions and values) that guide strategic choice and action (Harrigan, 1985; Lorsch, 1986; Mitroff and Mohrman, 1987; Porter, 1980; Waddock and Isabella, 1989). Moreover, the process of influencing such beliefs in developing and implementing strategies is a task that has an important behavioral, as well as technical analytical, component. Indeed, this task is often difficult for management consultants who are often quite sophisticated in using applied economic frameworks (see Caves, 1984; Oster, 1994; Porter, 1980, 1985) to diagnose competitive problems, but who still frequently encounter significant difficulty in using such diagnoses to facilitate strategic change in organizations (Argyris, 1985; Martin, 1993). Yet, consultants are typically hired specifically to help produce change, and thus are deeply involved in influencing competitive beliefs in organizations.

On a technical level, consultants conduct formal economic or competitive analyses of critical strategic problems and opportunities. These analyses entail a systematic examination of critical competitive beliefs. On a behavioral level, consultants undertake activities intended to ensure the implementation of recommendations emerging from a project (in other words, change). These activities necessarily include attempts to influence clients' competitive beliefs and behavior based on the technical analyses. Thus, the role and activities of strategy consultants create an ideal setting in which to study the phenomenon of interest because the consulting process involves: (1) explicit empirical examination of the validity of key competitive beliefs; and (2) systematic attempts to influence managers' competitive beliefs and assumptions as part of the implementation process. From this perspective, consultants' abilities to help clients reexamine the validity of their competitive beliefs and revise them appropriately – in effect to learn – are critical to their effectiveness.

One senior consultant described her experience on a major engagement:

> We had to prove [that our recommendation] was right many times before they believed us. Six months ago they thought we were dead wrong. We proved it fourteen different ways and they finally bought in, but it was an incredibly uphill battle . . . they have a lot of pat arguments which they kept bringing up until we finally put together enough [data and analysis] . . . after a while it is just having an answer to every argument.

Here, we see outside consultants hired at great expense to help a client organization that was in considerable financial difficulty – yet when the consultants challenged fundamental aspects of the client's conventional strategic wisdom, they encountered tremendous resistance from the managers they were hired to help. This puzzle is the practical impetus behind this research, which focuses on the secondary, more active form of inertia. Specifically, it examines explicit attempts by consultants to influence the competitive strategies and beliefs of managers in client organizations. The goal is to illuminate some of the mechanisms underlying the tendency for the beliefs and assumptions that shape strategic choices and actions to resist change.[1] This phenomenon was studied over a three-year period in a naturalistic context of consultant-facilitated strategy formulation and implementation efforts (Phills, 1994).

Below, I outline a general framework for understanding the process of strategic consulting. While there are both empirical and theoretical elements to this research, because of space limitations, I present only the theoretical component. The central elements of the framework are *Generic Analytical Activities* (GAAs). These activities were derived inductively from observations in a global strategy consulting firm which I will call Strategic Technology Associates (STA). Although this firm has a particular model of competitive strategy that is grounded in industrial economics, I believe GAAs are equally applicable to other consulting firms and models of strategy. Thus GAAs represent a kind of meta-model or *epistemology* of practice which is concerned with methods and standards for generating knowledge and determining its validity. This represents a fundamental concern in the philosophy of science (Kuhn, 1970; Popper, 1968) as well as in research methods in the behavioral sciences (Campbell and Stanley, 1966; Cook and Campbell, 1979; Kaplan, 1963; Rosenthal and Rosnow, 1984).

Consulting and Strategic Knowledge

Knowledge in the domain of strategy deals with the nature of competition in industries. This knowledge must first define the parameters and concepts that can be used to describe industries in general. Second, it must be specific in that its elements must be connectable to the particulars of an individual firm or industry. In addition, such knowledge must be normative and prescriptive (Bell et al., 1988) since it must be connectable to action, and be sufficiently comprehensive to deal with the effectiveness of action, where effectiveness derives from achieving desired outcomes at the organizational level (Argyris and Schön, 1978) – or, in the language of economics, at the level of the 'firm', where the primary desideratum is sustained above-average profitability or rents (Caves, 1984; Oster, 1994; Porter, 1980, 1985).

Consultants are brought in when there is some identifiable problem or opportunity that presents the client organization with a question of what action(s) to take. Typically, answering this question requires some understanding of causality in the client's business environment. This might involve determining why particular patterns of competitive or economic outcomes are observed in the industry (especially firm-level performance outcomes). There may also be issues of process, such as how the causal forces identified produced the outcomes observed. Often, there may be questions of extrapolation, such as what the industry will look like in the future. Ultimately, there will be questions about action such as: Given these competitive forces and trends, what should the company do? There may also be a series of more specific questions about how to concretize the general actions. For example, if a key action is to reduce costs, this presents managers with choices about which costs to reduce, what time frame to adopt, and how to assign responsibility for subtasks. Normally, such choices are considered part of the process of strategy implementation (Andrews, 1987; Galbraith and Kazanjian, 1986; Hrebiniak and Joyce, 1984). Collectively, these questions sketch the inquiry and problem-solving process that guides strategic consulting interventions.

To reiterate, the focus here is on understanding: (1) When and why are clients likely to accept or reject consultants' assertions? and (2) What leads to the difficulty that consultants and clients encounter in resolving differences productively, in the context of strategy formulation and implementation efforts (that is, what is it about the problems themselves, the consultants' diagnosis or advice, or the clients, that leads to differences in view and difficulty in resolving such differences)?[2] These questions represent an instance of the general problem of organizational learning (Argyris and Schön, 1978), where 'learning' involves reconciling conflicting competitive beliefs (or increasing consensus) while also increasing their validity and accuracy. This framing allows for the possibility that consultants as well as clients may revise their beliefs. Moreover, it shifts the focus from clients' acquiescence in the face of consultants' expertise and analyses (that is, the problem of persuasion) to the quality of the reasoning and action of both the clients and the consultants. As I will argue, the answer to the questions posed above lies partly in an understanding of the epistemology of consulting, particularly with respect to the GAAs that are outlined below and their attendant barriers to learning.

Generic Analytical Activities

GAAs Defined

As strategy consultants work with clients, they engage in four interrelated Generic Analytical Activities (GAAs): comparison, explanation, prediction and prescription. These GAAs are 'generic' in the sense that they can be observed across a broad range of strategic consulting engagements. GAAs are 'analytical' in the sense that they involve the systematic use of deductive or inductive reasoning to make inferences about competitive phenomena.[3] The notion of an 'activity' is broad; it encompasses everything from collecting data and performing analyses and experiments to communicating the conclusions of such investigations. The GAAs, in essence, represent the basic epistemic building blocks of competitive analysis. They are defined below in more detail:

- *Comparison* involves analyses that contrast two or more strategically relevant entities along one or more dimensions. For example, comparison would include: competitive cost analyses, analyses of customer perceptions, or evaluations of a company's products/services relative to a competitor's (differentiation).
- *Explanation* involves diagnoses of competitive phenomena (usually problems) that specify causal relationships among strategically important variables. For example, explanations would include assertions like 'profitability has declined because of increases in industry capacity and price cutting by new entrants'.
- *Prediction* involves forecasts and estimates of future events, quantities, relationships, or consequences of current actions. For example, predictions would include assertions like 'industry prices will decline' or 'industry sales will reach $3 billion within two years'.
- *Prescription* involves recommendations that a client implement specific decisions, initiatives, or policies intended to address a problem or an opportunity. For example, prescriptions would include assertions like 'you should consolidate your product line by thirty per cent' or 'capacity at Plant A should be expanded to 300 million pounds/year'.

Most of the competitive beliefs expressed or examined during a strategic consulting project are embedded within the context of one or more of these activities. Although I have separated GAAs for the conceptual purpose of identifying their distinctive features, in practice they are closely connected. Indeed, they typically occur as part of an integrated sequence of inferences, as I will illustrate shortly.

General Features of GAAs

Addressing strategic problems and opportunities necessarily involves all four GAAs. Each is essential to the process of strategic thinking and advising, and each is critical to the diagnostic and prescriptive reasoning that lies at the core of strategic consultation. In any particular consulting engagement, the elements of each GAA are derived from an overarching model of competition in industries and an understanding of the historical pattern of events connected with the particular client organization, its industry, and the strategic issue in question. In addition, there may be a kind of micro-causal model held by the client that can be characterized as the company's 'vision' (Collins and Porras, 1991; Senge, 1990), 'model of competitive advantage' (Martin, 1993), or 'organizational theory of action' (Argyris and Schön, 1978). This model will generally specify both a product-market concept and some type of organizational and managerial architecture for delivering the concept. Together, the overarching theory of competition and the organization specific information identify relevant variables and constructs, contain propositions about causal relationships among these variables, and detail a methodology for operationalizing these constructs. Consultants and clients draw on their respective models to assess the client organization's situation with respect to key variables (through analytic *comparisons*). They then *explain* the organization's past experience and current performance or industry outcomes, *predict* future outcomes resulting from current choices, and *prescribe* recommended strategic actions. Thus GAAs are ordinarily manifested as sequential steps in a line of reasoning that is similar to the series of inferences in Argyris and Schön's (1978) 'ladder of inference'. Such sequences appear within a single presentation as well as over the course of an engagement in the form of interrelated modules of work or analysis.

All four GAAs occur as part of attempts to structure and solve problems that are inherently very complex (Bower and Doz, 1979; Duncan, 1972; Schweiger et al., 1985). For example, strategic decisions are generally characterized by features such as uncertain outcomes, limited information and scarce resources. Competitive information is often difficult and costly to collect. Moreover, decision makers need to formulate modeling assumptions, estimate important parameters, and sample rather than collect data on entire populations of interest. Due to these sources of complexity and ambiguity, clients and consultants can develop conflicting beliefs for reasons that are primarily technical or cognitive. That is, these differences are based on informational or inferential factors and are thus rooted in the substance of the analysis.

A secondary feature of GAAs is that their implications often trigger emotional and motivational influences on behavior. This happens because GAAs diagnose problems and provide a guide for action. However, strategic choices and actions often entail shifts in allocation of power, resources and rewards. Because individuals have personal stakes and preferences around particular strategic choices and outcomes, GAAs can create a motivational basis for disagreement around competitive beliefs. I will expand on specific cognitive and motivational influences on learning in the discussion of each GAA.

GAAs and Barriers to Learning

When consultants and clients develop conflicting beliefs about strategic issues, these are situated in the context of GAAs. Each GAA is in turn associated with characteristic patterns of reasoning. Embedded in these patterns are predictable *barriers to learning*. The behavioral features of GAAs that are of interest here are those factors that contribute to initial differences in beliefs between consultants and clients, and make such differences more difficult to reconcile productively. These barriers to learning can be divided into two basic categories: *cognitive* and *motivational*. This distinction between cognitive and motivational influences corresponds closely to Abelson's (1963) seminal distinction between 'hot' and 'cold' cognition. In the domain of strategic decision making, there has been extensive treatment of the role of colder cognitive processes (Bazerman, 1986; Schwenk, 1988; Sims et al., 1986) as well as analyses that focus on motivational factors (Janis and Mann, 1977; Kets de Vries and Miller, 1984). In the organizational development literature, resistance to change has long been explained in terms of motivational mechanisms. These explanations reflect a broad set of inferred or imputed psychological motives such as maintaining control, reducing uncertainty, protecting self-esteem/impression management, minimizing effort or work demands; preventing disruption of social relationships (Ashforth and Lee, 1990; Kanter, 1985)

Although it is often difficult to distinguish between motivational and cognitive mechanisms, I use the distinction because of its heuristic value for understanding the challenge of learning in the context of GAAs and because it is pervasive in the literature.

In sum, each GAA is associated with identifiable barriers to learning. Some are unique to one, while others are applicable to multiple GAAs. The list of barriers discussed for each GAA is only partial. Nevertheless, it illustrates the connection between the cognitive and motivational features of GAAs and the difficulties consultants and clients have in reconciling divergent beliefs. In combination, these difficulties frequently act as a significant barrier to the implementation of major strategic changes. The challenge is to better understand how to enhance strategic adaptation in organizations, particularly by increasing the effectiveness of external consultants hired to intervene in these large social and economic systems.

Comparison

> The thing that was really hard . . . is we showed the clients their own inefficiencies. . . . You basically indict them by saying, 'I've been looking at five years of your costs, and I've cut them all these different ways, and I've run regression analyses. I've compared things, and talked to all of your managers; all of these graphs and quotes and implications that I've drawn out of this that say, this whole thing is not being managed very well'. That's a very hard thing for a manager to take. (A senior STA consultant)

Strategic analyses necessarily involve comparisons. They are critical to the reasoning process and *weltanschauung* of a strategic perspective. Indeed, a number of theoretical constructs central to strategic thinking, such as competitive advantage, differentiation, cost position (Porter, 1980, 1985), distinctive competence (Andrews, 1987) and core competence (Prahalad and Hamel, 1990) are relative and, therefore, have comparisons embedded in them. Furthermore, comparisons are an explicit part of many types of formal strategic analyses such as cost, customer positioning, and assessments of the sustainability or imitability of strategy (Ghemawat, 1991; Oster, 1994; Porter, 1985). The variables typically used in comparisons consist of various measures and determinants of performance such as product or business unit costs, product profitability, market share, customer satisfaction, customer profitability, product line or divisional profitability, growth, etc. As strategic analysts and advisors, consultants make extensive use of comparisons (see Zelazny, 1979).

In the real world of strategic decision making, comparisons contain inherent sources of *complexity* and *uncertainty*. They involve multiple, often interdependent, assumptions which are sensitive to implicit and explicit choices about sampling, reference points, measurement instruments and the operationalization of variables. In addition, clients and consultants typically bring different direct experiences (data) to bear on comparative analyses. Moreover, they often operate using different models of strategy, as well as styles and abilities. These potential sources of disagreement are primarily *cognitive*.

Multi-dimensional Reasoning

One of the primary cognitive barriers arises from the multi-dimensional nature of comparison. A critical feature of a comparison between two or more entities is the dimension(s) on which they are compared. In principle, entities have an infinite number of attributes and can be compared on multiple dimensions. Generally, they will be similar on some dimensions and dissimilar on others. For example, consider the proverbial injunction against comparing apples and oranges. Are they, or are they not, comparable? The answer depends on what dimensions are used. The two fruits might meaningfully be compared on dimensions such as caloric content, price, freshness, ease of consumption, fiber content and so on. Other dimensions such as 'peelability' or use for baking a pie, might be considered less meaningful because they are less relevant to one of the two. One could certainly argue that apples and oranges are 'different'. Nevertheless, if the purpose of the comparison was to decide which fruit to have for lunch, few would see the comparison as meaningless or somehow unfair. Yet, this appears to be precisely the reaction that managers often have to comparisons made for the purpose of evaluating and formulating strategy.

On one level, this is not surprising given that the terms 'different' and 'similar' are abstractions that can refer to a range of concrete attributes. In the case of strategic comparisons, people display a tendency to focus on whichever dimensions are most salient to them given their concerns, yet this selection occurs tacitly. Disagreement occurs over whether the entities are similar or different. It is unusual for explicit discussions to occur about which dimensions to consider and what inferences to make on the basis of the chosen dimensions.

Evaluation

Comparisons frequently contain implicit or explicit *evaluations* of past, present, and future competitive choices and performance. These evaluations are central to strategic thinking and necessary for decision making. Although on the surface most evaluations pertain to the firm, individuals are inevitably associated with strategic decisions and actions. This may be the result of formal responsibility or of informal roles in a particular strategic thrust. Consequently, any evaluation of competitive performance is frequently extrapolated to an evaluation of specific individuals. When negative or mixed, these can become (or appear to become) a *threat* to the material and/or psychological interests of those implicated. This introduces a *motivational* dimension that can exacerbate the difficulties and barriers consultants and clients already face as a result of the cognitive issues. Indeed, one feature of strategic comparisons that remains relatively consistent is the threat created by the public examination of such data. Thus, comparison is an activity fraught with all the perils and threats of performance evaluation in organization (cf. Beer, 1991). Nevertheless, while the task of performance evaluation is generally recognized as a behavioral and interpersonal task, comparison in the context of strategy formulation and implementation is primarily viewed as a technical challenge (Argyris, 1985).

Explanation

> Initially, the study was focused on the new Apollo product. We spent a month, and it became clear that [Apollo and the core] businesses were inextricably tied to one another. You make [both] products with the same capital. So the tremendous excess capacity was a problem for both. Second, there were dramatic changes in the industry that were attacking both businesses. Apollo was unique in that it had marketing problems – [the targeted] customers don't want it. But the industry forces were the same. The distinction in the clients' mind between this dog of a business and this cash cow was going to have to be broken down. (A senior STA consultant)

Addressing strategic problems and opportunities necessarily involves the development of explanations. They are critical to the diagnostic and prescriptive reasoning that lies at the core of strategic consultation. Drawing on their respective models of competition, consultants and clients assess the organization's situation and *explain* its past events, outcomes and especially performance. If the consultant's mission is to enhance their clients' performance, they must evaluate and identify the causes of poor or limited performance. As a result, the competence and decisions of managers responsible for the activities driving performance outcome can come into question. These explanations, and the models from which they stem, form the basis for future choices and actions.

Explanations share many sources of complexity common to all GAAs, but more importantly, they entail difficulties associated with making causal inferences about complex systems when it is impossible to conduct controlled experiments (Campbell and Stanley, 1966; Rosenthal and Rosnow, 1984) and especially when such systems are composed of human beings (Lincoln and Guba, 1985). In most instances, the strategic problems faced by clients involve a large number of variables and complex relationships (or 'interaction effects' in the language of multivariate statistics). Furthermore, both the value of variables and their relationship to one another are often changing in ways that are difficult to detect because they are not directly observable, or involve stochastic processes, or occur very gradually. These are conditions under which there is voluminous evidence of the fallibility of human judgment (Hogarth, 1980; Kahneman et al., 1982). Especially prone to error are inferential processes involved in judgments about correlation and causality that are at the heart of explanation (Jennings et al., 1982). As a result of these difficulties, conflicting interpretations of the causes of important outcomes can develop for reasons that are largely cognitive.

Comprehension and Abstraction

One of the major barriers to learning in the context of explanations lies in the constructs used as part of this GAA. The problem stems from the conceptually and analytically elaborate constructs used as part of explanations. These are frequently abstract and characterized by multiple attributes and nested (for example, Porter's (1980, 1985) notions of industry structure or the value chain). Since the constructs are second nature to the consultants, it may not occur to them that inertia may result from the different understandings of these constructs or a lack of comprehension.[4] Ironically, the very skillfulness and familiarity that consultants have with the constructs can blind them to clients' confusion. This difficulty can be understood in terms of the highly elaborate but tacit cognitive structures or 'schemata' (Bartlett, 1932; Bougon et al., 1977; Weick, 1979) that are invoked in solving difficult problems. The problem of comprehension and abstraction is exacerbated by the impact of stress, threat and embarrassment on human reasoning and action. Argyris (1991) has described how people tend: (1) to state their conclusions and beliefs at relatively high levels of inference, that is, without the data or the reasoning behind them; (2) to see these conclusions as concrete and obvious; and (3) to form assumptions about other actors' reactions which prevents them from inquiring into the reasoning behind these reactions. In the face of conflicting views, these tendencies lead to the escalation or polarization of disagreements. Finally, the sheer number of constructs and the volume of data associated with efforts to demonstrate relationships among them often preclude the detailed explicit reasoning required to resolve conflicting conclusions.

Control: The Retrospective Bias

Strategic explanations identify the key causal factors behind organizational performance. Two characteristics of these factors are the degree to which (1) they are (or were) controllable; and (2) they are (or were) foreseeable by managers. These are important because, like comparisons, explanations produce evaluations of past and present competitive decisions and actions – and therefore of individuals. Even though explanations may appear to be simple descriptions of a competitive situation, they can become a threat to individual clients when they imply a causal relationship between managerial action and negative performance outcomes. This introduces a motivational dimension that exacerbates the cognitive difficulties already inherent in the task of explaining competitive problems and opportunities.

Control is at the heart of what it means to manage. The American Heritage Dictionary (1992) defines 'manage' as to 'exert control over'. Explanation as an analytical activity is, in turn, intimately connected to control. The problem with learning in the context of explanation occurs because retrospectively, managers responsible for choices leading to negative outcomes often resist explanations focusing on controllable (or foreseeable) causes of these outcomes. In contrast to predictions, explanations deal with the causes of past (versus future) outcomes. This tendency is consistent with empirical evidence of bias in individual (Kunda, 1987; Riess and Taylor, 1984) and organizational (Bettman and Weitz, 1983; Staw et al., 1983) attributions about performance. However, controversy exists over the relative importance of cognitive versus motivational mechanisms in producing this bias (Tetlock and Levi, 1982; Zuckerman, 1979).

The retrospective attributional bias has been described in terms of individuals' propensity for self-justification and ego-defensiveness, which are in turn related to the drive to preserve self-esteem and the favorable impressions of others (Huber et al., 1986; Staw et al., 1983). Indeed, in actual consulting engagements, defensive behavior is particularly likely to occur in threatening or embarrassing situations (Argyris, 1985), as is often the case with explanations of poor performance. This often leads consultants to be concerned about offering explanations of negative outcomes that highlight controllable or foreseeable causes of these outcomes.

The core motivational dynamic around the retrospective bias is that explanations contain assertions about the causes of outcomes. When these are negative, attributing causal significance to variables that are controllable (for instance, actions, decisions, or inaction) or foreseeable produces an evaluation. In effect, explanations surface mistakes by providing direct empirical data on the effectiveness and logic of managerial choices. As with comparison, evaluations can threaten clients' reputations, careers, compensation and other interests.

Prediction

> The [client] had a report from an independent consultant that had predicted billions of dollars by 1995. . . . We didn't think the market was anywhere near [that]. . . . We came back and said, 'The market is really small, very profitable, with lots of inefficient pricing right now. As it grows, producers are going to

become more efficient. [At larger] quantities they are going to be able to make it cheaper and the price is going to fall. . . . Then we built a cost model of plants and figured out what the costs actually were. We figured they had to be making ridiculously high margins – thirty percent. And that is just not sustainable. . . . We did a lot of buyer analysis to figure out how much [buyers] would use and to what price it would have to fall. . . . The clients would agree, but when it came to the bottom line which was, 'This market is going to be $500 million, not $2 billion', all of a sudden, they did not want to hear anything any more. [Even though they agreed with all the pieces] they just didn't want to listen. It seemed irrational. (A senior STA consultant)

Predictions involve forecasts or estimates of future, events, quantities, or relationships.[5] Part of their significance arises from the fact that strategic problems and opportunities exist in a dynamic context, meaning decision makers must consider changes in relevant variables and relationships over time. In fact, competitive problems often stem from changes in the structure and nature of competition in an industry, such as the shift between rapid growth of emerging industries and the slow or negative growth and increasing competition that typically characterizes mature industries (Harrigan, 1985; Porter, 1985). Hence, strategy necessarily involves assumptions and beliefs about events that may occur in the future, what the industry will look like in the future, and the consequences that will result from an organization's actions.

Predictions about competitive phenomena, such as projections about industry demand or the behavior of competitors can be empirically based. For example, they might be direct or adjusted extrapolations of historical trends such as in conventional forecasting. Alternatively, predictions may be theoretically grounded. They might be derived from explicit models of competition such as game theoretic approaches to strategy (see Dixit and Nalebuff, 1991) or models of systematic and stochastic processes such as in scenario analysis (see Wack, 1985). Regardless of the mix of theoretical and empirical methods, the logic by which consultants or clients form predictions can be explicit or implicit. When the derivation is explicit, the prediction tends to be framed in the language of analysis and formal models. When the derivation is implicit, the prediction tends to be framed in the language of experience, judgment, or intuition. Either way, predictions are inherently complex because they must take into account many variables, relationships, and sources of uncertainty. Again, clients and consultants often reach conflicting conclusions about the future and have difficulty resolving these differences for reasons that are primarily cognitive.

Risk and Uncertainty

Predictions involve risk. Moreover, clients and consultants are affected differently by the range of possible outcomes of strategic actions and, therefore, have different interests, preferences and postures toward such uncertainty. Clients have to manage the future about which predictions are made. More importantly, they will be held accountable for the consequences of their strategic choices in the face of these predictions.

A common point of contention between clients and consultants involves differences over estimates of the likelihood of (or preferences for) undesired outcomes.[6] Sometimes conflict stems from the fact that they see the risks differently. Certain risks may be more salient for clients, and, therefore, clients may judge them as being more likely (Tversky and Kahneman, 1974). In instances where conflict is related to preferences for outcomes (rather than estimates of their probability), this is usually due to the implications such outcomes have for clients. Often, the real and perceived personal costs of negative outcomes carry a greater weight with the clients than does the probabilistic likelihood of such an outcome, especially when it concerns their accountability for future financial or operational results. This pattern is especially pronounced when clients view the outcomes as uncertain, and therefore risky. Consultants frame this behavior in terms of risk aversion (although there are different manifestations of risk aversion; see Hilton, 1989) or defensiveness. Nevertheless, in many circumstances, clients' fears may be quite reasonable, particularly in organizations where the culture and incentive systems punish failure to deliver predicted results. For their part, clients see consultants as overconfident, even cavalier, about predictions that they won't have to 'live with'. These differences may reflect a more general difference between consultants and clients with respect to their exposure to formal theoretical models and frameworks for analyzing uncertainty related to business decisions. Some evidence on decision-making suggests that risk aversion is attenuated through the application of formal models (Hammond, 1967).

Control: The Prospective Bias

Prediction is prey to a second bias around the issue of control that becomes apparent when the focus is on competitive beliefs about the future. More specifically, there is a peculiar duality to the way managers view their ability to control organizational outcomes. On one hand, *retrospectively*, managers responsible for choices leading to negative outcomes often resist explanations focusing on controllable (or foreseeable) causes of these outcomes. On the other hand, *prospectively*, they appear to have a bias toward believing they can control important outcomes. In the context of prediction this bias is manifested when predictions focus on the uncontrollable determinants of performance outcomes. This bias is consistent with evidence of the aversive nature of uncontrollability (Seligman, 1975) and the tendency for people to prefer and benefit from situations where they can (or believe they can) exert control (Langer, 1983).

One senior consultant noted the two sides of the control issue:

> If their business is doing well, clients want to believe it is because of their own brilliance. If they are doing poorly, they want to believe it is due to circumstances outside of their control. . . . These [biases] tend to be enduring because

they create a culture that either says, 'No matter what we do it is not going to help. So why should I change?' or swashbuckling like, 'Anything we try is great'.

This quotation aptly captures the classic ego-defensive or self-serving attribution bias postulated by Heider (1958) and observed in organizational attributions about performance (Bettman and Weitz, 1983; Staw et al., 1983).

The duality between retrospective vs prospective postures toward control could also be framed in terms of optimistic vs pessimistic explanatory style (Seligman and Schulman, 1986). In this line of research, the bias toward control is manifested in much the same way, although the beneficial aspects of attributional distortion for performance outcomes are emphasized. Notably, however, notions such as 'learning' and 'valid information' (Argyris and Schön, 1978) are not among the outcomes selected.

Prescription

> We were talking about taking four or five million dollars out of this plant. . . . That's two hundred people that Joe [the plant manager] knows personally. For Joe, that's his life. Those are his neighbors. If they lose their jobs, then they still live next door to him. So he's wild about [the recommendations]. . . . Joe can be very nice and pleasant most of the time. But now he just goes nuts. . . . He agrees that the numbers are right, but then he says, 'We're talking about two hundred people who work at this plant today, who are going to be out of work if we do this. Have you ever had to lay off two hundred people? Okay, fine. The analysis is right. The Japanese are coming. We've got all that. But I can't do this. You can't ask me to kill my children. You can't do that. Have you ever had to kill your children Peter? I bet you haven't.' (A senior STA consultant)

A prescription is a recommendation that clients implement a specific decision, initiative, or policy designed to address a strategic problem or opportunity. It is based on a conviction that the recommended action will either produce desired outcomes (for instance, reduced costs) or ameliorate undesired outcomes (such as poor product quality). As noted earlier, this is a particular type of prediction – one that deals with causal relationships between current actions and future outcomes. Correcting strategic problems or taking advantage of opportunities requires concrete choices and actions. Thus, consultants can only help clients improve their firm's competitive position and performance through the implementation of specific strategic and operational recommendations.

Prescriptions also represent attempts to design action while taking into account a complex array of economic and behavioral variables, the interrelationships among them, and the imperfect information and uncertainty associated with strategic problems and opportunities. Thus, prescriptions are necessarily incomplete. These sources of ambiguity and potential error constitute fertile soil for disagreements based primarily on cognitive or technical factors.

Risk and Feasibility

In the context of prescription, contention sometime arises between clients and consultants, not because clients doubt the underlying causal relationships or efficacy of recommendations, but because they see obstacles that could prevent them from implementing the recommendations derived from the analysis. The issue is not so much one of validity as it is one of *feasibility*. The risks connected with concerns about feasibility may involve the failure to produce desired consequences, or the occurrence of undesired consequences. In either case, risk stems from barriers that could prevent timely and/or effective implementation of strategic recommendations. In addition, differences can arise (1) over clients' and consultants' estimates of the likelihood of desired outcomes, (2) over their preferences for these outcomes, or (3) over their risk profile or preferences for various probability distributions for these outcomes.

These divergences should not be surprising given that the implications of the range of possible outcomes for the two parties may be quite different indeed. Common examples include the personal costs associated with the different types of errors: what are commonly distinguished as Type I versus Type II errors (cf. Kaplan, 1963) or 'errors of commission' versus 'errors of omission' (Ghemawat, 1991: 147–151). These distinctions correspond to strategic initiatives that are pursued and fail as opposed to those that would ultimately succeed, but are not pursued. Clients' judgments and preferences may lead them to be less willing to adopt changes in strategy that consultants see as beneficial, but which clients see as risky or infeasible.

Vested Interests and Organizational Politics

Because of their concrete links to change, prescriptions trigger motivational forces that exacerbate the barriers to learning consultants and clients already face as a result of cognitive factors. Prescriptions (if implemented) almost always lead to changes that affect the material and psychological interests of individuals and subgroups within the organization. In this sense, they present the most directly identifiable threats and opportunities to managers and employees of the client organization. Again, these threats and opportunities are usually a direct result of managers' preferences for, or vested interest in, particular strategic alternatives (Bower, 1970; Donaldson and Lorsch, 1983; Ghemawat, 1991). The interests and the behaviors manifested in pursuit of them are often characterized as organizational politics (Bower and Doz, 1979; Pettigrew, 1973; Pfeffer, 1992), although researchers' use of the term 'politics' varies with respect to whether it encompasses functional as well as dysfunctional processes and behavior (Drory and Romm, 1990; Mayes and Allen, 1977).

Perhaps the most frequently offered explanations of inertia have to do with 'client politics'. Consultants, in particular, use this term to refer to situations in which they believe clients' reasoning and actions are designed to protect vested interests or pursue hidden agendas. At the group level, clients may be seen as protecting or furthering local functional, departmental, or geographic interests. Often these involve deflecting responsibility for problems or gaining or preserving access to financial, material, or human resources. At the individual level, 'politics' is usually used to characterize behavior designed to protect or further personal interests such as job security, career advancement, rewards, power or to protect the interests of an organizational subunit, such as access to scarce resources.

These concerns are characteristic or illustrative of more general work-related motives or classes of outcomes which managers prefer and actively pursue in organizational settings (Vroom, 1964/1995). Structurally, they resemble and are probably closely related to more basic human motivations such as the needs for achievement, power and affiliation (McClelland and Steele, 1973) or self-efficacy (Bandura, 1977).

Often political motives and actions are covert, meaning that managers cannot legitimately pursue them publicly (Mayes and Allen, 1977) because they are likely to be seen as inconsistent with (or orthogonal to) the best interests of the organization. This is especially true for individuals' attempts to pursue self-interests (as opposed to parochial subgroup political behavior). This occurs because local organizational concerns are viewed as more legitimate, or at least as inevitable. Pursuit of individual goals (at the expense of organizational goals) is less likely to be organizationally sanctioned. Despite the pervasiveness of clandestine behavior and motives in discussions of politics, some treatments of the term frame the construct in neutral terms of power and influence (see Pfeffer, 1992).

To review, consultants' political interpretations of inertia hold that clients cling to pre-existing competitive beliefs about their business (1) to cover-up or deny past mistakes and poor decisions, (2) to conceal or minimize current performance deficiencies, (3) to protect their personal career opportunities or the careers of their subordinates, or (4) to justify opportunities that they want to pursue. Nevertheless, despite the ease with which political explanations are invoked, consultants appear to recognize the difficulty of validating them or ruling out alternative explanations of client behavior. Yet the domain (interpersonal and organizational behavior) is one in which their conventional epistemology fails. The consultant cannot measure objectively, cannot quantify, cannot conduct public tests without an epistemology and model of behavioral intervention to complement their applied economic theory.

Conclusions and Implications

The framework presented in this chapter has both theoretical and practical implications. Theoretically, the notion of GAAs provides a more detailed view of the epistemological foundations for strategy development efforts, particularly as conducted by management consultants. The activities of comparison, explanation, prediction and prescription capture the patterns of reasoning and inference observed in actual strategy development efforts. Conceptually, the process of formulating and modifying corporate and competitive strategies, particularly the initial stage of reexamining and reformulating the premises (beliefs), represents a critical form of organization learning.

Closely linked to GAAs are barriers to learning or traps that can arise in the context of these activities. Clearly, the list and descriptions of barriers outlined here are preliminary. Nevertheless, they begin to illustrate the cognitive and motivational mechanisms that can inhibit learning. Hence, these barriers are central to understanding the impact of consultants' interventions.

The theoretical contributions of this work lead directly to its implications for practice. GAAs can be linked to fundamental epistemological constructs, and hence point to new ways of reflecting on and talking more explicitly about the validity of strategic knowledge, the analyses that generate it, and the effectiveness of strategic action. Furthermore, by increasing their awareness of the source of potential barriers, consultants should be able to anticipate and intervene more effectively to facilitate learning in the face of inertia. This awareness might even inform the design of technical analyses and the structure of whole consulting engagements. For example, comparisons could include more exhaustive lists of the range of dimensions (qualitative and quantitative) of entities. They might also deal more explicitly with the controllability of such dimensions. This would begin to reduce the problematic aspects of multi-dimensional reasoning in comparison. Similarly, consultants might incorporate more education around critical concepts and tools into their engagements and also design ways of testing more explicitly the adequacy of both their own and their clients' understanding. These steps would begin to address the barrier of comprehension in the context of explanation.

Despite the potential utility of this framework, there are a number of important caveats. First, the interventions that deal with the motivational barriers to learning are more complex because of the interpersonal competence required (Argyris, 1989). While there are a variety of models for dealing with the behavioral aspects of strategic change (see Argyris and Schön, 1978; Beer et al., 1990; Floyd and Woolridge, 1992; Quinn, 1980; Tichy, 1983), the skills and organizational capabilities required tend to be difficult to learn and institutionalize. Second, there are a number of gaps in this framework that need to be addressed by future research. For example, it is important to explore the applicability of the framework in light of models of strategy other than that of STA. Additional GAAs may be necessary to encompass a broader range of analytical models of strategy. Another key area for exploration is that of expanding the list of barriers to learning for the four GAAs.

These caveats notwithstanding, the framework represents an important step in expanding knowledge about strategic change that integrates economic/strategic variables with behavioral/organizational constructs. More specifically, it begins to provide a more detailed understanding of the micro-processes that underlie the phenomenon of inertia that economically-oriented strategists have found so frustrating and bewildering (Harrigan, 1985; Porter, 1980). Moreover, the framework suggests ways to enhance learning that go beyond the 'great deal of convincing data and evidence' suggested by Porter (1980: xix) and illustrates the fundamental connection between organizational learning and competitive advantage – the theme of the current volume. In this regard, it builds on existing efforts to develop integrative and interdisciplinary perspectives on strategic change (see Argyris, 1985; Donaldson and Lorsch, 1983; Hinings and Greenwood, 1988; Kanter, 1989; Martin, 1993; Miller, 1990; Pettigrew, 1988; Porter, 1991; Starkey and McKinlay, 1988). Hopefully, future work will further advance our understanding of the relationships between technical management disciplines of economics, finance, accounting and strategy, and approaches to management grounded in the behavioral sciences such as organizational learning.

Notes

This research was supported in part by the Harvard Business School, Yale School of Management, and the consulting firm in which the field research was conducted. I am grateful for the helpful comments made on earlier drafts by Chris Argyris and Richard Hackman, and for the assistance of Tolan Steele and Mike Toffel.

1 In this chapter I set aside the normative question of whether consultants' advice is valid or usable. Admittedly, it is sometimes neither. The ability of researchers to resolve this question awaits a more robust and comprehensive model of strategy.

2 Following Nickerson (1986), the term 'assertion' is used to refer to the explicit expression of a belief as well as a basic element of an argument or line of reasoning.

3 Similar accounts of basic inferential tasks appear in the fields of cognitive and social psychology (Kahneman and Tversky, 1973; Kaplan, 1963; Nisbett and Ross, 1980), economics (Coats, 1989; Secord, 1986), organization theory (Cyert and Grunberg, 1963) and more general treatises on epistemology and methodology (Campbell and Stanley, 1966; Cook and Campbell, 1979; Kuhn, 1962/1970; Popper, 1968; Stinchcombe, 1968).

4 Again, I set aside the question of whether lack of comprehension is a function of the clients' or the consultants' attributes. These are instances where clients appear not to understand a construct.

5 Predictions can also involve the consequences of particular actions such as the assertion that building a new plant will reduce costs and/or increase productivity. When such consequences represent desired end-states or intended outcomes, these actions and predictions form the basis for prescriptions, which I will discuss in the next section. For the purposes of this discussion, predictions about consequences of actions that have clear normative implications will be treated as prescriptions.

6 In addition to concerns about outcomes that *might* occur (risk), there may be circumstances where consultants or clients are relatively certain about outcomes that will/will not occur. The problem is then one of *feasibility*, which is most relevant to the GAA of prescription and is discussed in the next section.

References

Abelson, R.P. (1963) 'Computer simulations of "hot" cognitions', in S.S. Tomkins and S. Messick (eds), *Computer Simulations of Personality*. New York: Wiley. pp. 277–298.

American Heritage Dictionary (1992) *American Heritage Dictionary*, 3rd edn. Boston, MA: Houghton Mifflin.

Andrews, K.R. (1987) *The Concept of Corporate Strategy*, 3rd edn. Homewood, IL: Irwin.

Argyris, C. (1985) *Strategy, Change and Defensive Routines*. Marshfield, MA: Pitman Publishing Inc.

Argyris, C. (1989) 'Strategy implementation: An experience in learning', *Organizational Dynamics*, 18(2): 5–15.

Argyris, C. (1991) *Overcoming Organizational Defenses*. Boston, MA: Allyn-Bacon.

Argyris, C. and Schön, D.A. (1978) *Organizational Learning*. Reading, MA: Addison-Wesley.

Ashforth, B.E. and Lee, R.T. (1990) 'Defensive behavior in organizations: A preliminary model', *Human Relations*, 43(7): 621–649.

Bandura, A. (1977) 'Toward a unifying theory of behavioral change', *Psychological Review*, 84(2): 191–215.

Bartlett, F.C. (1932) *Remembering*. Cambridge: Cambridge University Press.

Bazerman, M.H. (1986) *Judgment in Managerial Decision Making*. New York: John Wiley.

Beer, M. (1991) 'Making performance appraisal work', in J.J. Gabarro (ed.), *Managing People and Organizations*. Boston, MA: Harvard Business School Press. pp. 195-212.

Beer, M., Eisenstat, R.A. and Spector, B. (1990) *The Critical Path to Corporate Renewal*. Boston, MA: Harvard Business School Press.

Bell, D.E., Raiffa, H. and Tversky, A. (1988) 'Descriptive, normative, and prescriptive interactions in decision making', in D.E. Bell, H. Raiffa and A. Tversky (eds), *Decision Making: Descriptive, Normative, and Prescriptive Interactions*. Cambridge: Cambridge University Press. pp. 9–30.

Bettman, J.R. and Weitz, B.A. (1983) 'Attributions in the board room: Causal reasoning in corporate annual reports', *Administrative Science Quarterly*, 28(2): 165–183.

Boeker, W. (1989) 'Strategic change: The effects of founding and history', *Academy of Management Journal*, 32(3): 489–515.

Bonoma, T.V. (1981) 'Market success can breed marketing inertia', *Harvard Business Review*, 59(5): 115–121.

Bougon, M.G., Weick, K.E. and Binkhorst, D. (1977) 'Cognition in organizations: An analysis of the Utrecht Jazz Orchestra', *Administrative Science Quarterly*, 22(4): 606–639.

Bower, J.L. (1970) *Managing the Resource Allocation Process: A Study of Corporate Planning and Investment*. Boston, MA: Harvard Business School, Division of Research.

Bower, J.L. and Doz, Y. (1979) 'Strategy formulation: A social and political process', in D.E. Schendel and C.W. Hofer (eds), *Strategic Management: A New View of Business Policy and Planning*. Boston, MA: Little, Brown. pp. 152–166.

Burgelman, R.A. (1991) 'Intraorganizational ecology of strategy making and organizational adaptation', *Organization Science*, 2(3): 239–262.

Campbell, D.T. and Stanley, J.C. (1966) *Experimental and Quasi-experimental Designs for Research*. Chicago, IL: Rand McNally.

Caves, R.E. (1984) 'Economic analysis and the quest for competitive advantage', *American Economic Review*, 74(2): 127–132.

Coats, A.W.S. (1989) 'Explanations in history and economics', *Social Research*, 56(2): 331–360.

Collins, J.C. and Porras, J.I. (1991) 'Organizational vision and visionary organizations', *California Management Review*, 34(1): 30–52.

Cook, T.D. and Campbell, D.T. (1979) *Quasi-experimentation: Design and Analysis Issues for Field Settings*. Boston, MA: Houghton Mifflin.

Cyert, R. and Grunberg, E. (1963) 'Assumption, prediction, and explanation in economics', in R.M. Cyert and J.G. March (eds), *A Behavioral Theory of the Firm*. Englewood Cliffs, NJ: Prentice Hall. pp. 298–311.

Dixit, A.K. and Nalebuff, B.J. (1991) *Thinking Strategically: The Competitive Edge in Business, Politics, and Everyday Life*. New York: Norton.

Donaldson, G. and Lorsch, J.W. (1983) *Decision Making at the Top*. New York: Basic Books.

Drory, A. and Romm, T. (1990) 'The definition of organizational politics: A review', *Human Relations*, 43(11): 1133–1155.

Duncan, R.B. (1972) 'Characteristics of organizational environments and perceived environmental uncertainty', *Administrative Science Quarterly*, 17(3): 313–327.

Floyd, S.W. and Woolridge, B. (1992) 'Managing strategic consensus: The foundation of effective implementation', *Academy of Management Executive*, 6(4): 27–39.

Fombrun, C.J. (1992) *Turning Points: Creating Strategic Change in Corporations*. New York: McGraw-Hill.

Fredrickson, J.W. and Iaquinto, A. (1989) 'Inertia and creeping rationality in strategic decision processes', *Academy of Management Journal*, 32(3): 516–542.

Galbraith, J.R. and Kazanjian, R.K. (1986) *Strategy Implementation: Structure, Systems, and Process*. St. Paul, MN: West.

Gersick, C.J.G. (1994) 'Pacing strategic change: The case of a new venture', *Academy of Management Journal*, 37(1): 9–45.

Ghemawat, P. (1991) *Commitment: The Dynamic of Strategy*. New York: Free Press.

Hammond, J.S. (1967) 'Better decisions with preference theory', *Harvard Business Review*, 45(6): 123–141.

Hannan, M.T. and Freeman, J. (1984) 'Structural inertia and organizational change', *American Sociological Review*, 49(2): 149–164.

Harrigan, K.R. (1985) *Strategic Flexibility: A Management Guide for Changing Times*. Lexington, MA: Lexington Books.

Haveman, H.A. (1992) 'Between a rock and a hard place: Organizational change and performance under conditions of fundamental environmental transformation', *Administrative Science Quarterly*, 37(1): 48-75.

Heider, F. (1958) *The Psychology of Interpersonal Relations*. New York: Wiley.

Hilton, R.W. (1989) 'Risk attitude under random utility', *Journal of Mathematical Psychology*, 33(2): 206–222.

Hinings, C.R. and Greenwood, R. (1988) *The Dynamics of Strategic Change*. New York: Basil Blackwell.

Hogarth, R.M. (1980) *Judgment and Choice: The Psychology of Decision*. Chichester: Wiley.

Hrebiniak, L.G. and Joyce, W.F. (1984) *Implementing Strategy*. New York: Macmillan.

Huber, V.L., Podsakoff, P.M. and Todor, W.D. (1986) 'An investigation of biasing factors in the attributions of subordinates and their supervisors', *Journal of Business Research*, 14(1): 83–97.

Janis, I.L. and Mann, L. (1977) *Decision Making: A Psychological Analysis of Conflict, Choice and Commitment*. New York: Free Press.

Jennings, D.L., Amabile, T.M. and Ross, L. (1982) 'Informal covariation assessment: Data-based versus theory based judgments', in D. Kahneman, P. Slovic and A. Tversky (eds), *Judgment Under Uncertainty: Heuristics and Biases*. Cambridge: Cambridge University Press. pp. 211-230.

Johnson, G. (1987) *Strategic Change and the Management Process*. New York: Basil Blackwell.

Kahneman, D. and Tversky, A. (1973) 'On the psychology of prediction', *Psychological Review*, 80: 237–251.

Kahneman, D., Slovic, P. and Tversky, D. (eds) (1982) *Judgment Under Uncertainty: Heuristics and Biases*. Cambridge: Cambridge University Press.

Kanter, R.M. (1985) 'Managing the human side of change', *Management Review*, 74(4): 52–56.

Kanter, R.M. (1989) *When Giants Learn to Dance: Mastering the Challenges of Strategy, Management, and Careers in the 1990s*. New York: Simon and Schuster.

Kaplan, A. (1963) *The Conduct of Inquiry: Methodology for the Behavioral Sciences*. New York: Harper and Row.

Kets de Vries, M.F.R. and Miller, D. (1984) *The Neurotic Organization: Diagnosing and Changing Counterproductive Styles of Management*. San Francisco, CA: Jossey-Bass.

Kuhn, T. (1970) *The Structure of Scientific Revolutions*, 2nd edn. University of Chicago: Hackett.

Kuhn, T.S. (1962/1970) *The Structure of Scientific Revolutions*, vol. 2, 2nd edn. Chicago, IL: University of Chicago Press.

Kunda, Z. (1987) 'Motivated inference: Self-serving generation and evaluation of causal theories', *Journal of Personality and Social Psychology*, 53(4): 636–647.

Langer, E. (1983) *The Psychology of Control*. Beverly Hills, CA: Sage.

Lawrence, P.R. and Dyer, D. (1983) *Renewing American Industry: Organizing for Efficiency and Innovation*. New York: Free Press.

Lincoln, Y.S. and Guba, E.G. (1985) *Naturalistic Inquiry*. Beverly Hills, CA: Sage.

Loomis, C.J. and Mendes, J. (1993) 'Dinosaurs?' *Fortune*, 3 May: 32.

Lorsch, J.W. (1986) 'Managing culture: The invisible barrier to strategic change', *California Management Review*, 28(2): 95–109.

McClelland, D.C. and Steele, R.S. (1973) *Human Motivation: A Book of Readings*. Morristown, NJ: General Learning Press.

Martin, R. (1993) 'Changing the mind of the corporation', *Harvard Business Review*, 71(6): 81–89.

Mayes, B.T. and Allen, R.W. (1977) 'Toward a definition of organizational politics', *Academy of Management Review*, 2(4): 672–678.

Miller, D. (1990) *The Icarus Paradox: How Exceptional Companies Bring About Their Own Downfall*. New York: Harper.

Miller, D. and Chen, M.-J. (1994) 'Sources and consequences of competitive inertia: A study of the U.S. airline industry', *Administrative Science Quarterly*, 39(1): 1–24.

Mitroff, I.I. and Mohrman, S. (1987) 'Correcting tunnel vision', *Journal of Business Strategy*, 7(3): 49–59.

Nickerson, R.S. (1986) *Reflections on Reasoning*. Hillsdale, NJ: Lawrence Earlbaum.

Nisbett, R.E. and Ross, L. (1980) *Human Inference: Strategies and Shortcomings of Social Judgment*. Englewood Cliffs, NJ: Prentice Hall.

Oster, S. (1982) 'Intra-industry structure and the ease of strategic change', *Review of Economics and Statistics*, 64(3): 376–383.

Oster, S. (1994) *Modern Competitive Analysis*, 2nd edn. New York: Oxford University Press.

Pennings, J.M. (ed.) (1985) *Organizational Strategy and Change*. San Francisco, CA: Jossey Bass.

Pettigrew, A.M. (1973) *The Politics of Organizational Decision Making*. London: Tavistock.

Pettigrew, A.M. (1985) *The Awakening Giant: Continuity and Change in Imperial Chemical Industries*. New York: Basil Blackwell.

Pettigrew, A.M. (ed.) (1988) *The Management of Strategic Change*. New York: Basil Blackwell.

Pettigrew, A.M. and Whipp, R. (1991) *Managing Change for Competitive Success*. Cambridge, MA: Basil Blackwell.

Pfeffer, J. (1992) *Managing with Power: Politics and Influence in Organizations*. Boston, MA: Harvard Business School Press.

Phills, J.A. (1994) 'Competitive beliefs, organizational learning, and strategic change'. PhD dissertation, Harvard University.

Popper, K.R. (1968) *The Logic of Scientific Discovery*, 2nd edn. New York: Harper and Row.

Porter, M.E. (1980) *Competitive Strategy: Techniques for Analyzing Industries and Competitors*. New York: Free Press.

Porter, M.E. (1985) *Competitive Advantage: Creating and Sustaining Superior Performance*. New York: Free Press.

Porter, M.E. (1991) 'Towards a dynamic theory of strategy', *Strategic Management Journal*, 12: 95–117.

Prahalad, C.K. and Hamel, G.K. (1990) 'The core competence of the corporation', *Harvard Business Review*, 68(3): 79–91.

Quinn, J.B. (1978) 'Strategic change: Logical incrementalism', *Sloan Management Review*, 20(1): 7–21.

Quinn, J.B. (1980) *Strategies for Change: Logical Incrementalism*. Homewood, IL: Dorsey Press.

Riess, M. and Taylor, J. (1984) 'Ego-involvement and attributions for success and failure in a field setting', *Personality and Social Psychology Bulletin*, 10(4): 536–543.

Rosenthal, R. and Rosnow, R.L. (1984) *Essentials of Behavioral Research: Methods and Data Analysis*. New York: McGraw-Hill.

Schweiger, D.M., Anderson, C.R. and Locke, E.A. (1985) 'Complex decision making: A longitudinal study of process and performance', *Organizational Behavior and Human Decision Processes*, 36(2): 245–272.

Schwenk, C. (1988) 'The cognitive perspective on strategic decision making', *Journal of Management Studies*, 25(1): 41–55.

Secord, P.F. (1986) 'Explanation in the social sciences and in life situations', in D. Fiske and R. Shweder (eds), *Metatheory in Social Science: Pluralisms and Subjectivities*. Chicago, IL: University of Chicago Press. pp. 197–221.

Seligman, M.E. (1975) *Helplessness: On Depression, Development, and Death*. New York: W.H. Freeman.

Seligman, M.E. and Schulman, P. (1986) 'Explanatory style as a predictor of productivity and quitting among life insurance sales agents', *Journal of Personality and Social Psychology*, 50(4): 832–838.

Senge, P.M. (1990) *The Fifth Discipline: The Art and Practice of the Learning Organization*. New York: Doubleday.

Sims, H.P., Gioia, D.A. and Associates (1986) *The Thinking Organization*. San Francisco, CA: Jossey-Bass.

Solomon, J. and Underwood, A. (1993) 'The fall of the dinosaurs', *Newsweek*, 42.

Starkey, K. and McKinlay, A. (1988) *Organizational Innovation: Competitive Strategy and the Management of Change in Four Major Companies*. London: Economic and Social Research Council.

Staw, B.M., Mckenzie, P.I. and Puffer, S.M. (1983) 'The justifications of organizational performance', *Administrative Science Quarterly*, 28(4): 582–600.

Stinchcombe, A.L. (1968) *Constructing Social Theory*. New York: Harcourt, Brace and World.

Tetlock, P.E. and Levi, A. (1982) 'Attribution bias: On the inconclusiveness of the cognition-motivation debate', *Journal of Experimental Social Psychology*, 18(1): 68–88.

Tichy, N.M. (1983) *Managing Strategic Change: Technical, Political, and Cultural Dynamics*. New York: John Wiley.

Tversky, A. and Kahneman, D. (1974) 'Judgment under uncertainty: Heuristics and biases', *Science*, 185(4157): 1124–1131.

Vroom, V.H. (1964/1995) *Work and Motivation*. San Francisco, CA: Jossey Bass.

Wack, P. (1985) 'Scenarios: Shooting the rapids; how medium-term analysis illuminated the power of scenarios for Shell management', *Harvard Business Review*, 63(6): 139–151.

Waddock, S.A. and Isabella, L.A. (1989) 'Strategy, beliefs about the environment, and performance in a banking simulation', *Journal of Management*, 15(4): 617–632.

Weick, K.E. (1979) 'Cognitive processes in organizations', in B.M. Staw (ed.), *Research in Organizational Behavior*, vol. 1. Greenwich, CT: JAI Press. pp. 41–74.

Zelazny, G. (1979) *From Chart to Data*. New York: McKinsey.

Zuckerman, M. (1979) 'Attributions of success and failure revisited, or: The motivational bias is alive and well in attribution theory', *Journal of Personality*, 47(2): 245–287.

Index